CONTENTS

THE DARK PLACE IN A PSYCHEDELIC YEAR.	2
HEAD TO HEAD.	14
ON THE ROAD TO FURTHER.	21
THE SEA.	47
THE EDINBURGH HOTEL IN BRIGHTON.	63
A NIGHT SO ALIVE.	81
WAITING FOR THE BUS.	97
THE MERRY PRANKSTERS!	116
STONEHENGE AND KESEY.	145
PEACE AT LAST.	170
ONLY ONE WAY BACK!	199
THE GOLDEN TICKETS.	229
TOTAL ECLIPSE.	245
HIGH HEAD.	284
Kool Aid Acid test	310
TRIP OR TREAT TOO!	349
POSTSCRIPT	358

DAVIS JOHN

**Ken Kesey.
The Merry Pranksters.
The eclipse.
And three.**

THE DARK PLACE IN A PSYCHEDELIC YEAR.

Initially there had been at least ten of us who were supposed to have been traveling to Cornwall. The months passed by quickly and by the time we were finally ready to leave Vienna behind, it was down to just the three.

"The answer is never the answer. What's really interesting is the mystery. If you seek the mystery instead of the answer, you'll always be seeking. I've never seen anybody really find the answer, they think they have, so they stop thinking. But the job is to seek mystery, evoke mystery, plant a garden in which strange plants grow and mysteries bloom.

The need for mystery
is greater than the
need for an answer."
Ken Kesey

I had plenty of questions but there didn't seem to be many answers!!

1999 was a wholly manufactured panic, a form of mass hysteria that just swept us along that year. It may all seem rather comical in hindsight but to look back is to forget the feeling of the time, to forget how it felt to be on the edge of the unknown. The world was younger then, more naive somehow, but the lessons we learnt along that stormy path will never be forgotten. In fact, it strengthened us and prepared us for the future. It was a fine time of deft contradictions.

All in all things were getting serious and it felt like we the latest world were crumbling.
I mean we seemed to be constantly under fire.
It was 1999 and the early simmering of global warming had us fried.

We, the fresh-baked computerized generation, moved with little confidence and a foreboding reigned supreme. We were like a three minute old foal trying to balance on a tightrope, and below us were clouds of absolute uncertainty.

They told us it was time to stock pile and they told us it was a time to get in what you needed. Most of all though we were told it was a time to panic and a time to pray at the feet of whichever god you still believed in. Amidst all this, just when a soothing word was needed, comfort from anywhere, nature in her wisdom decided to throw in a total eclipse! Immediately the panicking types were in their

element.
"Just look at the numbers!" They told us.

"Numerology! It must mean something!" We were warned.

It was in ancient Cornwall, England that the eclipse was to first come to land, and more worryingly it was due to arrive at the eleventh minute after eleven o clock, on the eleventh of August.
11:11 a.m. on the 11th of August 1999.

"The longest duration of totality." They informed us bleakly.
Even the most skeptical amongst us caught the possible significance of it all and soon the whole nation was worried. This rising mysticism spread out like a stain and pretty soon most of the Northern Hemisphere lay in the grip of mild supernatural curiosity. Daily we all listened for the latest news of this doomsday morning, all of us increasingly mauled, weary and trapped with fear in our eyes.
Away, away, run away.

"Don't go to Cornwall, England." They threatened us.
Our parochial old government fought desperately to avoid an ecological disaster in one of England's least spoilt corners.
Day after day the national press was filled with paranoid outbursts of gloom.
"Cornwall's roads to be war zones.".
"Checkpoints and armed police."
"Two million expected to make the journey."
"Water and Food rationing."
They didn't want anyone there to witness the scene, but what scene?
Why the huge interest? It was probably down to the fact

that a thousand years were coming to an end and people were feeling the icy breath of mortality on their necks.

Even the computer kings and queens were in a lather about something they had christened the 'millennium bug'. Thousands of companies were investing hefty sums in preparing themselves for the possible meltdown disaster.
 They were busy telling anyone who would listen that everything was going to blow at midnight on the thirty first of December 1999.

They told us that computers across the world would implode. and that the only supposed hope lay in investing heavily in numerous anti-bug devices costing a lot of money. Of course, these very security services were being offered by the very same computer companies who were casting out all the warnings. It was a huge electronic heist, but to some degree or other, we all fell for it during those unsure, terrifying, almost. comical times.

Even the name Nostradamus was again a daily rider.
Of course they claimed that Nostradamus had claimed that the world would end in the year 2000.
Of course, it did not!

To me 1999 seemed liked a potent time because it was entertaining being. in amidst this all around chaos. I was on my summer vacation from teaching and there was nothing in the sky to darken my personal view. It was great too to be back in old Britain because most of the year I lived in Vienna.

I was about to join in the chaos and venture out to Cornwall for the TOTAL ECLIPSE OF THE SUN. The driving force was the arrival of the elderly, psychedelic American bandits known as the 'Merry Pranksters.'

The elderly who? You may ask.
The Merry Pranksters, I say again.

I harbored at that time in my life, I still do in fact, a fascination with anything vaguely questioning of authority. American literature was another huge passion of mine. Indeed, it was anything artistic with a hint of edge about it, anything that had the artists looking down at the swirling void below. I loved those creators that had been unsure of their calling but who had been always fascinated by a weird view. I was in fact addicted to hunting down the unusual.
The 'Merry Pranksters.'

They had been around since the early Sixties, and had been a group of outlaws in a entertainingly threatening sense. Ken Kesey the most prominent of the Pranksters had written the much celebrated 'One flew over the cuckoo's nest',, the one with the Chief, the madhouse and the nurse.

Ken Kesey's real life story however is probably a little less well known. At the age of twenty six Ken Kesey had written this enormous story of rebellion in a psychiatric hospital, he'd then written another epic, before, in true anarchic fashion, throwing it all in to become an underground menace named Captain America, or the 'Chief' or simply Kesey.

"I'm tired of being the seismograph, I'd rather be the lightning rod." He'd said at the time.
After running a wild campaign of crazed but seminal events called the 'Acid Tests', he had been chased by the FBI to Mexico, had faked his own suicide before returning to the USA as a fugitive. He was finally hunted down and caught after a Hollywood style chase along one of San Francisco's main highways. After being granted bail, Kesey went on to

hold more parties before finally being locked up on a one jail year sentence. He was twenty-nine years old.

To give it a context, you have to imagine anyone carrying this out in our times. A huge best selling novel then three years later you return not with a new story, but a plan to change the whole world!
This unlikely story was captured brilliantly by Tom Wolfe in his 'Electric Kool Aid Acid Test'.

Since first reading that most vivid of tales I've always wondered just what was driving these people. In my mind it somehow all didn't tie up. The Hippie ethic of the Nineteen Sixties seemed to be so blatantly naive whilst somehow Kesey's Merry Pranksters, seemed to be so obviously unhinged and lingering.

Good god, I mean Kesey, and the Pranksters had just always seemed to have been one step to the side of everyone else. One time, when invited to speak at an anti Vietnam rally in the mid sixties, Kesey and the Pranksters had been ruthlessly pilloried for turning up in painted army uniforms armed with plastic guns. Their message was clear, 'Don't play how they play!'.

Their kick was always causing ripples beyond the usual. Their instrumental role in instigating the rise and fall of the now lamented LSD counterculture, is well documented. The Merry Pranksters had then built up their notoriety by lashing around in controversy, innocently fixing up with the Hells Angels, and driving a painted school bus on missions of madness around the sleeping states of America. They were loved and loathed in equal measures and the enigma of Ken Kesey split camps in both the literary and underground worlds. Some argued that his literature had dried up as the psychedelics had taken over and by some he was forever perceived as the 'Tarnished Galahad'. The one who could have gone so far but instead chose to go further. "Too far?" Some said!

These Merry Pranksters, the original cast brought to life by Tom Wolfe's journalistic classic, were middle class, dissatisfied kids. In the Sixties they had 'done their thing` and had since died or stayed alive and gone through middle age to become old and gray.

Suddenly in 1999, out of the blue, the surviving Pranksters now just into their sixth decade, and accompanied by a wildly painted 1939 school bus they called "Further", were due to spend three weeks on a tour of the British Isles.

I, a modern day ship adrift, wanted to know why?
Just what was bringing these old age hustlers out of retirement for the final 'prank'?

Well, the claimed focus of the tour was a search for 'Merlin', and it was to Cornwall they were heading, and if it was a good enough reason to move them, well how in god's name could I, the fascinated one, refuse?
Suddenly in 2001, out of the blue, Ken Kesey died. This event in the midst of America's new war on the unseen enemy and the freak outs about Osama Bin Laden, went pretty much unnoticed by most.

Back in 1999 it was the night before the start of the journey and a long way away from Cornwall, Vienna, the United States of America or the year 2000.

I was at the time a thirty-something teacher, tall and thin, with long wayward dark hair, usually tied back in a pony tail. I had light grey spiral eyes, and virtually always wore dark shades against the day light. I was born in Wales and after a time spent in Liverpool had. descended on Vienna with madness and desire in my eyes.

At my side that night was Myrthin, then twenty-eight, a wild Welsh warrior of the jagged soul, with his boyish good looks and dark eyed excitement like a man born for internal adventure. He should have 'Chasing the Dawn' stenciled across his forehead.

He was a teacher of Welsh and was along with Sparks, an Australian friend from Vienna, to be part of the mission of discovery to Cornwall. His reasons for traveling were similar to mine. He too enjoyed the Kesey tale and being on vacation meant that he was also intent on having major fun.

Several others were in the bar that night, all old allies of ours and gently we pass the time and flow in and out of conversation.
We kill minutes with talk about dentists or marbles lost in ear drums and other such obtuse past exploits.

That I lived away in Austria meant that these nights were always a holy chance to catch up with the present Welsh constitution. That night as is quite often the case, a truly electrical storm of conversation was brewing.

The "Dark Place" is a small bar and Ruthin is a small town, the town in which I grew up. I remember it now as a place full of innocent moments of high trickery and for the fact that when the clouds cracked, there were stars in the sky. Legend has it that the town was once a stronghold of the Welsh bandit leader Owen Glyndwr and that the rebels had never really left. They had seemingly just passed their blood down through the generations. Anyhow, whatever the truth, this latest breed, which was namely us, didn't have anything left to fight against, so we'd simply laid war with ourselves in destructive sort of way.

Ruthin is a crazily group orientated town, everywhere one looks one sees a group. There are groups of men, groups of women and of course groups of children.
This collective ideal stays the intact until, as inevitably we all do, we fall in love, become more balanced, disappear, before returning some years later with lines under our eyes and the same pulse burning our souls.
Ruthin is a typical home for the reckless. A typical home for experimentation as escape which then becomes a permanent ethos for living.

And that night the neon bar lights advertising lager dip and sway in the greens of a mad fever, for nothing more makes sense. Rhyd, Myrthin's younger brother, the most clean-cut. guy you could ever wish to meet, at least on the outside. He is an intelligent conversationalist and that which he fails to understand he merely takes on his shoulders and questions.

"So, who are this band you're going to see?".

He asks, drinking slowly then turning to me for an answer to his bemused gaze. My thoughts drift off, away with the neon 'Cold Beer' sign. They leave this weird late night and out to where a 'question mark planet' stands alone as the symbol for uncertainty.

And I wonder about our impending trek across old Great Britain, and just what we hope to find and where we hope to find it.

"Well, they're not actually a band." I answered lamely, for it

10

was hard to explain just what the Merry Pranksters actually were and are.

"You know the film, 'One flew over the Cuckoo's Nest."

I continued desperately looking for a hook of understanding, any hook of understanding.

"Well Ken Kesey one of the Pranksters, wrote the book.".

Rhyd nodded earnestly enough, though he looked far from convinced. He was probably wondering just why anyone would bother traveling the length and breadth of the country in pursuit of a sixty four year old author.
It was a fair question, yet the main point was that I actually had the time and the possibility to follow my instinct, the summer vacation meant that I was free to come and go as we chose.

"In Nineteen Sixty Four they drove across America in a psychedelic bus.".

I continued to nothing like a reaction. But what had I expected? The talk of a psychedelic bus cut no real ice with anyone in the late Nineties. It was nothing new, in fact something commonplace, and often a thing with seriously negative vibrations.

The new-age esoteric of which I was also very skeptical, had sent the idea of group dynamics positively into old age. It seemed now to be all about self-discovery through being alone, meditating, contemplating and a great deal of navel gazing. That the Merry Pranksters were somewhat akin to a passive guerrilla movement meant little to most in the year 1999.

I began to wonder whether they were about to be perceived as another gang of crazy old hippies. Or worse still, as a nostalgia ridden crude 'Rolling Stones' kind of concept.
I pondered hard on just what tinge of indecent voyeurism was forcing 'us' on this perfect escapade. Us being them the Merry Pranksters and we the three.
Yet this was a gut feeling, some instinct driven idea to maybe laugh and witness the remains of what might have originated at the outset. A chance to taste something of that silly, rainbow colored decade that had brought in the man on the moon, the Beatles and indeed, the baby me.

Whatever the reason, I knew we had to be there.
Explain I could not but I knew as sure as gravity keeps us down that the whole adventure was to bring with it some form of vital learning.
And around me the mist began to swoop red and thicken in bubbles.
And Myrthin leaves to confront the beer foam.

And I turn to one Mad Phil to continue our previous conversation about chloroform dentists. Which if the recent government declarations are to be believed, might be the father spirit of my adventure. The reason why the following day we were about to hunt down the notorious psychedelic bus "Further", en route to searching for Merlin.

Why call a bus 'Further'? Because that is where the Merry Pranksters claimed that they were heading.

As a baby in the womb, I had spent three months on Valium and downers. They called it 'high class' Sixties pre-natal medication.

As a child in the Seventies I'd had several unnecessary general anesthetics for several minor dental drillings. They

called it 'high class' Seventies Dental medication.
It seems to me that the government always reaps what it sows.
Medicated children grow up to be anarchic lone rangers.
Just ask the C.I.A. and the Merry Pranksters.

HEAD TO HEAD.

The C.I.A. had kicked off the whole psychedelic revolution with their evil plans to dose the enemy into submission, or by interrogating the spies into speaking, or by bullying the world into being a better place. Just what the C.I.A. know about improving one's lot in life is an unanswerable question.

Soon their crazy acid child was out of the house and in the streets, fizzing. Men like Kesey and Leary took in on and soon it became the C.I.A versus LSD and in that fight there was always only going to be one winner. Or so they thought, for the fight continues, the battle is not over.

Things have changed irreversibly and as we drive wildly through a new time, there is a desperate need for a little hit of counter culture weirdness.

In the Sixties the Hippies were the downfall and in a way their failure brought in the spiteful Seventies and Nixon and Thatcher and dozens of other greed-head monsters. It was the curse of those who trusted, it was their failure. The Merry Pranksters were never to be trusted.

14

Trust me!

Our story really starts on a warm, summer morning in 1999, a Thursday, one week before the Total Eclipse.
We needed wheels to get to Cornwall and Myrthin in his wisdom had rented a car for the ridiculous price of fifty pounds for ten days. So after persuading a friend to drive us eight miles we were on our way to a neighboring town to meet with our vehicle.

The Vale of Clwyd is a goddess landscape and as you drive along the main road you are flanked down one side by the rolling mother hills of the Clwydian Range. Hills as smooth and undulating as one can get. On top of many are the iron age hill fort remains which can be made out as circular scars on the rounded summits. Growing up in constant sight of the range they stood as protectors of the humble valley in which we lived. A last gasp boundary between us and the real world which started just the other side of the hills.

These hunched giants allowed us a safe breeding ground in which we could practice our innocent psychedelic childlike magic. Nature tends to invokes the green in each of us.
England and the real world was what lay beyond. The world of muggings, murder and urban mayhem, at least that is what we were led to believe by our elders, the Daily Post and the Daily Mirror national tabloids.
Yet with our natural shield safely in place somehow all these wild stereotypes seemed to belong to another existence.

Though throughout it all there was that sneaking growing desire to go out and search. For just as port folk always have the sea as a reminder of greater things, we had the hills as proof that a mere six mile journey over and beyond would unleash the forces of a different form of freedom.

As a youngster I had often been dragged unwillingly on long Sunday walks on those hills.

My brother Dave and I walking behind our quick stepping parents, us lost playing the games of childhood, lost in the imagination of the childhood mind.

Now twenty years later, trekking silently along the eight mile journey with little being said, we moved towards the first step of our journey.

Soon we were in sight of the outskirts of Denbigh, a further small town in deepest North Wales. We could already see the crumbling castle squatting on a hill, which stood crash bang in the middle of the old market town. Denbigh was mainly famous for being the home of the former North Wales Hospital. A huge, sprawling Victorian lunatic asylum in the classic 'bars on windows' mould.

It had been a frightening place, a place which you would drive past and literally feel the misery leaking out of the narrow windows. Like a traffic accident in freezing snow it was one of those places one didn't linger at. It was however a truly fitting place to start this Kesey week, what with 'One flew over the Cuckoo's nest being heavy on our minds. The buildings are empty now though, with only lonely lost souls as occupants.

Anyhow it seemed strange to be beginning our intrepid mission in the midst of such notoriety. Insanity is a running theme with the anarchic within us. I quite remembered those horrific government films, those that highlighted the desire to leap out of windows and warned of the threat of madness and lethal paranoia. Terrible

propaganda told the world that LSD makes you believe you can fly!
I was about to find out whether the Ken Kesey the LSD renegade was any crazier than the next man, or whether just being oneself in one's own minor way can sometimes lead to major problems.

I now work with a group of teenagers labelled as being psychologically unfit by the powers that be in Vienna, twelve of them in all. At the time of the total eclipse in 1999 I didn't. Yet I digress.
Back in the car Myrthin in his madness says what he thinks.

"Stop and ask the first person we see.".
Within minutes we were stranded in the town square watching the Thursday morning shopping take place.
"Excuse me. Do you know where Jo Cars Rental might be?" Rods asks a middle aged guy walking past the driver's window.

"Jo Cars!!" The man paused to think, his face, ruddied by the sun, his eyes narrowed but looming large behind thick glasses. "Aren't they down on the new industrial estate. Yeah, I think so." His accent sounded so exotic, a rich Welsh deep tone that was at the same time so familiar yet so foreign. He was only too pleased to help and immediately called for assistance.
"June." He beckoned his rotund wife over. "Jo Cars isn't that down on the Rhyl road?".

His wife happily joined in on the superb desire to assist.
"Aye. By the old piano shop." She spoke sincerely and I felt the magic in these people on their daily round of groceries that were genuinely concerned that we found our destination. Simple communication is the most basic of our

magic tricks, too often undervalued, and in this computer age, dangerously under threat.

Good god will we all fall into this virtual society, of electronic mailing, gaming and worse without so much as a struggle? That would be a huge shame. Bringing people together yet driving people apart!

We were soon rising up the correct hill, it was flanked either side by units of different kinds of workplaces, one of which had been home to Rodders the welder for a good half dozen year. This was the bottom end of the great economic spiral into your pocket, these were the one man businesses, the tradesmen and women, the eager to succeed.

"See that gate there!" Says Rods, "My work that." He has a justifiable pride in seeing his work swirling its introduction to one 'Jacob's Office Machinery'.

Then we drove past 'Snow King Frozen foods', where my own mother had worked for fifteen years and even I had once for two dreary weeks. We continued past 'Lazner's Pianos', the place, the only place where one could buy guitar strings in the locality. A very special place, the guy that ran the place was an exiled old German, driven from his home at the outbreak of World War Two. All these businesses were insignificant in a way, yet for many they were a livelihood and a reason.

We had a reason too, the dubious pleasure of a commercial dealing with Jo Cars of Denbigh. Theirs was a tiny hut at the top of a hill, hardly a proud establishment, a real low rung company, scrapping for customers at the bottom end of the market. It has long since gone into receivership but that day they were the way and the means of us getting to

Cornwall.
I walked in through the door and spoke quietly.

"Hello. We've booked a car for today."

"Under what name?" Asks the proprietor, a woman whose peroxide hair was streaked with gray.

We answer uneasily and swat flies caught helpless in the draughts that leaked into the hill top cabin. The woman seemed uncomfortable, apparently unused to dealing with the driving public on such a formal level. At her side stood a girl that must have been her young daughter. She sang softly as she busily fiddled with her tiny seven-year-old fingers on a desk covered in drawings.

Suddenly the telephone rang and Myrthin and I caught each others eyes.

"Hello Jo Cars. How can I help you?".
In a ringing clarity the first sparkler of the great adventure burst into fizzing flame.
She'd said "Jo Cars", both of us had heard it.
Not Jo's Cars, or Jo Auto Hire.
No, it was 'Jo Cars.' And for 'Jo Cars' read 'Jo Kars' read 'Jo Kers' read 'JOKERS.'

We were renting a car for bottom dollar prices from a firm who openly went by the name of "Jokers". Now that was a bit of fun.
Soon and quickly the phone was down, and we returned with a new found faith to our financial dealing. A wad of notes rose from our pockets and it became obvious that both sides of this specific barter were serious "jokers".
"You want to have that one?". The flustered woman asked as an outstretched arm led us out through a side window.

A car is indeed a car, and renting a car is like playing poker, so of course we agreed to the red Ford saloon, what else could we do.

And money changed hands and Rodders paced around anxiously outside and the girl tidied paper clips and we stood proudly and everything was done. The woman filed away the cash and somehow I got the feeling that she trusted us no more than we trusted her, but anyhow with clenched teeth almost breaking into a smile she told us what we wanted to hear.

"The keys are in the ignition. Away you go. That's it."
She'd not even looked at our driving licenses.

We could hardly believe our luck, and we were away.
Two doors slammed shut in North Wales and it would be quite a while and a couple of hundred miles 'til we opened them once more.
In England in fact.

ON THE ROAD TO FURTHER.

The Doors music filled the car with control over the first miles of the journey. It was the end of 'The End', if you get my drift.

Jim Morrison, long gone and now in the new era, nothing like the presence he had been even ten years before. Had their music grown dated, less powerful?

Did the kids of today have no place for leather clad growling aggression? Or did they just not know about these things, these people or these events of earlier times? Context is I suppose, god, and hold on, America in the new era was nothing like America in the Nineteen Sixties.

There is no longer any war in Vietnam, just a violent war against terrorism. There is no longer any counter culture, just a swerving anti globalization movement..

There is no more C.I.A. infiltration, oh yes there is, and stronger than ever. You see the world hasn't really changed; it has just got more electronic.

The two chivalrous knights of the winding road cared not a lot as we talked a little over things on the quiet side of life. I was glued behind the steering wheel whilst Myrthin was spread across the passenger seat.

KEN KESEY. THE MERRY PRANKSTERS. THE ECLIPSE. AND THREE.

Our talk was gentle, it was as if we both needed to be polite as the wheels and the tarmac ran into their groove. Out towards a town called Wrexham we headed, out on a twisting narrow pedantic little road, bordered on either side by dense forest.

As I had lived away in Austria for over five years even this most familiar of routes was a pleasant memory lane experience. Other journeys long gone came alive as I sat gripping the steering wheel and curving the bends out. I remembered childhood Christmas shopping jaunts, I remembered trips to random international soccer matches and even the odd reluctant family of four visits to dull relatives. This spindly two lane track had not changed but my horizon certainly had.

At one point a tiny humble collection of flowers lay as a reminder, an indication that the traveling game sometimes has it's victims too. Only a week previously a young motorcyclist had overshot a corner and ended lost under the wheels of an oncoming bus.

It was that easy, to lose sight of the apex on any bend one comes to and what awaits then, what surprise has fate got in store for you? Well for that poor soul it was a big price he'd had to pay for a tiny loss of control. I sighed inside, I wished the person peace and instinctively my foot twitched down on the gas pedal to speed past the lonely roses. Soon the bends were only a green line in the rear view mirror.

22

Meanwhile Myrthin had already inevitably built the first joint of the journey.

'Oh no!' I thought earnestly. 'Here we go again!'

At times in those days, the late Nineties, the world was submerged in strong grass. He claimed it was probably a government technique to avoid too much panic. I felt personally that I had reached a point where the whole routine was dulling my senses. I remember the constant feeling of zest in the morning becoming a constant jolly confusion by the evening.

I used to like smoking dope, but I was after a steady decade of consumption, beginning to tire of the whole procedure of breaking up the jigsaw puzzle. I was half convinced that the longer you did it, the more pieces of the puzzle went missing.

.

"Twenty five pounds for a half thumb of dope, my god, we rented an engine and four wheels for only twice the price!!!!!". He happily announced whilst lost in the world of economics. Thick smoke poured from his lips as he blindly dug into a plastic bag of cassettes.

One was a compilation I'd called "Caution Weird Load!". This was a key phrase from the Kesey's earlier bus journeys. These were the words inscribed on the tail plate of the original 1964 bus. It was a jump with words on the usual 'Caution Wide Load' and a suitable starting point for raising questions in small town USA. Imagine the faces on these people coming slowly home from work in Dillon or Bigwick or Fulton.

There goes a huge bus, alive with color and noise. Remember this was the age of black and white living, suits, televisions and even segregated buses.

Not for the Pranksters though, they would explode with color into any town, playfully tooting flutes, chucking small red balls and relaying, delayed, delayed, delayed music from the streets back onto the streets.

"What in god's name was that?". You'd find yourself asking and the answer is the rear of the bus and what you are left with. "Well a weird load, that's what!".
Our own later version was no way as weird, but still to be treated with caution.

The Doors tape ejected its prime position to be replaced by a crazy collection of other songs from the permanent edge. Myrthin passed on the spliff and I shrugged my shoulders.

Outside, we were still surrounded by greenery but rapidly approaching Coedpoeth, a small township just outside Wrexham. Coedpoeth was the place where the thin road grew wider and evolved into a dual roadway.

I was contemplating the prospect of a bus load of Sixties veterans dealing with dying Nineties Britain. I was trying I guess, to secure myself that Kesey might know what he was letting he and his gang in for. Wondering whether without the zest of youth they would be able to pull anything off apart from some horrific version of a sad 'comeback' tour, or even worse, a mere nostalgia trip back to the Sixties.
Britain would not stand for that, Britain had no respect for any dewy eyed Sixties American shenanigans.
We'd stopped at the first traffic lights of the journey and there before us were angry eyes. You could just tell. Two guys crossing the road. We saw them and they certainly saw us in our stoned long hair stereotype. No one had long hair any longer, but we did.

Why? I have no idea, maybe it was just easier than cutting your hair, it was certainly not a statement of any kind, it was most probably laziness. These eyes outside glared and dribbled into the heat haze as they pounded the black and white stripes shimmering beneath their feet.

Glowering looks from the monsters turned the lights from red to green and we were off quickly.
Good god Ken Kesey, I felt worried for him, he was much older now, an old man, a man who had just survived a stroke the year before. Why was he doing this now? What was the point? I was totally unsure as to whether the world still had a place for such outdated ethos.

It was though clear even at that early point of the journey, that this inquisitive trip was going to be as much 'our' time for adventure. An important journey at a strange time, it was probably going to involve learning of some sort. As I sit here now I find it naive in the extreme that I should have actually been worrying for the welfare of these people. These people and Kesey in particular turned out to be as tough as they come. I found out later that nothing could phase them, nothing at all.

Coedpoeth vanished as quickly as it had arrived and the new dual carriageway was a freeway gift from the gods. It meant no more gear changing, or no looking to the next bend, but just a straight ahead burst down the fast lane. To me it had already become increasingly obvious that the faster we went the less complicated the driving was. So I let Norm clear his chest and let him gallop away.

Soon we were hightailing it in fast lane number one, heading towards the English border. The road we were on was a flat stretch through some of the most grandiose countryside anywhere. Bridges towered over valleys below as green stretched as far as the mind could see. It kind of reminded me of a place in Germany, a place that I'd never seen but somehow had either dreamt or seen televised.

Spiritualized and their amazing brand of music crashed the view and took centre stage. Spiritualized are an English band of huge underground stature and Spiritualized has always been a weird one. I'll try to explain.

A good seven years previously I'd been laid up with one of those shivering fevers, probably a result of too many speeding January nights, during a wild loveless phase in my early twenties. Suddenly as I lie under furnace blankets, I catch some television show and I hear something that stops my shaking.
A tune writhes out from the tinny speaker with this amazing melody. It was a sound that in no uncertain terms, forever changed my way ahead, it was as if something shifted within me.

Explain it I could not but the effect was overwhelming, I was gifted the first glimpses of a view clear around the world and a possibility that grew from that screen and has never since left.
It was a tune called 'Run! Run! Run!' and just like Forrest Gump, that's what I did. I ran out of bed and recovered immediately.
Spiritualized!

A while later we were approaching a town called Nesscliffe. A town or rather a village just beyond the border between England and Wales.
This place is weird.
Why? I don't really know.

It's just that the place is inevitably always empty and just

inevitably a little bit on the frightening side.
Nesscliffe gets me each and every time. On the face of it, it's probably something to do with the fact that the motorway is within touching distance and suddenly peace, quiet and whoosh, you have to slow down. It is at this unholy place that three lanes converge into a tight two-lane deal. Nesscliffe is also quite probably the slowest town in the world.

Immediately you feel paralyzed by the sudden surge of disturbing signs depicting children playing.
"Reduce your speed!" They tell you!
"Take care children!" They wail.

At some point in my life I would like to do a bit of hyper investigation into the background of this place, maybe involve one of those mystics that can sense these things.

Dowse the underground water channels and read the trees try to find out a deep version of this feeling. For as you sit grid locked moving at three miles an hour, some inexplicable something nags away at your subconscious. It's like a vision of some insanely awful road accident that washes over your mind, it is a real bad feeling.

It is as if you were moving onto the site of an ancient massacre. How I imagine it must feel in Auschwitz, Dachau or any of those most horrendous of places. But is it just imagination? Is it just wild panic? I have never found out, but I've never lost that suspicion about the place. Somehow it just seems miserable there, really miserable.

Of course I didn't mention it to Myrthin, he seemed ignorant to any bad vibrations because he was blissfully unaware.
Yet just as soon as it hits you this spooked little village, it's

gone, like a mirage. You suddenly find yourself approaching a farewell sign and the blood immediately begins to pump harder once more. All at once the sign reads in clear lettering.
"Thank you for driving carefully.".

It becomes clear that before each and every one of us in this temporary gypsy caravan of travelers, lies the chaos of three hundred miles of motorway.

"Farewell Nesscliffe!" We holler, both obviously frustrated at being held up in the messed-up village.

Our car chugs a little, it's already evident that he's a big road traveller and not at all into the stop start game of country traffic.

So I spread the accelerator out and the traffic thins as the ghost town becomes yet another blur in the rear view mirror.
Soon the village was recent history and before us spread the whole length and breadth of England.
England commences at the beginning of the smoky Midlands.

Hardly the most auspicious start to a legendary journey. There are gangs of abandoned factories and half fallen chimneys. It is vaguely depressing, the Black country I believe it is called, named after the soot from the factories that used to twitch and shake out tonnes of metal every day of the year. Yeah they used to and now they don't, for now the factories have long since gone.

Only to be replaced by hundreds of low lying, work units specializing in the computer hardware economy.

Progress they call it, some people call it a shame, whatever it must be said that there is little left of the countryside in this part of England.
Countryside was thin on the ground! Traffic though, there was enough on the road to make you think of turning back.

There were business boys and girls lost in the next deal as they drove perky motors whilst speaking rapidly on mobile phones. Their journeys were always dollar-driven, always under pressure to make time count, for there aren't enough hours in a day these days.

Arthur Miller's salesman and women still plugging the globe, endlessly. These guys would move from business to business like hungry sharks, but their hunt was not for the wounded at sea, no they were in search of bigger fish. These guys were after the tail of the American dream, the dream that there is a light at the top of the ladder, and a golden pot at the end of the rainbow.

It was the god of money that drove these people on, the desire to freeze their fingers on a slab of frozen energy.

Look!

There were truck drivers too, bearded guys perched up on high, looking down on the world below, moving slowly towards that never ending horizon. This was the way of the long-distance lorry driver. These guys drove rumbling motors with the patience of a saint yet had photos of topless blondes for company. Delissa, Saffron and Cherie to name just three!.

Look!

There were even coaches, coaches full of bored looking

holiday-makers. Mostly old, retired grandmas and grandpas returning from a North Wales break by the sea. Above us there were many sleeping with their heads resting on the glass of the windows, happily snoring their way home.
"Good God!" I say pointing up at the coach, "They are the same age as the Merry Pranksters!."
"On a different bus though!" Responds the man at my side.
"But still pensioners." I laugh.
"Old, old pensioners!".
It caught me cold and sent a twitch down my spine. The Merry Pranksters, as sixty-year-olds. Now the only photographs I had seen in my previous investigation were from the faded color Sixties shots of young clown costumed energetic madness.

You know the type, bare torsos, rippling muscles, and women floating beautifully beneath white chiffon and lace.

That was the Merry Pranksters.

Admittedly I had seen a recent picture of Ken Kesey and his main man, Ken Babbs on a stop off in London the summer before, and they looked tough, really tough. But not you know, the explosion of youth that had shone out of the few pictures that exist from their original time in the Sixties.
"But power is always power!" Adds Myrthin after a break of silence. "Age is in the mind! Those guys!" He says pointing at the cuddly holiday makers, "Have probably always looked like that, always!".

I took his point, I really did, but niggling doubts rode up for attention at that stage of the journey.
'Where we really going to travel a thousand miles to witness an outdated freak show?'.

"So they're at the train station at ten o' clock, then in Brighton all day?"

He was speaking of Kesey and the Prankster's fabled non-itinerary and their non plans for the summer trip.

You see, the Pranksters were big into the idea of defying language. They had non-leaders, non-mechanics, and even non-plans. It was a way of disrespecting any convention. In the world of the Pranksters, nothing seemed to have a label attached to it, and everything was open to interpretation.

Kesey was a non-leader, he didn't and did give the orders on the bus. Babbs was the non-navigator, he did and didn't give directions on the bus.

So, their non-itinerary was something we would have to get used to. It existed and didn't exist, if you get my drift or non-drift.

"Yeah, the schedule says that they're landing at Gatwick at nine thirty and meeting the bus in Brighton at about ten."

This was non-information that had been posted on the Merry Pranksters home page for some months. They had even posted a daily schedule that had been formulated but as their motto was "Never trust a Prankster.", it all seemed somehow a little too darn easy.

Myrthin shook his head. This was a man that had once painted the walls of his flat with various quotes of Prankster wisdom. He'd even once color chalked the toilet door in the Dark Place bar in Ruthin. Acid was to blame and Bill the owner had fairly freaked. "You silly bugger, you can't do that!"

Well Bill he had, and Bill had then left the collage untouched for at least five years. He was in probably too in awe to clean it off, or more likely too lazy. No matter, it had stayed and probably confused many, many customers over the years.
There is I suppose a need for such mindless fun. We as a generation suffer from a serious lack of adventure in most of our lives, a lack of pilgrim spirit.

In you and me both. Often a painful lack of desire to push boundaries.

So, it really didn't matter whether the toilet door was clean or whether the Pranksters were actually to grace Great Britain that summer, because for me it was already high magic to have Sparks the Australian flying over from Vienna and to be already in a car traveling South. The idea of 'our' trip within 'their' trip was taking priority. We didn't even realize at that point that it might become the same trip.

A place called Telford had been and gone and it was the M6 motorway that was next on the horizon. Ominously the countdown had begun many miles before.

In the shape of blue painted Old Testament tablets we had been shown at irregular intervals just how many miles lay until the madness. Now the madness on the M6 certainly isn't my kind of madness. It takes the shape of the most cluttered collection of junctions, flyovers and traffic cones in the whole of the good old United Kingdom, probably the world. That ill conceived tarmac whirlpool was always on fast rinse. But Christ almighty, it was only a Thursday.

Surely, we'd be in and out of the horrendous traffic web before we had had any time to notice. I looked carefully, outside the flow continued pretty much unchanged. Sure there were a couple more caravans and maybe the extra truck or two. Though all in all it was the same concentration of road-hogs as there had been over the last dozen or so miles.

A sign grew blue from the green bush embankment and we were told that the M6 was six miles away. Progress is a drug of the highest order, and this was a moment of success to be cherished. We were cruising at high speed towards the mayhem. I truly hoped that we would drift in and out of the Birmingham situation as quickly and as humanely as possible, too many car corpses already litter that pitiless stretch of highway.

Ten minutes later the intersection that led onto the motorway was a hellish scene.
Herds of trucks that had been traveling together since Northern Scotland were in no mood to let new arrivals bustle their way onto the motorway.
Our mighty procession trundled forward in first gear and we moved fifty yards further.

A billion travelers on a road that went for a hundred miles before converging on the next track, the M1 to London. We moved forward another twenty yards. The usual filter service of letting one car in was slowly beginning to work.

The hard-bitten Scottish truck masters finally conceded defeat and allowed the Welsh whacked connection some space in their big boys game. Soon we were running parallel with the beasts and indicating with lights and hand signals. We were there. We were on. First gear chugging onto one of the British Isles' finest hook up roadways.

As soon as we'd made it onto fresh tarmac it became obvious that the inside lane was for dawdlers and that we had to move on up if any significant progress was to be made. So, with smoke obscuring the view I waited for a free space to take us into the middle lane.

"Whoa, watch this man, we're breaking through.'. I screamed.
It was a word to the wise and the wise were watching through their closed circuit cameras or in helicopters way above our heads.

"Quick there! Go go go go." Myrthin had scared off the latest approaching vehicle with a flash of the eyes beneath the purple heart sunglasses. Just as a Super Furry Animals song dove off into the instrumental section, we looked our way into second then third gear as the momentum picked up.
"We're away. Birmingham. Food then Brighton by sundown."

"But who knows where we'll be when the shit hits the fun." I retorted eyeing my spliff as I inhaled and blew out and chucked the gear into fifth ready to move into our home lane number three.

"Here man grab this." I said as the smoke danced an eerie dance over the space between driver and passenger and soon, we were up to forty miles per hour and in the fast lane.

In a seminal instant the cluttered mayhem out on the road cleared up to provide an unspectacular typical midweek afternoon on Britain's highways. Space grew between each truck, caravan, coach, car and us and before long the blue signs began sparkling with information of Birmingham's imminent arrival. Some thirty miles or so.

Outside the car window middle industrial England began to take control and there was gradually more and more concrete. A city called Wolverhampton offered its services at an exit we were coming to. We ignored the pleasant invitation and drove on, drove onto a road system that had governed pretty much unchanged from it's earliest days. It had been designed in its heyday to cope with tinkling 1950's Dinky toy traffic but was now absurdly overburdened and always, just always, ram packed with fuming drivers of all types.

A sense of foreboding began to saturate our movement. I glanced at the faces of some of the fellow travelers, and always saw the same fear. The fear of being late. The fear of being trapped. The fear of being caught in the net. We were all to be equal, the fastest and the slowest, the old and the young. We would be all projected as one in the slow moving crawl through Birmingham.

We cars winked hopefully towards the skies. The skies winked back brimming with evil for they knew better.

They knew what was ahead.
They were feeling benevolent.

Unbelievably they let us through Birmingham as easily as physically possible. Before turning to check, it was us pushing relentlessly onwards and coming towards the tail end of the conurbation. On the mile counter, the numbers confirmed that our intrepid trip was already approaching a hundred and fifty deep. On the cassette up came a monster classic by the German psychedelic kings 'Can'.

The song was called 'Mother Sky' and is a driving anthem, that afternoon it was about to drive us close to insanity. The song had been originally used as a soundtrack to a late night early Seventies autobahn police frenzy on German television. It must have been a long mysterious television program as the song was really, incredibly long, touching beyond fifteen minutes.

Can.
Can you dig it?
Can you boogie?
Can the can.

Relentless at the best of times, absolutely crazy at the worst. Can the band.

As we moved effortlessly out of the not so leafy lands of Birmingham's suburbs the tinkling introduction leaked out of the speakers. A leak that came out as a heartbeat, then as a thunderstorm, and finally a disintegrating rainbow.

It took a minute for the song to disturb our progress. Out of nowhere, suddenly there was cause for concern. A sign above our heads read of danger up ahead.
"Traffic delays on the M6 for the next ten, yeah ten, miles.".
"Oh no!" says Myrthin "Not now!"
It was a shock after sailing swiftly through the usual hoodoo voodoo trap of Big Hat Birmingham.

 My god, we'd let ourselves float off into complacency, we had been caught by the shirt tails, caught just where the road was about to open up and fly. A real shame but for a while nothing extraordinary crashed our dash board. The music got deeper, then louder and further out than at any other time of the journey, but that was typical Can, so hardly a shock. Then, suddenly as we came over the brow of a hill there before our eyes lay the gruesome beast itself .

A fearful sight, it was a snarling dinosaur three miles long, a wild flashing Brontosaurus of poisoned red lights, lights all backed up for as far as we could see.
A hundred cars all reluctantly pulled up to a stop, all one in a seething, violent, turgid standstill.

"Shit." Say I beginning to feel the initial rush of the journey in my non cramped bones. We were left having to suck hard and to look to the short term achievement of moving forward in tiny advances.

It was even fun that Can were beginning to freak both us out for that was their specific purpose and we knew that turning down the music was somehow admitting defeat.

Myrthin was already taking the situation further busy layering the cigarette papers with a thin crumbling of his high butane hash. Whilst outside it was still the same old view. But each tiny move forward was greeted with howls of cheering from within. We were surrounded on all sides but to our right, across the central barrier, was a free flowing top speed normal motorway scenario.

These were the lucky ones, all heading North to where we'd just left. It was a time to 'see' and not to 'look'. Don Juan of Carlos Castaneda fame had once claimed that. He'd claimed it was important to 'see' what you chose to and not to let the mind drift into horror images of what might be. We knew that 'looking' at our situation would be to open up the doors to the old classic enemy "Panic".

The car we were moving in was ancient. The journey we had to travel was long. There was a lot to lose in failure. But we couldn't afford to lose sight, not at this early stage in the huge trip.

It was our car that finally chose to take the panic game one step further. It was I who first spotted the situation. The situation that would ultimately name our vehicle and set the week on it's crazy paving course.

We were surrounded on all sides and crawling up a never ending hill. Grim enough but then I notice something really worrying.
"Man!", I say, then pause, fearful and breathless, "Has that needle always been that high up?". I was pointing at the temperature gauge.

Myrthin leant over between his skinning up to register his shock. "Jesus Christ."
And yeah immediately things on our test dipped a little closer to the old panic side of the equation.
"Watch out." Screams my fellow journeyman, "It's going to explode."

Can had played havoc with the radiator and that was not good, not in this steaming anal dinosaur ride up a never ending hill. The needle was suckling the tiny red block of paint on the predominantly black dial and that meant that we were definitely over heating. We were about to explode in a frothing lava of filthy boiling water. In the fast lane and with no way of escape. It couldn't have been much worse.

"Maybe it's been stuck like that the whole journey." I quickly add trying to appease myself, our world and all around us.

Throwing a bit of illogical common sense on a hot situation does no real good, but still, what else could we do. The pointer was already leaving the 'Norm' and heading towards where red spelt danger.

Oh woe, and there we were in the midst of a traffic hell, in the fast lane as well. Should our old engine have decided to give up the ghost at that inopportune moment then it would be us causing the next ten mile traffic hold up.
Us, two stoned teacher fools in a fifty pound rent-a-car on the way to meet the acid kings of the Sixties. Yeah us! Us, with our bag of extra curriculum, illegal, chemical eternity would be left trying to explain away our situation to some fuming team of Midlands traffic cops. Good god it didn't bear too much thinking about.

Myrthin was already nearly on my lap in his investigation as we left the 'Norm' way behind.
Each millimeter's progress upwards was like a sickly body blow.
"Norm. Come on!!!!!!". Implored my friend trying to will the temperature downwards but no, the engine was getting hotter and only one thing responded to his pleas.

Can!!

They were now reaching relentless levels of madness and they didn't look like easing off.
Listen!
A lilting Japanese voice of thinly disguised desperation invokes the gods, all acid and inspiration imploring all the time to the "Mother Sky", Can were no help, they were a danger.

Listen!

A bombastic drum sound as driven as an exploding piston hammering us senseless and guitars electric on a wildcat wail through a far distant sound. It completely saturated our increasingly stone drenched dilemma. We needed to send the temperature downwards and Can were inclined to hit us to new highs.

"Turn the heating on." Yells Myrthin. "It sends the temperature down!"

It was a common enough solution on the face of things, but on the fifth of August in a traffic jam!!! Reluctantly I twisted the heat control and soon we were being buffeted by blasts of tropical intensity that smelt of a ten-year-old engine giving up the ghost.
He was immediately busy, he'd been caught out in the breeze. Cigarette papers and hash particles were being instantly deposited across the back seat.

"Shit. Shit. Shit." He screams, all arms and legs and half in the front half in the back whilst Can thrash on mercilessly. I move in screeching first gear forwards a further dozen yards as the Mistral blows and blows and the needle continues upwards.

"Stop. Norm. Too hot. Too hot."

This test was getting serious and my thoughts began to creep over to the dark side called worry. Ideas of how much more money we should have spent in securing a real road worthy vehicle pounded at my brain.

I mean we were still nearer home than Brighton, and Sparks was arriving a day later and we may soon be back in the humble Vale of Clwyd completely defeated in our search for Merlin. A screaming voice of Papal reason told me to kill the music but somehow that seemed like the worst thing to do.

Myrthin had already recovered his cigarette papers and was busy building a wind barrier.

"What's going on? What's going on?".
"You don't want to know man. It's getting higher and higher"

The news was not good.
"The heater has done nothing but burn our eyebrows." I reply moodily.
"Then turn it off.". He said, he'd had enough of the electric wind.

So there we sat, about to implode on the M6 but despite Can's best efforts we were still out of control and in the hands of higher magic.

It was crazy but it was true, but as soon as the heater slowed it's fans, the needle twitched a tiny touch back on itself, back towards the "Norm", and outside suddenly as if by a miracle the traffic took up to moving once more.

Sure, only a Sunday afternoon crawl in third gear but movement all the same. All three lanes headed on slowly up the hill. Soon we were up into fourth and hitting thirty miles per hour. Incredible. It was a miracle, no more, no less, a holy miracle of synchronicity. Our pilgrimage had thrown itself a lifeline.

A new dawning arose as the dinosaur disappeared.

A painted petrol pump sign post indicated a service station

in six miles, and this was a sign of hope, six miles. A new monumental dilemma led us by the nose. The engine was still violently overheating and we still had six miles to drive.

Should we now cut the revs and move painstakingly slowly to our possible marginal Valhalla? Or, and it was an 'or' the size of an engine, should we speed as quickly as possible down the increasingly freed up motorway?

One needle twitch too many would leave us stranded in a plastic supermarket complex. It was a big one to deal with. Sure we could pitch our tents near the toilet block and spend seven days blitzed on dope and alcohol in the Midlands, but somehow that wasn't the bag. It was to Cornwall we were going and it was to Cornwall or bust.

"Crank the the beast up to eighty!" howled Myrthin just as Can began to fade out.

Can fading out meant six minutes more of their madness as they always had one hell of a fade out. And I quickly check the needle and was hardly surprised to see no positive inverse reaction to our increased speed.

'What the hell?"

I thought quietly to myself. It was far better to go out with all guns blazing than with a whimper, and soon we were up to eighty miles an hour. We held our breath. We toked on the new spliff. Having less than six miles to go at eighty miles an hour meant that we had about four minutes to survive.

We cranked the music up until the speakers leapt up and down in their housing and we prayed to some god or other.

Like a test pilot pushing the shackles out of a new rattling construction we fired down the heart of England counting the seconds and spinning out in our minds. A clear road ahead meant that eighty was soon ninety and that the needle was beyond the red and back into the molten white.

Signs shot past our roller coaster ride towards explosion and some informed us of the distance to our oasis and some not. It was my idea to hide the needle behind a rolled up newspaper. Myrthin duly provided the shield. The next time we would see the needle would probably be when the engine exploded and sent the damn thing spiraling into the rear seat.

"Come on Norm. COME ON!!!!!!" screamed my friend like a medicine man at an exorcism.

He was willing the engine, pistons, cogs and wheels to stay as a unit at least for a further two miles.

And the car officially had a name. It was Norm from that point onwards. We were willing the needle to head back into the 'normal', but you know what there was no returning, no turning back. It was if we two, the car and the whole of our worlds were about to leave the 'normal' behind forever.

I guess neither of us had thought of what we were leaving behind, you tend not to when your driving in a bomb.

"Come on Norm!!!!!!"

A sign informed us that we had fifteen hundred meters to go. FIFTEEN HUNDRED METERS IS LESS THAN TWO MILES.

We'd almost made it. The white-knuckle ride was almost over. I took my foot off the accelerator and the newspaper off the dashboard. It was clear that the needle was still having a seizure at the top of the scale. Can tinkled into their last verse and before us lay the enormous sign stating with absolutely total irony.

You soon will be entering a "WELCOME BREAK!" service station, they weren't kidding!!!!!!!

Relief, pounding hearts, and within the mayhem my first job was to secure the inside lanes. The last thing on god's almighty earth we needed to do was to miss the turn off and be left on the motorway for another thirty miles. So with as much care and consideration allowed by my heightened perspective, I jumped the whole shambling wreck into the middle lane as soon as a gap appeared. I watched him busy finishing off the dying embers of the victorious smoke, too busy to think any further.

He'd been quite shaken by the whole experience because it was after all his genius that had led us to this bargain deal of the week.

Even Can were down to the bare bones of their "Mother Sky" and as we pulled into the slow lane the feeling was one of having survived a run in with a psychedelic lawn mower.

No thoughts were wasted on the fact that we still had about two hundred miles to go, not even half way to the first of our several destinations. It was a time for easing off and soon the slip road that led into our oasis was sliding off the snarling motorway.

We glided onto the fresh tarmac almost freewheeling. In

my knees a twanging sensation rose as the clutch became necessary once more whilst in front of us a coach load of carefree tourists stopping for postcards, darted left, leaving us with no option but to pull to the right. In the post Can silence we followed the signs indicating a neon bright knife and fork.

Now sure, we, we merely needed feeding, but the newly christened Norm, well, they don't I believe, have a Lourdes for engines.
Norm and his engine pinged silent then refused to start again. It seemed as if he needed a long, long sleep.

Oh, cruel twist of fate. Oh, sad old dreams. It was all over.

In absolute silence, for now even the music had been turned off, I rolled the car into an empty gap. Words were inadequate. We two intrepid travelers hitched off our seat belts and burst into a thousand pieces.

The red doors slammed shut behind us and I was sure I could hear a death rattle from under the bonnet.
Had we really travelled our last mile in the cheap chariot?

Would we be back in Wales before nightfall?
Would the Pranksters miss us?

These worries, these worries they slowed you down to a virtual standstill, like quicksand s-s-s-s-sucking at your sandals.

Beyond the worrying lay a huge super-shop with its shelves of vibrating possibility like some unearthly choir of frozen angels. Piles of rainbow tinted places and dreams rose like Disney hills from the floor to the ceiling.

Onwards we went, we kept on going.

Onwards we went, we kept on going. Our journey still in its infancy was potentially doomed.Our journey still in it's infancy was about to get going

THE SEA.

Myrthin was busy working at unscrewing the radiator cap and a leaking radiator I knew from experience meant crash, the end of the road.

"Got it!!." He shouted as he held aloft the small round obstacle and I turned to face the water music. Like detectives over a missing clue we both peered into the rusty cuckoo chick-like opening of the water container.

There was not a drop of condensation to be seen anywhere. "Jesus Christ!" we both exhaled in shock. No wonder the temperature had been on the hot side of an exploding sun.

"Are you sure it isn't the container for the windscreen?." I asked non-professionally.
"No, it's definitely for the radiator, see the pipe leads into the front there.". Expert mechanics we were not.

We had, it seemed, been moving on fresh air for some sixty miles and hadn't even noticed. "Give Jo Cars a ring and ask if they filled the water before we left.." Myrthin's request made sense but as it was just silence and a blank digital display on the infernal mobile phone that I was holding, there was no real hope.

So, we gazed at the amazing sight of the empty water holder, both realizing that we may well have just escaped a severe inferno on the blessed M6.
"Let's go and get some water." He was looking quite as shocked as I'd ever seen him but determined too in a frazzled kind of way.

We quickly left Norm tipping it's bonnet to the sky in an attempt to cool down the situation and headed back to the infernal shopping center that was becoming far more than a "Welcome Break". More like purgatory.

"Let's get a big bottle of Evian." Says Myrthin whilst standing in a shop surrounded by plastic bottles, "Give Norm a treat.". Evian is expensive mineral water with carbon dioxide, the idea was so ludicrous that we burst into immediate giggles.
It was a classic twist to happily pour French spring water deep into the recesses of a collapsing motor engine, as visionary as it gets. There was a Lourdes for cars after all.

"But do you reckon, it's ok?".

I wasn't a hundred percent sure.

"Man, it's only water, it must be all right.".

He coughs pinging with confidence.

I was somehow more doubtful but only because in the giggles the phone in my hand had gone pinging onto the floor.

Whilst carefully dusting off the mobile and still sniggering at the monstrous plan I quickly see that we may after all just about to survive this first super test. Zap, we each grab a bottle of French sparkling water and head towards the cash desk triumphant in our wisdom.

Now the plan was to pour the holy water into the gaping hole in our friend then fill up the bottles from the nearby toilets. So after paying a thin young guy we were back out into the late afternoon, ready to spoil the car on the best drink ever guzzled. My bottle went in first, the whole litter bubbled and vanished without a trace. William's duly followed with exactly the same outcome, the water level rose not a millimeter. Anxiously we checked the floor for a leaking burst of liquid but joy oh joy there was none. The two liters were gone, thirstily lapped up.

On the engine's water container we eyed two marker lines carefully marked out. One, the higher line read "FULL", the other, the lower line read more ominously "EMPTY". It seemed almost unbelievable but the two liters we'd just dispatched had left the level still somewhere deep in the pipes and at least a full three inches below the danger point. It was if you will, less than empty!!!! Incredible!!!!

We'd been driving at eighty miles per hour a whole two liters and a further pack of inches below the absolute minimum level of water required to make Norm tick.

Gulp.

No wonder. No wonder at all.

Finally, after several minutes we had the kettle filled. The cap was carefully screwed back as tight as our fingers would allow and it was time to see if life had returned to the poisoned engine.

Myrthin surprisingly decided he wanted to drive us all the way to Brighton.
"Give you a break man. My Grandmother used to have one of these you know. It'll be like old times." It was too good to refuse and a significant moment.
The idea of playing away the next two hundred miles safely in the passenger seat filled me with glee.

"Yeah cool. Are you sure though?".

"As sure as damn." Myrthin says in his element in the midst of the whole water episode.

So that was that. I'd finished for the day and all that was to take place between that moment and the English Channel was in the other Welshman's hands. One thing though remained well and truly under my command, my non-functioning cell phone. One I'd borrowed from a relative, yet had never thought of finding out how it worked. Yeah, life does throw up unlikely moments at times.

As I paced delicately back and forwards around the red vehicle, thoughts flew around like lazy eagles. Just what were we going to do should the Evian miracle not click the ignition into place? Just where would this evening lead us? I quickly acknowledged that thinking had never solved anything. It was already pre-destined anyhow. A smile etched it's way onto my burning face and suddenly there was the unusual sight of my partner in adventure sitting keyless at the steering wheel of the as yet impotent motor car.

In earlier times, years before we would often as a gang of adventurers head on up to mystic forests for evenings of fire and smoke. We would all take it in turns to drive on these almost nightly experiences and as he was the only one without a car of his own he would invariably borrow his grandmother's saloon.

Now it sure was strange to see the man back in position some nine years later. To see the man now back next to me at the wheel, us journeying alone together for the first time in at least eight years expanded the happy smile right across my face.
Of course, the car would start.

"Let's hit Brighton?" I suggested cheekily as I opened the passenger door to take up the relaxing position of guest.

"Give us the keys and we'll be away man."

I handed over the control of the trip to the man at my side.

Time stops, dramatic Hitchcock tension, edge of your seat. In slid the phallic scenario of key into slot and deep breathing reverberated around . Would the engine start or would it dud off into the sound of choking silence? Myrthin glanced over to me and turned the key.

The Merry Pranksters and their 1939 International Harvester school bus had been experts on the dangers of inappropriate road travel.

In 1964 they had set off into the wild unknown, a journey that was to take unplanned hold ups into an art form. They learnt how to take the inconvenient at face value, hey there is after all no rush, no great plan, merely an adventure.

During that trip, in a slow, shuddering vehicle that was intended for minor journeys to and from school, the Pranksters had been forced to face adversity with a smile. Countless times the bus would hit a mechanical question mark and out would leap Cassady, all high pitched and in a professional road voice would assess the damage.

"Let me see, let me see! Something not hitting the wheel to the gravel, or the gravel to the wheel, a steal, depending on which way is up or down. It is as hot as Antoinette could get. We need to look and not lose our heads, calm I say. Lift up the hood and look. Steam pouring out of the steam, see what I mean. You have to look. Interesting combination!"

Then there would be a wait at the side of the road until, well until something took them on, further.
The lost instant bounced back in the surging power of an engine firing into life.

In 1999 we waited and then, "YAAAAAAAAAAGH!!!!" we both exalted.

The Evian had worked, and the lifeless collection of cogs was once more a functioning unit. Smiles the size of California pierced the windscreen.
"Kesey watch out, here we come."

It was a holy miracle and soon the gears were connected and we rolled backwards to continue the holy journey.

I've never seen a happier version of my dear friend, magician and ally. Now all that could hold us back was a return to rising away from the 'Norm' which we both knew would not happen., as once you've left the norm, it is impossible to find your way back.

Actually we now felt so confident that we suspected that nothing could stop us and down the slip lane we moved as I fished around in the bag of tricks for the next tape of music and came up with one. The sight of freely moving traffic back on the highway was the final proof. Old Norm glided into the stream and was soon drifting along in top gear.

Myrthin hailed me over. "Look at this. Look!" The temperature gauge was well and truly stuck in the zone marked blue, the cold zone. I decided to get back to work on the mobile phone.
Immediately and I promise it is no lie, the digital display exploded in a row of options that had never previously existed.

"MAN!! The phone, it's working."

It felt like some kind of exorcism and a step forward.
As the Super Furry Animals blasted forth on the stereo, we left what had truly been a "Welcome Break.".

Just down the road lay Brighton and the Merry Pranksters. And shadows slowly began to lengthen on that track, as afternoon slowly fell towards evening, our worries lay eased, in front of us a plainly normal temperature.

The devilish needle sat safely at mid point on the dial, the water had obviously worked. The heat chaos had all been down to the jokers at Jo Cars, they had obviously not filled the car with water.

So there we were cruising at speed along the snail end of the motorway, just about to drive onto the next path on our journey, onto the M1. He was happy in his new guise and took great pleasure in constantly informing me of the remarkably well behaved temperature gauge.

We were now approaching the near two hundred miles mark and outside strange masts grew skywards, up

from the unbearable flatlands of middle England and as the Super Furry Animals reminded us, we were indeed 'Mountain People.'.
London was already in the air.
I've always believed that you can feel the presence of the huge metropolis from a long way away.

It seems to growl unseen on the horizon for miles.
We were over two hundred miles into the journey and running like never before. It was as if the old boy had shaken off a hundred timid safe weekend specials to finally return in full spirit. I was certain that our chariot had been one of those abused company cars that get constantly raged around the country in search of deals.

It was somehow I felt, for this intrepid trip that our Norm had been welded together over ten years earlier, I was almost sure of it. This could quite possibly be the trip of the car's lifetime, this thousand-mile drift around the veins and arteries of Britain's transport network. This could quite possibly be the car's last ever trip, I mean age wasn't on his side and there was neglect in his mileage.

He would never make it through another year, and if his value then was a mere fifty pound a week, then in a year he would be valueless and on the way to the junkyard, heaven or hell.

 See the metaphor. See the Merry Pranksters, out on only their second ever truly major Bus trip, two in thirty five years, see their ages, see the point. The Merry Pranksters were approaching old age gracelessly, but time waits for no man and just as Norm was relishing this last trip, so too were Kesey and the Pranksters. That it turned out to be Kesey's last expedition, none of us could have known. The man looked as strong as an ox and in full eager health, but somehow there was that awareness of time and the pressure of a ticking clock.

Outside, signs for the M25 began to emerge from the embankments.

It was approaching six o'clock. Six o'clock, a time when all over the island, good people were returning from a hard day's work at a million different workplaces, eager to dive into Thursday evening. A time when traditions deemed it right that kettles across the land would be bubbling to the tune of the evening news and knives and forks would be carefully positioned aside an empty space.

I lit a cigarette in acknowledgement of our making it this far. It was a pleasant change to pull on the insanely harmless buzz of a government backed narcotic. I often forgot that I smoked cigarettes and in a weird kind of way was always pleasantly surprised to remember that particular vice.

So "safe" smoke to the wind and here comes the M25. I recalled once reading about the mad types who saw fit to try and lay the fastest time for a complete lap of the motorway. To be the fastest. To spiral around the nation's capital at great velocity must be one rather large high. A game of huge risk except that one would be quicker around the circular monster on a scooter. For the M25 was yet another of Britain's ludicrously overburdened highways.
"You need Heathrow man." I announced with that classic air of wisdom
borne out of ignorance.

An hour later it was quite the most joyous of experiences to be rattling at speed along the almost deserted road, deep in the heart of Sussex. The M25 had given us little cause for concern and approaching half past seven it was us a mere twenty miles away from the shingle and the tide. Myrthin was still at the wheel and me still deep in the passenger seat watching dusk envelope the rolling green landscape. Under a slow unfurling blanket that the sun enhanced, we were well into evening and approaching the wild time called darkness.

Now the first night's living quarters were still unspecified but that was something we'd sort out in due time. For the moment it was just a lilting eighty miles per hour romp through the three hundred miles boundary with the radio in vogue.

Brighton was a place I'd heard much about but had only once visited and even then, had not stopped. My brother and I were on our way to a midnight ferry leaving from nearby Newhaven.

Brighton was closing in and the end I realized was now a matter of miles away. The Merry Pranksters were already aboard an airliner circumnavigating this wonderful old globe of ours. Sparks was busy doing his DJ thing at some wedding in Northern Austria, no doubt with a head full of passionate expectation and a room full of revelry.

We'd finished the last spliff a good three quarters of an hour ago, and though washed out under the combined influence of smoking our way through two countries and numerous counties, it was a clear head that was on my shoulders. We'd been six hours on the road and the prospect of standing tall was a fascinating one.

"Myrthin man.". My voice cracked the silent atmosphere in two. "We're nearly there. Nearly home." He smiled though failed to speak. It was still the journey to him, as he was the driver and only then when the wheels would come to a stop would his eyes refocus. Soon afterwards we were into the outskirts of this South Coast city, Brighton, our temporary oasis.

You could see darkened lawns that stretched away from large, detached houses. You could see where windows glowed with warm light peeking through illuminating the branches of carefully pruned bushes and trees.

The signposts standing guard at the roadside diverged messages of places unknown to either of us, yet there was suddenly one destination that trapped us, the sea front.

It was to the ocean we were heading.
Now as things got together more coherently than at any other time so far that wayward day, something grew in my mind as a reason to panic. It was one of those dangerous thoughts that chip away at your good sense yet are so illogical it becomes impossible to voice your fear.

My worry was that the man to my side was so into his motorway mindset, that even though we were now plainly in an urban zone of traffic restriction, it was at high speed we were traveling through and beyond. We must have been flying at over seventy miles per hour and in my head a jagged sense stabbed at my left brain.

"Tell him to slow down. Slow. Slow. Slow."

I could visualize a traffic light, or a cat, or a push chair, or worst of all a sharp bend that would send us spinning into some late night casualty ward. But I realized that there was no point in airing any of these feelings for the road fried man at the wheel had not driven this far to foul up.

He was so close to our checkered flag that he could smell the champagne. So no matter what tickled away at my fizzing brain it was silence that was to remain and it was back to the grace of god. It was back to taking in the flashing traces of folk on pavements that were there, then gone, then there, then gone again. I mentally gripped the dash board and wished I'd sneaked my safety belt on at some point much earlier in the journey.

As big a friend as Norm was becoming, all of god's creatures need their space and being cramped knees to chin, balanced on the pedals for six hours is as close as you should get to anyone. Norm felt the same, you could sense it in the rattling hum that rose from the engine. He too was in desperate need of letting his hair down, a night on the town as such.
"The seafront, straight on!" I yelled not knowing for sure if the boy to my right had seen the tiny sign growing out of a hedge.

"Just straight on for another two miles man. Keep on going straight."

Somehow it was all the driver needed, he eased off the accelerator. A mere comforting word of encouragement and assurance had ensured him that there was an end to his tense two hundred mile runway.

See, it was possible now to feel the sea and taste the end of his driving duties for in brutal reality these were to be the last two handsome, crucial, righteous miles of his total shift at the wheel. Well if you discount a later spin around a camp site in Taunton which nearly killed three innocent passers by.

No these were his final miles on the driving side of the

road trip and freedom was close at hand. Now the fact that buildings had well and truly taken control other doubts began to nibble away at my consciousness. It now seemed optimistic in the extreme that the likelihood of a camping site should rise from somewhere in the midst of this urban settlement.

I'd been too busy drifting away on the idealistic seaside scenario. I hadn't allowed enough reality to seep through and I had failed to realize that in fact Brighton was a city and that not too many cities have tenting facilities close to the main strip. The action we were searching for defied the concept of camping for it was urban action that we demanded of the night. Huge, circus trapeze, neon lit kind of action. Countryside bingo would not be sufficient!!!!

Somehow a hotel had always seemed likely but realistically we had to keep within our budget, we needed a limitation on our spending in some way or other.

Myrthin had earlier mentioned either sleeping in old Norm or staying up all night as possibilities to which I had scoffed due to the level of responsibility my age brings.
As the soon to be arriving Sparks of Australia had once so wisely said,

"A bed is in fact the least we deserve for polishing the hours until dawn.."

So, a bed would be ideal if only for the feeling of vaguely tangible affluence it allows a thirty year old teacher by trade. It is of little relevance to divulge at this stage that my sleep for the night eventually totaled a whacking great big zero hours, nil minutes and less than a second. At that specific point it was simply the security of perceived financial ability that was the golden key.

"Just carry on straight!." I urge. "The seafront is only a mile away."

It was necessary to appease my partner in crime who'd taken to squinting out at each and every signpost planted by the obviously diligent local council. Jesus, there were dozens of signs. They had signs for swimming pools, churches, car parks and even one for a 'Norwegian Fishermen's lodge', I kid you not.

"Not right or left, just keep on going."

Whether he knew why it was to the sea-front we were going, I know not.

On my behalf it was just an instinctive impulse to see the ocean, to prove that there was no further to go and that we'd reached the edge.

I had noticed that the bigger vehicles were playing close attention to our minor progress and soon buses vied for position with taxis in pulsating packs.

They travelled in a shimmering glow pasted as reflections against the now huge storefront windows and an ever larger numbers of revelers. It was getting obvious that we were way downtown and approaching where the seagulls flew. I thanked a relevant god that it was only with a moderate pace that we were now involved in, for there were few hiding places in this new spinning world.

Eventually a traffic light stopped us solid in our tracks, a red light. Myrthin leant back in his seat and tried to stretch his arms to the heavens only to be stopped by the soft padded ceiling inches above his head.

"Nearly there now, nearly there." I said encouraging the weary traveller.

"Thank god!" Says a bored, tired Welshman.

Though if either of us would have cared to stop to think about the specific nature of the "where" we were coming up to, we may have taken little or no solace in our situation. Luckily though we had already been spellbound by the journey and trusted the old magic of fairness implicitly.

Red turned to green and on we moved. Signposts became immediately obsolete for at the end of this latest street there were no further buildings, no dark shapes splattered with squared eruptions of light. No there was only a dark, star shot sky ahead of us, a dark star shot sky and the sea.

We had travelled over three hundred miles to witness this sight. It was a vision to behold and it was supreme to know that we'd beaten the road into ultimate submission. The knowledge of which immediately filled the car with light colored relief.

The 'sea is my brother', Jack Kerouac had once written and I suddenly knew what he had meant.

 A true Celtic journey had been undertaken and we were once more close to the waves.

There was a sense of overwhelming achievement against all odds. Rolling the last hundred yards to where a junction offered only left or right options, each bordered by the hissing brilliance of the rolling tide was to arrive at destination zero, the real starting point of our journey. We the two explorers turned to smile at each other and a sense of victorious euphoria enveloped the three of us. I suspect that Norm knew it too.

Norm knew it too, I figured that he'd really never seen Brighton before.

Some kindly old king in the traffic headquarters then allowed us a red light at the very top of the road. It was a gift. It gave us time to revel in the moment of arrival. There was little else to do other than hug each other wildly and fight back the tears in our eyes. Somehow the three most unlikely journeymen had traversed the country in search of wisdom and made it.
It was time to find our feet!!!!!!!!!!!!!!

THE EDINBURGH HOTEL IN BRIGHTON.

"**R**ocket, Rocket U.S.A."
Pale and proud, and only a decade earlier the scene of a bomb under the evil Queen Margaret of the Falklands' bed of nails.
It was Brighton's Grand Hotel.

Iridescent in its floodlit majesty, all curving pillars and pouting balconies behind which rooms lie naked and alive with light. A light that merely leaks opulently out through slashed gaps in velvet curtains.

Light escaping from within the golden palace. It was in fact beautiful in its elegance yet no, under no circumstance was this to be our specific tent for the night, no matter how appealing the whole idea seemed. Later though we did try successfully in a highly zoomed amphetamine frenzy to purchase a drink at one of the hotel's luxurious lounges. We even managed to get comfortable in their softest of seats before two burly professionals ended that specific jape with well meaning smiles.

They fully understood our cavalier intentions and were ultimately only doing their job after all. You and me, him and her out! Out now!

But that's a leap forward, a leap in time to a later place long after we'd well and truly laid roots in old Brighton town.

One of the things as we drove along the promenade road towards an area called Hove was trying to persuade Myrthin into the urgency of finding a room. He was not seemingly willing to empty out the wallet in big dollars for a bed for an hour, neither was I, but Christ even mad Merry Prankster investigators have to sleep somewhere.

It was becoming increasingly obvious that no camping site would save us from filling out a hotel registration form. My hopes had begun to lay with some crazy, beat Y.M.C.A hostel possibility, but none reared its ugly head, so along the promenade we rode. Norm all jittery and eager to turn in and Myrthin in the thirteenth throe of thigh cramp, and all of us absolutely desperate for relief of some kind.

"There's one over there!" I shout. "The Gala. See it? Looks pretty cheap.". I enthuse.

Then, "Look over there, The Edinburgh Hotel. It looks really run down." Me with more hopeful enthusing.
Now, Brighton is an affluent neighborhood and we were probably only half a mile from being smack bang in the town center, so 'really run down' it may well have looked but I was fooling no-one but the seagulls that wove spirals above the moon.

These places were going to cost us a hundred dollars, no question.

"Let's give it a shot. It can't do any harm." I said ready to break the bank as long as the journey finally wound to a stop.

He flinched but, in the end, though it was the guru Norm that finally took control. He simply decided to stall and roll us quietly without so much as an engine noise into the fringes of a 'Taxi Only' zone.
"Enough is enough you fools, I am ready for bed.". Is what the car might have said.
His ignition refused to respond so that was that, we were finished for the day.
The end of our journey was parked at an indiscreet angle in a forbidden spot, and it was just how it always should have ended. After a second's subdued confusion out we sprang just 'oh so happy' to be using our legs once more.

Myrthin did a feline stretch to the skies and sucked in on the salty air, warm gusts came breezing up gently from the shore some fifty yards to our left.

"Damn it!" I curse. "We'll leave the car here."

I was having no more.

"Shit, any fines will be sent to Jo Cars anyhow.". I stated optimistically.

"Let's go and check out The Edinburgh, it's got to be worth a shot?".

Norm had already slipped into dreams of a thousand

journeys.

He shrugged his shoulders so off we went. The man was a war veteran returning home with too many vivid "Road" memories to be worrying about banalities. Inside I knew our own four walls were imperative for the well being of mankind in general and specifically us.

We both shot across the almost empty wide lanes of road talking gibberish about the journey, each of us lost in different aspects of life behind the wheel.

"Nesscliffe man. Then the end of civilization. Then five hours in the presence of mania.".

"Yeah, but the M25 was the worst. Good god those lunatics in their vans, trucks and cars doing a daily torture trip. Having to keep the throttle revving just in case it cuts out, it's all insane.".

Reminiscences of the road exploded around us as we walked powerfully up a flight of stone steps towards where a dimly lit buzzer was supposed to allow us entry to the 'Edinburgh hotel'.

I recall hoping beyond hope for some cute special deal to save our spending for as sure as eggs are ominous, there was no way we'd get the chance to run on a flyer from this place without paying cash up front.

I pressed on the magic button and in an instant a friendly face appeared at the other side of a semi frosted pane of glass. The man was in his fifties, the picture of control, with carefully combed gray hair running short to his ears. Ears which jauntily housed the straight lines of his spectacles. Four dark eyes glowered suspiciously out at us the bedraggled highly "motor weary" wild men. Amazingly he let us in.

"Evening??" I asked. "We're looking for a room with two beds for one night.."

He led us through to where the reception desk hovered in a mild citric light. Even the carpet beneath our feet felt unusual and watching it run in soothing, lilac flower patterns upstairs to the rooms!!! The possibilities had me transfixed.

"Yes, we do have a double room vacant."

My head leapt at the information.

"It's forty pounds per person per night."

Myrthin gripped onto the desk as defense against the shock. Forty pounds, good god!!! It was almost the same amount that we'd paid for Norm. But that was for seven days, and between the two of us the hotel was thirty pounds more expensive. My head spun as it looked for a hook of comparison.

"It is that the kind of going rate around these parts?" I stammered desperately trying to find a valuable perspective, "Does that include breakfast and a television?"

"Certainly sir, breakfast is from seven until eight thirty and each room has a television. En suite bathroom too and a view of the sea."

I couldn't decide whether the guy was deliberately confusing me. He could undoubtedly see the shock in my eyes and I worried that he was probably taking the bluff as far as he could.

It struck me that not the view, breakfast or even the television would be of much use to us once the evening's "speed" slid down our senses but still!!

"You can't do it for thirty five a piece can you?". My man from Wales queries through clenched teeth as his fingernails gripped deeper into the oak desk top.

"Sorry sir, I'm only the manager and our prices are fixed."

I turned whispering to the pale roadster at my side.

"What do you think? There's not going to be anywhere cheaper."

For a moment the silence was deafening. There was a pause in time, a choice to be made.

The air hung heavy with our brain waves on full swing. I twitched, the old guy coughed and suddenly two old ladies emerged from the carpet to bid us all a "Good night.."
In an instant he went for his wallet as a gunfighter goes for his pistol. Instinctively I went for mine. Billy the kid and Jesse James had found a room for a night, but only because the ghosts had spooked us into action.
"Okay we'll take it. One night only." My voice almost choked on the implications and I expected him to faint but somehow a sickly grin began to stretch across his features.

We bustled into busy action filling out forms with false names and addresses. I fished out the huge wallet I had with me containing my funds for a four week stay in Britain and dealt out two crisp twenty pound notes. I felt sad to see them go. Myrthin extracted the same amount from some hidden recess and that was that we were proud owners of a box room for an evening.

Brighton was to be 'it' for the next day and a half so we had no need for movement beyond a gentle local skip to and from. We crawled smiling past the latest ghosts, a pair of middle aged men looking at a map on a wall.

"Lovely out there tonight." Myrthin says on his forever polite weather trip and some minutes later we had flopped onto two separate beds and were horizontal for the first time in close on three hundred and fifty miles! But not for long though!

Oh no! We were soon to unleash the powerful amphetamine that we were carrying, enough to speed up an elephant. Sometimes it is the only way one can survive. An hour later we were in a bar listening to a Country and Western band leaving for Abilene. There we were talking, chewing, drinking and fighting the rising shivers up the spine that the "Speed" monster was sending us. Enthusiastic about everything to the point that sitting still was impossible and twitching became the game.

Twitch the toes, then flex the ankles, then tap to the music which is only music we ourselves interpret to be the music of Hank Williamson and his Red Rodgers.

Our version was twice as fast and a sound like an airplane.

"It"s just that it's not like any other job." I say excitedly about suddenly realizing I'm a teacher and that the summer holidays are in their infancy.

"It's a privilege to hang out with the kids. You know they're always there, always up for it. Always brilliant, brilliant,

brilliant."

Then whoosh, we are out on the streets moving like the wind. So powerful so untouchable.

"Listen to the sea man. Wow. It's just amazing."
It was so hard not to sprint down to the shore just for a closer look and listen.

"You ever heard about the seventh wave? You know the one that is always bigger than the six before it. Then crash just washes up and along come six more. But why seven man, that's what I've never understood. I mean it is a mystical kind of number isn't it. The seven dwarves.
Lucky number seven.
The Magnificent seven.
Seven colors in a rainbow.
Crazy huh."

"Yeah, but twenty-three is also a weird one." He answers laconically.

"I know, I know. Twenty-three. Man, that's Wilson's thing in the Cosmic Trigger right. Christ maybe there's a twenty third wave that outdoes all the sevens before it. And imagine Snow White and the Twenty-three dwarves. They'd still only need a normal sized house man."

I burst into giggles at the idea. "Twenty-three dwarves!"

"They would need one huge car though.". Replies the sniggering man.

"Or a bus!"

Our strides leapt us through the dark empty streets

towards where we knew of clubs. We were going dancing. In the distance, about a mile away a glow of colored lights blinked off the ocean in gentle explosions. Club land where these wonderful legs of mine would be able to loop, bend, stomp, all night long. Club land where thousands of wonderful beings would cast spirits to the air and weave spells in dark corners.

It was the perfect antidote for the road trip, mindless movement was the way to ease away the creases.
"I haven't danced for a long time." I said imitating Muhammad Ali. "I'm going to dance, I'm going to dance.." The monster "Speed" had us running rings around the George Foreman of Brighton's streets and before we could deliver the knockout punch, another drink.

"Let's go for a quick one in The Grand Hotel.". We suggest putting a further touch of the unusual into the evening.

It was a fine idea so we sped our way right up to the entrance of one of Britain's noblest hotels. Somehow, we were very thirsty for adventure and beer.

We the two kings of the lonesome road strode confidently up towards the lavish golden entrance. It looked like one of those doors that always trickle into a dangerous furnace of some kind. We both knew that there was no reason to be pestering the goodly folk at the bar of the Grand Hotel.

No reason other than the urgent need for a drink and a total disrespect for Britain's awful class system.

 We knew we were not upper-class people, but we knew we were high, very high.

High enough that he and I breezed past the door man

dressed up as a penguin without so much as a glance over our shoulders!
You've got to look confident in these places, Christ the first show of fear and boy those old walls would be tumbling down before you'd even had a chance to smile.

We strode in like politicians. Into the eye of a hurricane as we moved across the carpet that was so deep that we felt like we were sinking or as if the texture was jumping up to grab us by our necks. Grab us by our necks and pull us under like crocodiles do. I looked down to check for large reptiles and saw my feet disappear in a purple jungle.

The atmosphere all around us was one of sweet smelling affluence, a perfumed stench of overt wealth. We didn't belong in there but there was not so much as a slight muscle movement of resistance from anyone.

Not from the small group of well dressed old Lords and Ladies. Not from the desk clerks. Not from the restaurant staff. Myrthin and I snuggled up against each other in an attempt to stay inconspicuous. Us, we could have chosen to have walked inside anywhere it seemed.
"It is important to keep your eyes on the ceiling!". I whispered to the man at my side. "We don't want to risk being taken by surprise."

Bounce, bounce, bounce! We knew this place was ours for a short slice of time only, one beer if we were quick. The trappings of wealth would undoubtedly eventually rise up to meet us as a Titanic proportioned beast. We would be tossed to the wolves, once they realized we were inside the building.

"We have to be quick, very quick!". I said secretively.

Me soaring on the monster speed with a cigarette glued to my lips and my hair pinned back in a tight respectable ponytail.

Myrthin there floating up in one of his psychedelic shirts with his hair flopping in the purified air. It didn't take long to feel the intense weight of the pressure building up around us. There were people with weapons just waiting for the likes of us. Why though?

We were not dangerous, merely psychedelic terrorists with a leaning for fun! On our way to hook up with Ken Kesey. We were harmless! There were probably other things going on in that doomed hotel that night that would make even George Bush blush. I imagined that behind some of the closed doors there were innocents dying, huge money changing hands and quite probably sex games the likes of which would embarrass Clinton too! Goldfish were probably swimming to their death along tunnels made of razor blades. Whilst rabid, rent dogs, dragged off the streets of Brighton probably lolled helplessly and nibbled Sir Balkam's ears until morning came.

We were surrounded by extremes zoned out in only the way the untouchably rich could fathom. We however, were mere innocents in the midst of this hundred room millionaire's paradise. Our madness revolved around taking a peek at the ways of the moneyed eyes whilst securing a beer. No more no less. So with legs that sizzled, we moved into some opulent bar. In we went through swinging heavy doors that made not a sound as they swooned our way into the luxurious velvet lounge.

I became aware of tepid piped music filtering through the scene, a type of string quartet lilt one would associate with Nineteen Thirties ocean liners.

It was hard if not impossible to avoid my amphetamine induced swinging baboon dance as we walked through the softest looking furniture in the Western world. This bar was not especially exciting. Only a couple of tables were occupied. I could see a couple of painted mouths deep in conversation. I could see a whole table of monsters with bow ties.

"Look!" I say quietly. "Look at the walruses!"
Above us the walruses were huge chandeliers hanging like crystal fruit from a cream colored ceiling.

"There's a table over there." Says Myrthin pointing to a far corner of relative safety.

"Fine. You get the drinks I'll save the space.". I say almost breathlessly. "A suitable energy site which we could call home."

He left with his cigarette ash tumbling towards the carpet and I grimaced as I leapt up two steps that led to a raised platform.

It seemed perfect insanity to be hopping between the tables, but in my drift towards the corner lounge suite, I'd forgotten where I was.

Only a pair of bloodshot eyes followed my progress, eyes which then looked over to Myrthin, and then around to the large doors. I'm sure the rich and not too beautiful folk of the Grand Hotel were worried, concerned that we were in fact the scouting troop of a larger scraggly band of undesirables. It was possible to taste the growing unease amongst these desperate patrons.

But what was this fear that they were swinging around their head? It frightened me not as I sat down in the warm womb of an easy chair. I immediately felt uncomfortable. The whole sitting concept was too soft, there were not enough edges!! It was too rigid so I pushed my weight forward and sat with my twitching knees finding unholy rhythm in the gentle music no one else could hear.

Speed, speed, speed! I dipped my finger carefully into my pocket just to check I hadn't lost my drive. I could see him over at the bar in animated conversation of some kind, no big deal, the man was always animated. The smartly dressed bar-tender's bald palette gleamed in the powerful light. I noticed some olden people barely alive on an adjacent table. They seemed to be taking an unhealthy interest in my welfare, unhealthy in as much as I was only sitting and merrily twitching.

"Good evening! Lovely place. Lovely." I would like to have said to these inquisitive patrons. I was surrounded by silence but soon even that got quieter. The two rich old folks stopped their staring, which was a shame because I would have quite happily shared a minute or two with the unholy twosome. The man looked like an ill William Burroughs clone and his female companion looked uncannily like Klaus Kinski. I fell in love with both of them immediately.

Love though was lost before it had had the chance to blossom for look out here comes Myrthin with two foaming beers.

"Cost over seven pounds man." He says loudly as he slides past the two shadows on the adjacent table. "But!" He said secretively and with a wicked grin across his pale features, "It's great huh, like a scene from the Godfather.".

The fun lasted only approximately three minutes for suddenly above us were sets of strange eyes, glowering down from the ceiling. It was three heavy guys, and they didn't seem to be too impressed with our free form of expression.

"I'm afraid you're going to have to leave." The voice said in a professional tone that made it obvious that trying to argue our case would be a complete waste of time.

"Fine." I replied, happy to be on the move again. "We are just about finished anyhow!" The security dudes seemed impatient yet far from mean minded, they even let us finish off the beers as we rose rocket-like to our feet.

Myrthin to my side found it all very amusing and kept reassuring our escorts.

"We mean no harm, we're only here to investigate the Merry Pranksters. We've driven all the way down from Wales for the show."

The two guys showed absolutely no interest in my friend's information and soon we were walking out.
"Hey do you know any good clubs around here?" We ask defiantly. "We're looking to dance our legs off.".
The security guys loosened a little then told us quickly of a range of excellent venues that lay on the sea front. They were seemingly anxious to move the 'weird load', us, out of their hair and get back to other less precarious scenarios.

"Try the Roxy on the sea front. It's a good 'House' night on Thursdays."

Now an expert I was not. I'd long since lost track of the

splintering fractions of the dying on it's feet rave scene, but house sounded fine.

"If the Roxy is anywhere near as good as its Prague namesake then 'house' it should be." I said illogically.

"See what you think fellas!". Said one of the security guys as we moved away from the hotel's entrance.

We wished the three reasonable security types a pleasant evening then burst out into the night.
It was time for a further dab of the monster speed, so I fished around in my pockets and retrieved an untouched gram.

In front of where Margaret Thatcher was blown out of her bed we both dipped into the crystal lucky dip and shivered at the bitter taste of power. I quickly followed up with a cigarette to kill off the atrocious swallow and in an instant we were bursting across the highway towards where the beach called us forward. It was almost pitch black on the promenade but the beach was lit up with fires and groups of party-goers toasting the ocean with potions unclear from our distance.

Free and high, we blinked at the sea, and saw a rippled reflection on the dark ocean which soon let us catch up with a gang of fellows. Myrthin was never slow at moving forwards.

"Hi, how ya doing?" He says to the dark shapes in front of us, and three men, and three women turn to face us. In Austria no-one speaks to strangers on the street so in my confusion I held back and let the man do the talking.

"Do you know of any good clubs around here?"

The gang of six immediately began listing names of valuable places interspersed with good humored questions of our origin.

Me though, I was suddenly trapped. A shiver had shot down my spine the shape of a barbed wire fence. One of the faces in the darkness was the face of an American that had captured my soul a couple of years earlier.

Billie Parker, it couldn't be. But it was, it was her, but it wasn't. Absolutely identical. I didn't know what was going on. Omens and such stuff play a big role in my time, and this was a big one.
Billie Parker with her killer smile, her doped out eyes and kooky view of the world.

Billie Parker one of the weirdest persons I'd ever met and maybe would ever meet. She'd appeared out of some bushes one May the First and changed the world forever. She was the most complicated human being of all time, she was the biggest blocked dimension ever. Here's what she once wrote me.

"Einstein's unfinished revolutionary thought implies, refines, decreases and clarifies through its most confusing reality that motion is relative. We tell a body is moving through comparison by comparing its position with or against the position of others. Although through electrodynamics(value for the speed of light) relative motion is contradictory."

"Einstein's theories prove to be undeniable and contradictory. If motion is relative then a pulse of light should have speed that varies relative to the motion of the observer, having then no constant speed. The only way to effect reconciliation is to give up something assumed since the beginning of science, universality of time and space, the only way two observers can see the same pulse of light moving at the same speed relative to themselves.."

I'd last seen Billie a year before, she was stoned on the hash I'd brought with me, and I'd refused to go home with her and left her sitting on a bus, looking bedraggled at five in the morning. The next day I was leaving for an intrepid trip to Berlin. A year later she was married, three years later so was I.

Billie should you ever read this, I once loved you and sincerely hope that your pulse of light is brighter than ever, and it was scary to meet someone so hugely confusing. You end up fearing for the curve and end up acting like kids in a zoo.

So, as we walked speeding along the promenade, me staring blindly at this Billie replica thinking of the original and wondering and thinking and falling in love once more with the picture in my mind. It was almost imperative that I keep away from this person. I let Myrthin talk and I just goof out looking for the non existent halo above this latest vision's beautiful head.

"If there's something inside you want to say, say it out loud it'll be okay. I will be all right, I will be all right. I will be all right . I will be all right." The Beta Band 1998.

I hadn't told Billie anything I really knew and expected her to get it anyhow.

As I walked I realized that I sometimes put this huge expectation of the sub-conscious on the people I love and sometimes it works and well, sometimes it doesn't. Maybe the Beta Band had it right, or maybe the fear of losing prevents one from fully stating the truth. Truth, whatever that might be at any specific time in history. Castaneda's writings had led me safely away from Billie Parker and somehow it had even made sense at the time.

If it is wrong.

Castaneda had warned of a danger, and it had confirmed my suspicions. Billie could have captured me for the whole of this plane called life and I'd always instinctively felt that there was more to dig for in this gold-mine called existence than weirdness from all angles.

Though she still did travel with me daily through the whole of three years and Ken Kesey was to lay it all out in black and white a mere week later.

Remember Billie!

Remember the chess game, remember that chess game!

For one afternoon you were moving the queen and I was moving the king.

A NIGHT SO ALIVE.

A thousand light bulbs exploding in rainbows had me aghast in the corner. The Billie Parker look-alike crowd had led us into the Roxy and had left for another place, I was hugely relieved.

It had all been too surreal just looking and seeing her image so clearly before my eyes. So the music soon took me to the place where good music can and it was a joy to have legs that felt like flexible steel. I soon got to my position and within in seconds I was off, dancing to truly great music, feeling like sixteen and totally aware of the bounding nature in my spring like ankles.

Myrthin was quickly gone on a round of the club. I would catch glimpses of him over the next five hours, always smiling, always communing in his own style then as if linked by an unseen bond, a bang as he disappears into some alcove or hidden recess.

I felt ecstatic just spinning on my thing, smiling at strangers who would smile back at the great unspoken, we are here together for this night in our lives and this night only.
See the beautiful girl in dread-lock heaven as her hair leaves traces in the powder blue light that only comes on when the sneaky keyboard-line jumps beyond the bass. Or

see the beautiful guy, shirtless, pumping to the sky in a red shadow as the bass takes over once more.

The boom, the heartbeat alive against the thin treble of a brain-wave tune. Smiling, a community. The latest generation hammering the hidden ceiling under the intoxicating rhythm of tribal confusion. See the beautiful, sixteen-year-old, shaved head, dangerous dude as he pulsates in an iridescent orange, then hands me water when I fear I need to drink.

No words, no words, just communication, just me dancing with eyes shut, just lost in the absolute power of the music, as the god speed sends shivers down from the top of my head to the tips of my toes. Remembering other such times and realizing why amphetamine could be a god and how god shouldn't be a weekly item. Then thinking that no sleep will be hitting my forehead this evening. There were big thoughts in that shapely, small corner. Big times in the fizz of the show.

Big movements from the open fingers of my hands, open out, open out.

Expression takes on many forms, but all make sense in the specific moment.

My senses were open to everything as behind a glass front some stranger ran amok with his digital magic. His music the electricity that plugged through the floor and pushed my limbs in inconceivable directions.

Then pulling on a cigarette and watching the smoke dance in a dozen shades before my very eyes. Then gratefully lapping up some god given water from yet another stranger on a waltz around the room handing out the Jesus vibe.

I quickly knew that alcohol had no place in such a religious setting, it was to be water from now on in, at least until breakfast.

Then smiling at the water carrier as only a mad speed freak can and wishing her the best of luck before back onto the stomp of another build up to a crescendo electronic crash-out. Then, out of the scattered colored raindrops here he comes with a bottle of lager in his hand smiling with no words or worries in the world before moving off on his unending communion. Then feeling warm and deciding to return to a Grand hotel vibe and stripping off the shirt that was damper than ever and feeling free of all hang ups as a smile from a nearby manic bodybuilder assures me that it's cool.

He ripples his muscles and I bend my twigs, but the body is beautiful, and the rules are self orientated. My sweat bubbled palm meets his flooded shoulder and we connect with a wink at sixty miles an hour and he is on his way and I'm still pumping.

Then a time with eyes closed once more when holy alone knows what images if any ride in the front reign of the cerebellum rear. Just sound as a guide and comfort as a carpet. No fear in here, no fear. No angry testosterone freak boys on the search of violence. Just fun and high summer and the pure joy.

Eyes open once more and a colored waterfall before my

rotating arms as the strobe swings and bends ten times the reds into greens.

It's a long way from the automotive beginnings of this enormous day but somehow all the same.

No dope for a good three hours, new chemicals were now in charge as I could feel the beer subside and the spiky amphetamine high rising up like a placid tornado. I dabbled into my pocket trying to be ever so discreet and topped off some more with the sharp tasting powder.
No sleep this evening I now know.

It would have to be the Merry Pranksters through sun-glassed blasted eyes, but Christ why not? These were no church wardens of the old faith, these were wizards of the chemical age. I expected that they expected no less of the expectant second generation.

And as I danced the speed down the throat it struck me just who we were coming into contact with. I did a dance for each of these strangers surrounding me.
Soon it was time to think of the ultimate speed-freak, the time. to think of Neal Cassady.

Now he was in no uncertain terms a lost legend. He'd been a muscle jerking king of the American Highway and his main unbelievable thing was to have been a central figure in both Kerouac's beat generation and Kesey's later beater generation.

As a child he'd travelled with his barber father across the depression torn cowboy cactus lands and had by his own account once been left on a freight train at the age of four with a gang of hobos as company. His father had disappeared for water at a random stop and missed the leaving train.

Now most four-year-olds are loath to even leave their push-chairs let alone be riding a train with wine drinking brothers of the forever hope.

Yet as the great man himself said later "It was like having an endless supply of caring uncles.". Sure a comfortable family home would have led to a smoother path but Neal Cassady was born to be the beacon to thirty years of adventuring and in his own way went further than the three hundred years earlier Columbus and his ship sailing dudes.

In the Sixties he'd become famous for his non-stop rapping, huge speed consumption and dancing with a hammer whilst hanging his bare-chest under a strobe.

A hammer I didn't have. The muscular build failed me as well but what the hell, I had the speed, now. the bare-chest and I had just travelled three hundred odd miles in a psychedelic Ford Escort.

 I blinked through my totally released wild. mane of hair and watched the sweat sparkle against the most appropriate strobe light I could find.

My arms pumped towards the sky beyond the ceiling, all the time fingers splayed open weaving patterns between my hair, eyes and the psychotic strobe. My legs felt stronger with each movement, it was just the greatest feeling to be driving into the early hours on a rocket to the moon.

More water soon arrived on the scene, another gulp from a passing stranger and a smile and the crystal features of another new friend disappears into the pulsing-colored

horizon. A shiver eels its way down my backbone and I think in raptures that already the whole trip has been worth while, no matter what. But Christ the day after the Merry Pranksters were due in town. It's early August. I have five weeks holiday left.
Myrthin is somewhere in the room blissfully enjoying the whole game as much as myself.

Ecstatic, speeding, dancing on an ice floor. A cigarette would just be perfect. But I can't stop dancing, no big deal, just waltz over to where my shirt lies crumbled in a pool of chemical blue. And a dabble of the potion just to keep on rising.

Within a time-spread I'm under a new light and bathed in yellow watching the dancing glow of the orange headed cigarette flies in traces before me. Spirals into spirals then round it off with a circle. I turned left then spun behind a light and returned to being a flying version of myself.

A twitch to the left and a jerk to the right on powerful legs. It was as a tide this music, just constantly washing over the rainbow on the dark background. The room was now a seething mass of dancing movement.

Hundreds on the freedom trip on a Thursday come Friday in the middle of summer. No tension, no hang ups just all out front. So far from the old days of horror disco trips when I would feel like a cardboard box as some trashy music squeaked out from tinny speakers the shape of flowerpots. Maybe we were actually in a new age. A new age without 'new agers', just a room full of gods for an evening and as 'now' is the thing, wow, what a 'thing'.

Suddenly out of an erupting volcanic eruption here comes Myrthin, beer in hand, mad grin across his chops, and eyes that start at his forehead to finish at his chin.

"Hell, man, it's amazing." I shout across the beautiful din.

"I've just got some grass from a guy over there." He hollers back pointing somewhere into the strobe.

I recall him rambling on about more cushions and keeping a big stock, I was unable to prevent wild movement in all my god-given limbs and soon he was gone. A shaggy apparition disappearing into a mass of skin. 'What a desperate hero of the modern age.' I remember thinking to myself.

So it was back once more to the beat and the surroundings and the modern age in one huge flash of energetic experience. Time was on hold for the god speed defied any aspect of tiring which on the whole was quite a majestic truth. Jesus I'd been on the go for a whole day and felt like a spring leaping lamb.

The feeling one gets at times such as these is that holy freak of weightlessness and not only the drug induced times but even beyond. To feel like a feather was something I'd always recognized was the feeling of greatness, when the spirit just flies and leaves gravity behind.

The latest vitamin powder was creasing my soul as yet another unknown classic rode through from the speaker above my head. And away and away and away went the sway. It was eyes closed once more and trip, trick and deftly move the limbs to the swaying rhythm.

Billie Parker was once more back in place as Mickey Mouse in the Disney world of brain-scope and it was just a blast to move, move, move.

The winner is clear, one needs as much space as one can possibly find at any given moment of time in any situation. My space in the corner was enormous, just as a dog can find a bone five hours entertainment so the joy in driving the feet to the floor whilst spearing the head into outer space. Neil Armstrong is not alone.

"If there's something inside that you want to say…………". Screams Myrthin.

"Lemonade and I went walking.". I shout back. "Another man down the path. He said it was 'Donk' the feast giver, whoa this can't last. Oh no, yes it can. It is luck. You know the feast was good."

Thirty minutes later it was us walking, walking against the first splash of color rising from somewhere behind the sea. The Roxy had thrown us through night with the ease that sleep can only dream of. We'd spent countless hours with me in my corner and my fellow explorer on his endless rounds of experience seeking and now it was approaching five o clock.

"Come on man. Let's go and have a spliff with the people." He says pointing to the beach as we move through the pebbles and sand.

"Christ let's get back and get ready for the morning." I answer with two eyes firmly on the imminent arrival of our mentors, morning and daylight.

"We'll have a couple of spliffs and relax in the hotel.".
It felt almost ridiculous to blast a severe amount of money on temporary accommodation and only return to pick up our bags.

He grudgingly agreed.

"Yeah but……..".

"Jesus' tomorrow." Was all I could squeeze out and that was it. Soon we were back on the solid ground of the wide as a football pitch promenade heading off between the seagulls through the deserted street of a twilight seaside resort.

Onwards and onwards we walked and I began to be convinced that we'd walked straight past our luxury lodgings, nothing looked at all familiar. Sure we had made the initial journey in darkness and in the first flash of an amphetamine snowstorm, but Christ, it all looked more like St. Petersburg than Brighton.

And I had never even been to Russia. For all I knew we could have slipped dimensions.

At least we kept on going and if I suddenly felt that the speed was wearing off then whoa, the next shivering buzz would quickly quash my theories.

It was beginning to look so desperate that even Myrthin was beginning to question our whereabouts.
"Are you sure it's up this way?". He asks staring blindly at a block of public toilets that clearly had him fascinated.

"Around here somewhere lies the Norm we only hours ago left behind.

Keep your eyes open and your wits about you!" Was the only sensible reply I could come up with.

We had eyes as dark as deep sea squids, though our legs numbered only four, in total.

Slowly an electric milk float crawled passed us rattling it's nutrition as it went. Almost as if to pass on a gentle rebuke from the world of corn flakes. Though it did somehow feel good that at least people were stirring, it was a perverse relief that the day was coming once more to join the night in busy action. I looked above our heads to where some people see the sky, it was obvious that the day would be a blue, blast, summertime special. I momentarily felt great again and forgot the walk completely.

The milk-cart disappeared on its trip and we were flanked either side by strangely familiar hotels that we had past eight hours earlier.

Suddenly there before us lay a twenty four hour garage stocked to the ceiling with a vital array of goods. We crossed the forecourt suspiciously, looking like the refugees that we were.

Strangely enough there was no direct admittance into the hallowed store room, there was only a small window through which you were supposed to place your order.

Order, my god, what order? I quickly thought of what I needed. Peanuts? Orange juice? Cigarettes? Chocolate? A thousand hapless products descended in one huge mesh of confusion.

Eventually we managed to secure a variety of pseudo vitamin-based drinks, cigarettes and an apple each. We were soon on our way back on the search for the elusive hotel.

My funny plastic bottle was called "Sunshine Delight" and tasted likes rusty nails. As a counterpoint I quickly reached for my freshly acquired Marlboro Lights and sparked a thin unhealthy plume of smoke into the sky. Myrthin, he was drinking Lucozade. This was a weird pretend health-drink that I remembered getting as a sickly seven-year-old child in the grip of a fever.

The boy to my side was using it to dowse his later somewhat more enjoyable man-made delirium.

So there we were armed with juice and finally approaching the Edinburgh Hotel. I had spotted the snoozing Norm just as my fellow traveller had spotted the hotel. It was pure relief for the walk was reaching the non amusing phase.

We yelped and hugged each other and bolted across the empty road at speed.

Now just who was carrying the hotel key I must admit I have no idea, but in an instant we were giggling our way through the empty reception area still remembering our arrival some serious hours earlier.

Everything was oppressively silent as all the other holiday makers had been in bed safely since long before even our Grand hotel debacle. Something inside me envied their peace. Then something inside me roared back approval for our amazing degree for illogical adventure. Like kids at church, we stifled our hysterics up the staircase and burst into room eleven. It was great to be home. The tiny clock radio on the cupboard glowed in an evil red and told us it was closing in on six.

It was at this point that the Ku Klux Klan took over.
One of us switched on the television in the corner and low and behold, there before our very eyes, was a documentary about the good old boys of the burning cross, the Ku Klux

Klan.

We were captured immediately by the insane slogan droning of some high-wizard of some lodge or other as he prepared his speech for a forthcoming anti-everything festival at his weekend. Both of us took to skinning up as soon as the foul freak on the screen commenced his awful rhetoric for the cameras.

This man, in his fifties, overweight and perspiring profusely had the look of a well fed sea lion in a three piece suit. He was clearly overjoyed to be the subject of the television program. It was somehow ironic that his Warhol fifteen minutes was destined for a screening at six in the morning to an audience of just Myrthin and I. We watched and were speechless.

I would have been even more embarrassed, had I realized what would then happen a mere six months later in my adopted home Austria, when their specific version of the white hoods, the blue suits, came into governmental power.

Back in 1999 though it was just a really strange feeling to be listening to the ignorance driven lunacy. This pompous prick with his negative head on full swing in his absolute prejudice was against everything apart from his wife, daughter, dog and three other pink skinned comrades. Something came to my mind that I'd read on a toilet wall in Vienna.

"When a white guy is embarrassed, he is red.
When a black guy is embarrassed he is black.
When a white guy is sick he is yellow.
When a black guy is sick he is black.
When a white guy has measles he is spotted.
When a black guy has measles he is black.
When a white guy is cold he is blue.

When a black guy is cold he is black.

And you have the cheek to call us colored!!!!!!!!!"

Mr. Lynch Mob was coming across as the nauseous color of dirty snow or pale vomit and somehow it suited.

The grass quickly hit me for six and soon I was stretched out fully clothed on the soft mattress pretending to be courting sleep. Behind my eyes a stream of images from an amphetamine cinema played at a curious version of thinking.

It was still being interrupted at regular intervals by the foul mouthed heathen and his racist tirade. It was getting lighter by the moment in the world beyond the curtains, probably approaching breakfast and the weight of a nation of refreshed well slept millions pulled hard at my semi-conscious.
There was somehow no denying the extent of this hedonistic madness at that point of the first morning of the journey. We were already fully under it's swing but hold on, if that's not Myrthin snoring somewhere close to my shoulder!!! I squinted through half closed eyelids to see the man's contour rest against the cancerous sea lion from the deep south. It was a huge relief to be able to reach across and turn off the television crazies and to lie in silence.

"Enjoy your two hours rest my friend". I said mainly to myself but meaning the shape of Myrthin, lost in twitching dreams whilst asleep in his boots.

Now came the problem of killing two to three hours in silence whilst saving at least some natural energy for the day ahead. Reading was out of the question for my eyes were already burning. A walk would be stupid and would only heighten the drain so I decided to lie and figure out as much of whatever I could. It was a time to reach deep into the library of memory, expectation and the sensory now.

A kind of lost zone of pretense, the pretense that one was readying oneself for sleep, yet in the deep knowledge that the time for such basic brain functions had long since been and gone. Instead I thought about several crucial non aspects of my life in no particular order.

Of course the forthcoming intrepid trip filled a large part of those sleepless hours and just what if anything was waiting for us in the swirl of the week to come? I thought of Sparks who was busy winding his own sleepless way to join us and still in Austria.

I thought of Fabian, the Londoner, who was probably lost in deep dreams those sixty or so miles up the road in the metropolis. Then of Lenny from Northern Ireland who was in London too and due to join us for one night and one night only.

Lenny was a gentle, gay mystic who also lived in our colony of repossessed in the Austrian capital. Twelve hours later we would all be together romping away in an early evening survival course with the Merry Pranksters.

Only Sparks was due to stay for the extended pilgrimage as Fabian and his brother Fab Junior were off to Uganda in two days, whilst Lenny was going home to Ireland for the summer. So, ultimately it would be the three of us, the triumvirate in search of the trees, fields and ancient kicks.

I look up and the gap in the curtain meets the gap between my eyelids and no there is little doubt that morning is well and truly growing. Myrthin snores, yeah snores, while

I bury my head deep into the pillow knowing that it is too late to sleep and that sleep would now only mystery the thing down to a negative. It is with speed sizzling my system that this day is to begin and slowly I plan out the strategy of rebirth.
Beers must be an absolute, for there is no option this day. Christ, the clock on the cupboard blinks away stating an hour past six o clock. Breakfast-time across the country and time to rise.

So rise I do quietly, not wishing to disturb the man in the confined space next to me and move towards a map we'd picked up from the reception desk on arrival. Sitting in a T-shirt and boxer shorts combination I open out the Brighton map before me. I see the sea that is out of the window and before me.

The two piers are there but wait, wait a moment, there's a camping site, the municipal camping site of the kingdom of Sussex.

Man, there had been one all the time, close to the center too.

Wow? I felt like the discoverer of an ancient pyramid in the long gone past. My finger traced the road line of red along the sea-front to our oasis of green. My god, what joy at breakfast time. It meant that the next night's sleep would be under canvas and a mere fraction of the price of the lovely old Edinburgh hotel. I thought of waking the sleeping giant with the information but quickly decided it was a highly personal moment. As celebration, a trip to the toilet became the thing.

Myrthin was still asleep and I had no desire to watch early morning television so I took up position at the window to gaze out at the ocean versus horizon battle that was frothing up over old Norm's head. It was a time to marvel, a time to count the waves and to number the seabirds.

Green railings ran along the promenade and reminded me immediately of my early childhood and playing endless summer soccer matches against the sand-dunes. All summer my brother and I would hang out as children on the beach, meeting endless numbers of tourist kids each on their own specific pilgrimages to the sea.

I remember being constantly freaked at the thought of the transient nature of those endless week long friendships as Friday would bring goodbye and love would be lost forever, at least until the next Monday brought the latest new faces.

"You know the feast was good.".

WAITING FOR THE BUS.

I started panicking a little at nine o clock, I mean one can not just sit counting grains of sand for the thirteenth time, it's unlucky. Brighton and its morning had clothed itself before my very eyes and from road sweeper to the first child to the swinging traffic, I had seen it all. Sure my eyes were hurting but you know what, I wasn't even tired as such, just hideously high and still crackling on the buzz of the night before and the day to come.

"Myrthin, Myrthin, get up, get up. It's nine o clock." I half whisper as I tug on his bed clothes to rouse him from his three-hour sleep. The man rose out of his dreams effortlessly without so much as a grumble or moan.

It was indeed useful that we'd already been given a ten-o clock check out time, so five after nine was only fifty five minutes too early and the same time away from the Merry Pranksters arrival at Brighton railway station.

It was at the station that it all was supposed to happen. The main body of Americans were arriving by train from Gatwick airport and the bus, which had been shipped over already, was supposed to take them on from there.

"I've found a camp site." I announce to the flailing image

before me who must have wondered just how I'd pulled that off. "No sleep man, not a single second, just been thinking and relaxing and watching the sun.." Myrthin looks at me with a curious gaze before heading off to the toilet.

"You've been awake all night?" He asks between scattering finely toxic water into and beyond the toilet bowl.

"You know me, I never can sleep on speed." I reply whilst stuffing the travel bag with whatever lay around that was mine.

A cough echoed around the room and the man was awake. His coughs are like jump leads, they kick the engine into life and fire away the spark plugs. Soon the boy was tying his hair back in a ponytail and ready to roll.
In no time at all we were wishing the new desk attendant a good day, a curious young arty type with carefully groomed hair. This reminded me of the unholy state of our disrepair so out we stumbled into the blinding sunlight. This was the very same sunlight that had only just begun to peep out from behind its own soft blankets on our walk home a matter of hours earlier. But day was now complete and blazing in its high summer feast.

Across the road Norm gleamed in the haze looking all the stronger for his twelve hour rest. Beyond him the sea glistened like a frosted mirror, calm without a wave to speak of. Its atmosphere rose to meet us as a sweep of sweet aromas.

You know the smell, that salty dampness that is the waves forming in tiny droplets at the beginning of any summer's day.

The trip was to really begin once more after a couple of hours hiatus lost in the hotel room. I slumped into the driver's seat and Myrthin took up the role of passenger and guide. To our surprise the car's motor started sweetly and even at the first time of asking and before long we were jostling with cake vans, taxis and motor-bikes.

"So do you know where the station is?". Asks Myrthin as he turns on the tail end of a radio breakfast show.

"No idea, but it'll be sign-posted, there's always a little red sign somewhere." I somewhat vacantly replied.
So, there we were, both flying on drugs, happy and about to meet the Merry Pranksters. It was certainly not just another day in the existence of our kind, most certainly not.

The excitement borne out of curiosity was tangible as we drove along the long journey of the night before. There look, the Grand Hotel was still standing, as were the piers, whilst on the pebbles smoldering remains of the fires of the night still smoked. Alone now, now that the revelers had fled to sleep.

We quickly tracked down the ignominious station signpost and were soon rolling up a steep hill towards the meeting point.

KEN KESEY. THE MERRY PRANKSTERS. THE ECLIPSE. AND THREE.

We planned to leave Norm safely in a multi-Level car park and trip up to meet Ken Kesey on foot.

It was already getting on towards nine forty five as we pulled off the street and into a dark cave. It already felt as if we had been in holiday mode for days, just free, free, free! We were in a good state of mind in which to run into the Merry Pranksters of all people.
We two non-heroes rode the lift to the street with two uncomfortable pairs of shoppers but on the bell, the doors opened and the street before them was the drag up to the station.

We began striding in bounds the last steps up the incline. Just as a Buddhist monk would, just as a mountain climber would, just as two speeding maniacs should. It was appropriate, for it somehow rang of the typical religious pilgrimage, you know, that aspect of the final mile being up into the clouds. Both of us craned their necks to spot the first view of 'Further' the Prankster's magic bus, but we needn't have bothered.

The whole train station scene couldn't have possibly been more ordinary.

In my mind I'd expected maybe hundreds of stereotypically stoned-out 'Heads' all camped out in tents on the station courtyard, and right down the street. I'd feared some corny, late Millennium Woodstock for the Generation X. Well nothing in that frightening scale awaited, the Heads were nowhere to be seen.

Though wait, we were almost around a pesky corner that blocked off the view of the bus. I pulled hard on a raucous cigarette to cleanse my soul as Myrthin tried to roll his own

100

as he walked in a tunnel of calm. Something, somehow just did not seem right.
And then, and then, just as I tossed my half finished smoke under the wheels of a parked van, there before us in shimmering beauty, was the station.

But just a station, just a red bricked semi-Victorian building just like a hundred others across the British Isles. There was no bus other than the public service kind and, get this, not a crowd of any type whatsoever. My spirits swirled a little then rose with a different expectation.

"Everybody must be inside." I said half in jest.
"But where's the bus?" asks the disappointed Myrthin.
I swallowed hard fearing the worst. Good God he was right, not only was the station doing merely a normal Friday morning trade, but there was no psychedelic bus anywhere. Suddenly the remaining amphetamine began to deflate itself in my system And above the station rode the ten o clock eye, a digital eye, the clock. We were on time so just where was everyone?

'Oh no,' I thought, 'the Pranksters', 'We've already been pranked.'

Myrthin god bless him, decides to buy one of those disposable cameras, he was still convinced they would show and in fact, Christ, so was I.

Suddenly an instant vision of important significance rose up, no not a bus painted in swirls, or even a thousand bongo playing fans, no just an odd looking group of old Grateful Dead T-shirts. It was a really weird mix of three men and one woman, in Stetsons and all in sandals. I didn't have time to think about the irony of such a measly representation of the Nineteen Ninety-Nine LSD generation for I was on their shoulders in a flash.

"Hi. Are you waiting for Kesey and the gang?" I ask to surprised but friendly interest. These were original Sixties types that had somehow not thrown off the memories of over thirty years living on.

"Yeah, they've probably missed their train." Says the guy with a Stetson, flowing gray locks and a huge handlebar mustache. He answers without ever taking his eyes from the arrival board. Myrthin came to join us fiddling with the plastic packaging of his new Kodak throwaway.

"Hello there, any sign of them yet?"

"No!"

So there we stood the six of us as welcoming committee for the one time greatest collection of underground bandits of the Twentieth Century. Ahem!

I felt a little embarrassed for this generation if this is what Ken Kesey represented to them. But hey, this was great somehow, a really entertaining beginning to a new day. I was glad to be awake but looking at Myrthin I saw that it was a personal thing.
We'd been tossed into this homely little scene, and it slowly began to make perfect sense. We were told that there was to be some kind of proposed get together later that evening at something called the 'Peace Memorial'.

"Down at the beach fella, that's where it is at, yes, yes!"

One of the waiting committee was talking to himself.

Myrthin then paced around examining his camera whilst

I did likewise examining the people around us. It was a human zoo of young mothers, businessmen, teenagers and pensioned couples.

There was still no sign of either the bus or the multi-colored gang from Oregon though we had been joined by yet another cowboy hat.

This latest cowboy was an American who claimed to Kesey's publisher. The guy weighed down with bags was dressed like a Safari hunter of Hemmingway's era which I illogically felt validated his claim.

He quickly commenced chewing the cud with the Dead-Heads whilst I chewed on my gums and spotted a bar in the corner of the foyer. Checking the arrivals board informed us groupies that the next train from London Gatwick was not for thirty minutes.

Myrthin and I gave up the waiting game in favor of the drinking equivalent and in no time we were sitting on high stools on a make believe terrace, sipping sweetly on English Bitter, a liquid breakfast.

"I feared there would be hundreds of people at least.".

I say to Myrthin blowing the froth across the table and onto the floor.

"You never know with these things, I didn't know what to expect." He replies from behind his purple heart sunglasses.

He busies himself rolling a stubby cigarette.

"The publisher guy said that he'd already spoken to Kesey and that they're on their way. Jesus knows where's the bus though!." He added.

The beer soon tasted brilliant, it was an inevitable survival technique after such a night of excess. There was no other way to maintain the fuzz and by god did we need to keep the eagle on the wing for the day was going to be long and disjointed. The rest of our own happy Vienna gang were due to arrive at about four thirty armed and ready to attack another night's darkness with spray color heads.

I immediately thought of Sparks who as we sat and drank was probably making his way to Vienna airport as sleepless as myself and probably cruising in fourth gear of pure biting sleep deprivation.
His today was our yesterday, but I was happy to already be in place at the station bar staring out at the world through the stained darkness of my sunglasses.
Mission Improbable was now alive with the news that the Merry Pranksters were definitely coming and that the beer was three quarters empty.

It was a time to relax and reflect on a view different to the one out of the hotel room window. Scurrying people would rush through the main door to stop in their tracks then stare up at the travel information, transfixed before continuing their treks onwards at a further haste. Haste was something we'd decided to let go of that holy week, our schedule existed but in only our own time and at our own or rather Norm's chosen pace.

Slurping casually on the beer with nothing to do other than to watch and disseminate, is a kind of past-time of mine when the chance allows, just blissful. Look as the mother struggles with a push-chair and toddler!! On her way in my mind to reunite with her sister for a day of being together. Watch as three teenagers head up to

London in the search of kicks, clothes and risky music! Look as the old man, a pensioner slowly steps each step patiently, aware that his legs only move at their own speed and that there is no rush anyhow.

Stereotypes were on my mind, which is good when you live away from the British Isles, it's beautiful to watch your folk doing what only your folk do. It's the same reason I freak out at supermarkets in Britain, the familiar unfamiliarity of it all.

"You want another one?" I ask Myrthin rather pointlessly as I head off back into the bar, failing to even wait for an answer.

The barman couldn't quite make us out, I could see that much, but it was okay for I was in no mood for explaining. I ordered another round and watched patiently as the pints frothed up over the rim before being handed to me as fully formed.

Paying with pounds is another great trip when your daily dealings are normally done in other currencies. Out came a blue note and a golden nugget and the deal was done.

I laughed as I remembered the useless but nonetheless imaginative scam that my brother Dave and I had once tried to pull off as kids. It involved two pennies, a tube of super glue and some gold paint. You had to stick the two pennies together and then spray them gold and bang, a totally unconvincing one-pound coin.

It never worked but it kept us busy for one week of some specific summer holiday. I giggled to myself as I returned to our high table. The giggling stopped dead.
Myrthin had somehow attracted what we call a **'Loose**

Canon', and this particular version was armed and dangerous.
Good god, we were here for peace and understanding, and this Broad-moor escapee was here to test us,

"Yeah, left me, the bitch. I should have killed her!."

The guy speaking was a shaven-headed, wrong cardigan, cheap-lager drinking, 'lost' classic. He spoke with an accent that I found hard to make out but greetings were exchanged and that was that, we had company for as long as we wanted.

"Guess where I'm from. Go on guess!" He challenged with a threatening air that made it dangerous to misplace the whereabouts of the man's infancy.

"MIDDLESBOROUGH!!" he announced with definitive pride.

Now I remembered Middlesborough from the late Eighties and the soccer. Jesus they were a desperate breed, and several times we'd had clashes with them and they somehow all looked like this guy, even the teenagers.

He was soon busy fishing around in a plastic shopping bag at his side and another can joined us. He flicked the booze open with a scarred well trained hand and continued his incessant ramble.

"My girl, my girl, she's Spanish but not anymore, she's gone home. Five years together, five years and then she decides she's got to go. Spain for Christ's sake. Spain." He spoke with a mixture of sadness and serious intent. Good god, five years must have been an eternity for the Señorita living with Mr. Middlesborough.

"How old do you think I am?" He fires out of nowhere. "Go on how old? You'll never guess."

My beer began to lose some of its taste and the prospect of running into the Merry pranksters with this maniac at our side didn't bear thinking about.

"We'll have to shoot after this one.". I said looking to Myrthin, who had indeed once spent a year working as a Care assistant and seemed to be unwilling to become too familiar with the jagged, hugging man at his side.

"We'll have to be moving along man.". Myrthin says to the Middlesborough man, "It's been nice talking.".

We then set about rising to our feet whilst ensuring him that we really had to go. Suddenly we were offered warm handshakes as he too rose to his feet before shuffling away in another direction out into the sunny, doomed streets of his Brighton.

"Take Care!" We both shouted after him and we both meant it. We both meant it with every sinew in our bodies.
And there were still no Merry Pranksters, just us, just us and our tired shadows. We left the station and quickly got lost.

I thought we'd never get back, a car park is not exactly the place, in which to be illogical! With Myrthin plotting on the map and me at the wheel we eventually found ourselves turning into a weird housing estate on a hill. It was not exactly the most picturesque scenario but hey, it was money we were supposed to be saving not idyllic views to be watching.

Parking in the arrivals camping site car park surrounded

by the Adventurer caravan types was the weirdest thing. We stumbled out of Norm and into the office with a determination that only comes from highly refined nonchalance. We were at the next point of dealing with people.

Couples in matching jackets swarmed around the office whispering glee at pamphlets of information whilst we zig-zagged into position at the counter.

"Hi, we need a pitch for one tent for one night!" I proclaimed with total reasonableness.

We were told that it was impossible to bring the car into the compound as all the spaces were taken, but we could carry all the shit and pitch our tent in block 36 A.
"36 A, yeah the right number, cool!". I answered with relief having been told that the price was a mere tenth of the virtually unused Edinburgh Hotel. We paid the price of two beers each and had a home for the night.

"You have to leave by ten o'clock tomorrow.". says Mrs. Camping Site.

"Ten o' clock is fine!" I answer knowing that once the sun pings into full volume you're gone, no camper ever lies in late, not in a tent, never.

We were given a disc and we carried our bags and we perspired and swore and had the blessed tent up in ten minutes.

Our fellow campers eyed us with suspicion, understandable I suppose, two guys in their thirties moving like stick insects on speed. Draw your own conclusions. Anyhow as soon as we'd arrived we were gone, leaving the barbecues, soft-tennis games, sunbathers and families to their own devices. We wouldn't be back for another fourteen hours so they needn't have worried.

Norm was left carefully parked on a hill leading to the camp site and that was that.
Away we walked in intense heat across a rolling school playing field trying to get back to the sea front that was now beginning to take on monumentally significant proportions.
"Let's have a spliff!" suggests a roasting Myrthin.

"Yeah, great idea." I reply with just the faintest of worries that the dreaded dope might kill off some of the chemical glide in my step. But man, it was no time for shirking additives, they were keeping us alive, so we sat with a view across the sea and talked, talked like warriors do when the battle subsides and a break allows a gathering of impressions.

We talked of the trip, and we talked of the day to come, and we talked of the view and halt, we even talked about food but mostly we talked of the combination of drugs to take us through the night.

I had five grams of amphetamine still with me, Myrthin for his sins had seven tabs of blotter acid. Somehow the speed would make sense but two nights running would obviously polish some of the stuff's potency, so L.S.D. seemed to be the hot runner and under the circumstances, who could argue?

Certainly not the Merry Pranksters huh!!!

Soon after with the sun blistering a hole between my eyes we got on a bus, funny huh, a bus, but not the real Merry

Prankster bus, no, just the one that travels open top along the Brighton sea road. We'd tried to walk but in the face of a severe fainting threat we jumped happily onto a thirty five pence ambulance heading towards the shops.

At the train station we left the bus and walked down the hill for the second time in our lives and were soon hitting a two o clock empty Chinese restaurant.

The trip was now hitting a slow survival pattern, it was just keeping on, and the speed was gone and three hundred miles and thirty odd waking hours in the bones was just not going to be loosened with Chop Suey and rice. No way, but the beer's remarkable tonic nature was clean and the drugs in our pockets would have to be left out until later.

So in silence we hit a minor slump of energy and saw the soup steaming around the corner. It was soon being spooned down our respective dried throats until I freaked out about some lumps in the liquid which just made no sense and that was the end of my starter for four.

Paranoid tinges began flaming away like candle fire tips in the snow.
Yet it was all right, for hold on here comes the chicken.

So in the order of things this was to be a loose time, a time between two mountains, one of which is the day come morning before and the other being the night and morning after. We'd sorted out the night's sleeping quarters and were now in place to drift the next few hours through whilst waiting for both our Vienna connection and the more elusive Oregon boys and girls. Inevitably it would be a time spent drinking away the tiredness but more, a holy time for conserving what little natural energy we still had.

Now Myrthin plays cricket and I don't, but I had as a child spent hours watching the laconic game with my brother Dave and our Grandfather. During the summer of Ninety Nine, England were involved in a fascinating test series with New Zealand, or at least so we were told by the media.

Little did we know then that cricket would take on an increasingly holy aspect during the intrepid trip, with Sparks at the helm, busy teaching various Merry Pranksters and children the rules of the game. So it was kind of apt that the decision made between chewing was to find a pub to watch the cricket and to rest on clotted cream beers.
It didn't take long.

Though somehow the pub had more of a boozed out library atmosphere about it. At the bar stood a battered small-town Richard Burton and his latest wife, a long suffering downbeat soap extra. He kept intending to leave.

"No I've got to go, no really." He would say, his words rolling ever so slightly angled off his tongue.

"Work calls!" He would tell his weary girlfriend.
She would then plead that he really should leave, then he, full of bravado and nonsense, would scoop down another short.
Richard Burton and his wife represented the bitter end of the road of lost dreams. The Merry Pranksters though, despite being in their pension-aged sixtieth year, had obviously somehow managed to maintain their spirit for adventure. There and then in the pub with the cricket I realized exactly what the trip was all about. It was about redefining magic and building a commitment to the unexpected, it was about eclipsing a routine.

Just as I put a full stop on the chill of this sentence,

Richard decided to leave and with a genuine affectionate kiss was gone. Suddenly the world seemed a little more positive Disney once more. England hit a four and I couldn't have cared less. It was to the bar I was heading full of light and feeling like an infant once more, a wise infant in search of a bottle.

With a smile I took the latest drink and caught some action on the television screen before deciding I needed a newspaper, sometimes cricket really is just thirteen men in night clothes and the tiniest ball in the world. So out I strode into the Sargasso sea of people swimming happily in the summer sun. Unfortunately, a newsagents was just across the road so any plans of a little solo jaunt were quickly dismissed.

It would have been perfect to do a little wandering and wondering in this strange new place, still a mere eighteen hours old to my eyes. Alas, it was into the shop that my feet took me and to the newspaper shelf I was heading.
"Anything happened?" I ask on returning. The almost trance-like Myrthin was lost in the clockwork process of over after over, over and out.

"No but they need a wicket pretty quickly, these two are beginning to look too comfortable." He answers looking more than comfortable himself. I forgot that Myrthin was actually something of a cricket expert.
"Right!" I said to no-one in particular sitting down ready to plough into beer and news with equal determination.

For two hours time stood still and drifted in a left to right motion called reading. I read of terrorists, super models, the 'up and coming' stars of the new English soccer season, an air crash in Peru, a dog called 'Jack' that had survived a fire, a murder in Manchester, the Queen's latest trip, the weather forecast, the eclipse build up and loved it all. Just to let the mind go and to drift in and out of iron consciousness is one of a holiday's greatest gifts.

Though by the end my eyes felt as if they needed refitting. I knew not whether it was the beer, the lack of sleep or the thousands of words I'd digested. Anyhow by the time I looked up another four empty glasses stood before me and the comfortable cricket partnership was looking more like a marriage made in heaven.
We eventually decided to leave the cricket to wind on its way to an inevitable tea-break and began our move to the sea front and the Peace Monument and next wait for it, the MERRY PRANKSTERS!!!

The curiosity was yet again seeping through, the stop off in the slumber pub had obviously worked. We were raring to go once more. So, after descending the hill to the beach it was a sharp left along the promenade in the direction of, yes you guessed it the freaking Edinburgh Hotel. We didn't quite get that far as another bar beckoned us into it's evil ways, or at least it's balcony's evil ways.

It was all quite the opposite of what we'd just left behind.

This place was leaden with a rowdy collection of different stag parties which had the place positively fizzing with energy. We both took a long look around before collapsing into the comfortable cushioned cane chairs with a view across to the beach.

This was the perfect place to watch for a sneaky psychedelic bus or to wait for a carload of ex-Viennese dispossessed.

Myrthin got two bottles from the bar and I switched on

my mobile phone in readiness. It was all getting pretty close and I felt like a cross between a gangster and an infant under a glowing Christmas tree. Myrthin and I began talking of the peace monument.

"Probably a dove or something." He says.
"Or a two fingers in a Victory sign.".

"No it'll be a soldier with a gun.".

Whatever it was we had no idea of it's whereabouts other than what Charlie the Dead Head had told us.

"Down on the promenade, you can't miss it fellas.".

So that was good, Charlie seemed to know everything. But by that point the morning's hanging around at the station seemed like three days earlier. Time was on its own peculiar trip that afternoon, good god it was only five o' clock yet in fact closer to double midnight on our own recently developed concept of the thirty-three-hour day. Yet tiredness was not really an issue for the old adrenaline rocket boosters were working severe overtime, and on the back of the day before and the hash blitz down through England, it was a relief that we'd stayed almost dope free all day. Beer was king for us non-sleeping types.

I thought of Sparks, who had been doing the same all night scenario as us, in a different country though, It was certain that he would turn up in some wild frenzy or other.

I checked the phone for no reason, then we looked out to the sea and sipped on the beer.

Our fellow revelers the Stag boys, were getting rowdy in their carefully considered skinhead no hair way. Though that was to be expected for it was after all Friday in high summer and euphoria seemed to be in. Another small beer arrived in Myrthin hands and sip we did like thirsty babes. We talked of the imminent arrival of the band of other brothers. "Sparks is supposed to arrive at four in Gatwick, so they should be here by five thirty." I said concerned that they all should be in place for the arrival of the bus and Kesey's gang.

"Who's actually coming all told?" Asks Myrthin for probably the first time.

"Well Sparks the Australian who's coming for the whole trip and Lenny who you once met in Vienna and Fabian the Wimbledon fan." I answer with sufficient information for the man to allow him a return with a nod to his beer.

"Fabian read the Kool Aid Acid Test and devoured it quicker than anyone I've ever met."

I add probably unnecessarily.

It was true though, Fabian at the age of twenty-two had become a form of born again Prankster overnight, complete with his favored outfit, a crazy flowered shirt, purple shorts and cowboy boots.

His name was Fabian, we called him Fab.

THE MERRY PRANKSTERS!

There had been still no phone call from the boys on their way, and it's now gone five o clock, just an hour before the proposed arrival of Kesey and the pranksters.

On the balcony overlooking the sea, things are heating up. Both sets of stag gangs have found their voices and are singing various London soccer songs. It's the last thing we need. So, off we go, out onto the promenade to find the peace statue. It was weird to be walking the walk of the early morning once more.

Out on the beach, happy families sit on rugs in squares of sandwich eating normality. Swimmers too, out there fighting with the waves and whooping out yells of joy in mock panic as the undertow takes them to the seabed. An ice cream van, the typical pink and white pastel shades, with the obligatory giant plastic cone on the front. It struck me that this scene could have been from anytime in the previous forty years and in the state of disrepair that I found myself, it was nice to have some proof of continuation. The seaside is a long standing but somehow wilting tradition, and Hardy swoops into my mind as I remember the closing chapters of Tess of the D'Urbevilles.

Good god, we were to be at Stonehenge in the morrow!!!

I then checked the mobile phone for the correct time and yes it was still on.

"No idea where they are man." I say to Myrthin.

The man shrugs.

"They'll be here."

Then continues staring out into the horizon.

"Hey there's the olden, golden, Dead Head family, look!"

It was the station waiting gang and they were seated on the grass next to what must have been the Peace monument. It was all in all quite a bigger scene than the one at the station. There were around a hundred bodies gathered in little groups on the grass.
All kinds of freaks, punks and New Age drifters.
"There we go. The Peace has found its statue." I say making not too much sense.

There was even a television crew juggling with thick wires that snaked across the lawn like thin oil slicks. Our interest bubbled up to a further level.

"Well, they must be coming if the television's here!" Myrthin says finally convinced that this crazily unlikely scenario is actually about to happen. We greet the few faces we recognized from the morning and find out that the bus has already been doing the rounds.

"Yeah fellas, fish and chips! Then they went back to the hotel for a couple of hours!."

The idea of the Merry Pranksters eating a British newspaper meal twists me out a bit.

"So, you've seen them?" I ask seeking ultimate proof.

"No, but Des has."

Not knowing who Des was meant that it was still second-hand confirmation, but better than nothing.
"Huh, Myrthin!!! Good old Des. Better than nothing!" I giggle as we find our own little magical place on the grass and my friend immediately commences rolling a joint.

The view down the sea road meant that one could see a good mile in either direction so the bus' arrival would be one encompassed within quite enormous proportions of clarity. Though somehow deep down I still felt it might all be a big scam.

I mean the peace monument, what was that all about? A phallic concrete pillar with a green angel of some sort holding what looked like a dove in its right hand.
Yet around us sat a growing number of groups of anticipation.

Now although long hair was king on the grass there were several 'cleaner cut types' too. These were probably fans of Kesey the writer as opposed to Kesey the bandit, but appearances can be very deceiving.

We all smiled happily in our own space as some street

musicians kicked up a racket on acoustic guitars and a shoeless hippie dances as her billowing skirt, mushrooms out in her spin, and kids laugh merrily.

"Shit we forgot to get beers!" says the unquenchable man from. North Wales.

He was right so I volunteer to hunt down a liquor store as he finishes the joint. I knew there was no point in letting up the drinking for it was the elixir of life that day. Off I bolted eager to not miss a minute of this festival atmosphere and within a hundred yards had found not a liquor store but a hotel willing to off-load several bottles of French Lager at ludicrous prices. I think we were paying for the fact that they were ice cold.

"Great they're cold. Ten pounds, fine."

The bemused bar tender watched me leave suspicious of the Peace Monument circus.

"What's going on with all those people?" He asks squinting through his glasses out to the growing mass outside.

"Ken Kesey's coming!" I inform him with great, wild-eyed enthusiasm. "Ken Kesey the American!."

With which I'm out and across the street juggling the beers back to Myrthin and his smoke.

"No sign?" I ask like a child in anticipation of Christmas.

"No, but apparently they're going to do something at a club later. Brighton's first acid test!" He laughed.

I was off once again checking the phone and I freed the

beer and guzzled down what seemed to be the juice of the day. Behind us some young guys were speaking in French. I turned to be showered in visions of dreadlocks and saw a dog running after a tattered red plastic ball.

Behind this bunch were a group of paisley shirt beatnik boys and girls. Behind them was a shirtless wanderer in denim shorts and no shoes. He was desperately trying to get a cigarette off anybody he could find.
There were kids chasing kids and the dog chasing them. The television crew were testing microphones, with red lights blinking in the sun and more and more people, a lot just stopping out of curiosity, it is amazing how magnetic a film crew can be.

Suddenly all in all, the one hundred had doubled and quite a merry, nostalgic scene was happening all around us.

I checked the road, both left and right, then the phone, pull on the joint and drink my beer. A process I repeat at regular intervals for the next ten minutes. A drummer joins in the musicians and the cameras are busy filming the folk for some reason. I knew that one of the National film channels were due to broadcast daily from the whole trip and as Sparks was later to say we got the whole intrepid trip on video, a priceless holiday memento, courtesy of the U.K.'s Channel Four.

Still no sign of anybody's bus though, just the circus like atmosphere increasing as some skateboard gurus put on a show of flips, bench riding and how to fall gracefully. Brighton truly was quite a place.

Myrthin passed the joint on to the nearest group and smiles were exchanged between two puffs of smoke. By the by, the atmosphere was getting tenser. Many people had taken to standing and staring in anticipation of the arrival of Further, the Sixties bus icon.

It was still the status quo though, there was not so much as a trill from the cursed phone in my pocket and it was so important that we were all together for the arrival of Kesey. A couple of empty beer bottles mark out our territory as the guitarists Irish jig to the cameras and young kids are busy pushing their faces into the lens. Myrthin has begun talking to a group of smiling teenagers to our right.

"Yeah they're supposed to be in Stonehenge tomorrow and then off to Cornwall!". He explains.
I find it impossible to talk in what I could only describe as tension.

"What are they looking for?" Asks one of the gang, a short guy wearing a Prodigy T-shirt.

"Merlin the magician!". Answers Myrthin to an immediate burst of laughter.

"Well, I hope they find him!" Says the only female in the group.
"Of course, they'll find him." Replies my companion "They've got special maps!"

Again, laughter and amidst the joviality there was a strange high-pitched chime.

"Jesus Christ! The telephone!" I scream before diving head first into my pocket.

"Hello! Hello! Where are you?" I ask Fabian who's voice it is on the other side of the line.

"Where? I know you're in a phone box, but where!"

"On the sea front near the pier!" He answers on a crackling connection.

"Well keep driving left out away from the town, but quickly man, the bus is due any moment!." I could hardly speak in the intensity of the moment. The sleep deprivation and the drinks and the drugs had me spinning intensely at everything.

"You can't miss us, there are about a thousand people."

I say, being always prone to exaggeration if the need is speed. With which Fab hightails it back to the car where sitting anxiously are Sparks, newly arrived from Austria, all blond lion hair and sunglasses. Also there is Lenny, tall and thin with short, neat David Bowie hair, sunglasses also there is Fab Junior, the younger brother who has short hair, is eighteen and has no sunglasses.

"What's the story?" asks Sparks with his tired Australian twang.

"Apparently the bus is on it's way!."

And I put the phone away and now have two vehicles to watch out for. Jesus the tension.

"Look out for a clapped out Volkswagen with Viennese number plates ." I tell Myrthin.

"They're coming from that direction."

We both turn to look back from whence we came. There was no Austrian bundle coming down the road. What there was however was one of the freakiest sights in the world, for there in a translucent heat-haze, came the shimmering vision of a floating bus.

The vibrating, gyrating, hallucinating bus 'Further.'

My world stood trapped in a weird dimension as cheers rippled through the crowd, and an open mouthed Myrthin takes off his sunglasses. For once he is struck dumb.

The snub-nosed vehicle moves forward in amidst the Nineteen Ninety-Nine traffic.

It was the Merry Pranksters!!!!

Somehow it was all quite unbelievable!! This was beginning to feel like running into Christopher Columbus or Alexander the Great. It was like history coming alive before your very eyes. I immediately stood up to get a better view of the approaching piece of legendary transport and marvel that despite the mass of colored collage painted onto the bus, it all comes across as some form of neon-yellow. It was as if the bus' original school mustard shade had been replaced by the same color from another realm, like a yellow from Sirius.

Instinctively the crowd move closer to the road as the bus approaches.

"Ken Kesey's on there!" I find myself telling whoever was closest to my left shoulder, "Ken Kesey!!"

It all seemed a little too surreal in the glow of my Christmas tree head of sleep deprivation and fairy lights. Yet it was indeed all true, the men and women on that bus were indeed the men and women who had been "ON THE

BUS!".

On that bus that Tom Wolfe had seen fit to write a three hundred page novel about. On that bus that the legendary real life Dean Moriarty had rolled around America with petulant ease. The lineage that was riding in that apparition of a vehicle was positively remarkable.
But hold on, the bus pulled away without even stopping, sure there had been a full-blown version of Dylan's corny epic "Everybody must get stoned!." Though somehow singing that song was like bringing a turkey to a Christmas party, plainly an 'unnecessary' gift.

'Was that it?' I wondered to myself, 'Was it a look but don't touch presence?.' Or was it the typical 'We are famous, and you are not, so look and behold, for that's as close as it gets', story-board.

Surely not! But as I look to Myrthin and he looks to me the bus disappears in a rumble off down the promenade in the opposite direction.

"Who was that young guy?" I asked cynically of some wildly dressed definitely non original Prankster that had surfed the roof of the bus in trails of blue fabric flying to the wind.

"No idea!" Replies Myrthin glumly.

Basically, it was confusion, and I was airing the huge egoistic voice of 'me, me, me.' demanding to be acknowledged for 'my' great effort in reaching this specific point. I was disappointed too I suppose, disappointed mainly that it was still 'us' down here and 'them' up there still on the bus. I'd imagined the Merry Pranksters to carry their notoriety with a bit more grace.

I had a lot of learning to do and that much is now obvious. Back then I suppose, I was just completely off my head and on my own minor, metaphysical trip.

I slugged some more beer and snuffled out another cigarette, good god, those were the survival days of just staying alive through any means possible.
Around us stand the now five hundred or so gathered various heads of dismay, a feeling of an altogether bummer in the summer rode a non wave!

A collective 'Was that it?' hovered above our heads.

Myrthin sits silently, lost in thought, no look of disappointment as such but then how could you when your eyes are hidden by purple hearts? I took to watching the bus disappear then to watching the hundreds of swirling seabirds following whatever trawled their minds, and I then cursed something for the stupidity of my expectation.

Old expectation the downfall of a generation of hope. Why always this expectancy? Why not just simple satisfaction in the idea of finding out when the time presents itself? It kills the future this idea of expecting some kind of outcome.

I was so busy wallowing on the lack of a vibe that I failed to notice that along the lower part of the promenade, on the road closest to the beach, the wonderful old hulking bus called 'Further' was slowly coming back towards us all. We had to a man, woman and child just had our first taste of close contact with the Merry Pranksters. We'd been well and truly tricked clean!
Rule one was and seemed to remain still! "Never trust a Prankster!"

I began to feel that I was in urgent need of a personal redefinition. A lot that I thought I knew about myself was from that point onwards about to be replaced by a far different non knowledge. We were in the hands of great people, not just specifically the Merry Pranksters but with them a whole host of awkward ghosts of the Nineteen Sixties as well.

Closer the bus came and soon it pulled up right next to the weird monument to peace and the engine noise died as the cheering rose into the late afternoon air.
In all the excitement and self doubt I'd completely forgotten about the imminent arrival of our own rag tag bunch of travelers. It was quite a surprise to see them emerge from just behind where the bus had come to rest.

Sparks was already two feet off the floor. Lenny was gliding on ice and the Fab brothers, for there were two of them, were in a progressive huddle. I ran to meet the foursome with as much enthusiasm as others were greeting the bus, but I was clear in the knowledge that it was all one big picture of perfect synchronicity. Strange memories now of that old long gone mystical Friday and way back in Nineteen Ninety-Nine.
"Yeah! Oh Yeah, boys and men!" I screamed making no sense but conveying the correct feeling.

Soon we were in one huddle of introductions, hugs and handshakes.

"They're here, they're here!" Someone was saying and they were right, we really were all there!

Sparks was dressed in his usual flamboyant over the top pseudo Las Vegas garb and seemed to be none the worse for his insomniac Austrian experience. He was big into the wilderness ways of one Hunter S. Thompson, he of a 'Fear and loathing in Las Vegas' fame, well actually we all were.

Yet it was only he that saw fit to dress in the most garish colored outfits that he could find. Think of a guy member of the old band Abba, dress him up in lurid shirts, paste on a doped smile, huge sunglasses, then you've roughly got Sparks, then twenty seven, now older.

As he once said "I am half Italian, half Australian, half Austrian!".

Indeed!!!!!!!!!!!!!

The others.
Myrthin had only met Lenny once before so the rest were all new fish to his ocean but within seconds our focus shifted outwards and we began paying attention to the men and women of the famous bus family.

"Look that must be Kesey!" We all said of several different correctly aged guys as they walked off the bus and onto Brighton's promenade.

The real Kesey though was easily identifiable, you just had to follow the spotlight and the cameras. There he was, there was Ken Kesey!

He was looking brilliant. His strong sun-tanned face looked lean, leathery and was framed by huge bushy white sideburns. On his head he wore a trademark flat hat and hiding beneath the rim shone quite the most amazing eyes. They pulsated like blue lasers out into the waiting chaotic admiration. His shirt was a blue and short sleeved covered in tiny white stars, the red stripes were his braces, and this was Captain America in person.

It was at this point that Sparks took on his new Persona as the trainee 'Roving Reporter'. There he was hustling and bustling camera in hand getting as close to the action as possible. It was obviously going to be the media boy's big task to get all the information in as many different recorded forms as possible.

We non-Australians stayed back, maintaining a healthy distance which allowed us to take in the whole picture.
"There's Mountain Girl!" Says Myrthin and we all immediately turn to where the vivid figure of the prankster called Carolyn Adams steps into the sunlight. She was still beautiful in her now gray hair irreverence. She was still loud too, just as we imagined Mountain Girl would be!

Mountain Girl had been a teenager when she'd turned up at Kesey's place in California in 1964. She'd left her home in the East to find what lay on the golden shores of the West. She'd then quickly become an integral part of the prankster's scene. Always pushing things, a step further by laying down challenges that were hard to run from. In Tom Wolfe's book she comes across as an amazingly defiant, confident explosion of a woman. In fact, she was famous for being the only Merry Prankster that didn't freak out at one of the last ever Beatles' concerts of all time. The others had all begun seeing demons and cancer in the cavernous arena, not Mountain Girl, no she'd just seen a pop band and berated the other Merry Pranksters for their lack of cool in panicking out.

Mountain Girl and Kesey had had a child together then later in the same decade she had married Jerry Garcia of the Grateful Dead. Carolyn Adams was a strong woman in the dying age of a truly man's world.
"There's Ken Babbs!." Say I all matter of fact as a tall guy

with shoulders of steel and a barrel chested stance walks off the bus. Busy laughing this deepest, craziest laugh in the whole world! Ken Babbs was also a key Prankster, again one who along with Kesey and Carolyn Adams had really driven the whole early crazy crusade and still does.

Ken Babbs had been a writer in the late fifties, studying on the same program as his long time friend Kesey. The guy whose prankster moniker was the 'Intrepid Traveller' had then left for Vietnam where he as a marine flew helicopters in and out of some of the violent jungle killing fields.

On returning to the United States in Nineteen Sixty-Three he'd jumped body and soul into the madcap birth of the psychedelic age. He and Kesey had then bought the school bus to travel to New York from San Francisco. Ken Babbs just continued flying, as an inner space astronaut though.

In front of us the same man thirty-five years later is now signing autographs and sipping whiskey from a plastic beaker.

On the top of the bus was the blue apparition, the young guy we'd already noticed. He was in his mid thirties and was busy rapping along to 'Green Onions' by Booker T and the Mg's.

Although we only recognize Kesey's brother Chuck and no-one else, it was all in all one of the most unusual experiences we'd probably ever singularly or collectively ever lived through. In our eyes these people were living proof of a thing we couldn't yet define. They were walking out of musty old pages and into the bright sunlight called August, Nineteen, Ninety Nine.

And Sparks comes rushing back talking about some great

pictures and Kesey settles to start answering questions and signing books. The rest of us, well we look on in bemusement realizing slowly at first, then all of a sudden in one fell swoop, that it was going to be quite possibly a very interesting week of changing roads and waysides.

We looked at the bus more closely. It wasn't the original bus of the 'Sixty-Four' pan-America trek, that was now a mossy covered relic back on Kesey's farm in Oregon, the 'ghost bus' it was called.

This newer version in it's amazing collage of artwork more than matched up as a bus for the new Millennium. Where the original may have been Stonehenge, this new one was like a swirling Sydney Opera House. Both buses were beautiful and it is truly not every day you get to hear psychedelic wisdom sung at a movable feast.

There we sat not really part of the scene but soaking it all in. By sitting on our own patch of ground it was just the most surprising thing to see these survivors of another age in such sprightly head out form. I acknowledged that it is important when you run the rim yourself to know that others have actually toppled off the gate and are still around to tell you how great it is to be able to float. This gang of three generations were the most outlaw bandit breed psychedelic America had ever produced. That they'd managed to continue the same perspective for so long through glorious ups and heinous downs and still be coming on, coming on, coming on, was to put it bluntly, something to admire, breathtaking in fact.

You just don't normally have legends as fully accessible as these guys were.

Kesey sits placidly signing book after book with a huge

black marker pen as Babbs the tower stands glass in hand booming something to whoever is there to listen. I begin to realize something called the 'Power of Babbs'. This is an observation that during that following week became more and more prevalent and it suddenly struck me as obvious.

If you have a dynamic three pointed arrow head made up of people with the energies of Ken Babbs, Ken Kesey and Neal Cassady, then there's not going to be much that can stop you.

The 'Power of Babbs' was then a steam train laugh and a slurp of some liquid from a sliced plastic water container.

"Well weird!" I said turning to Myrthin and he simply nods with a huge smile. None of us were talking, none of needed to, we were open empty pages letting events do the writing. The sea joined us with some respectable waves and the crowd got bigger and dustier as tired seaside families pushing kids and pulling push chairs came to join the swinging happy scene.
It was back up to adrenaline level one again instantly and that the evening of fun and games lay ahead of us no longer seemed daunting, just the greatest thing imaginable. Back at the now maybe thousand strong gathering, the Merry Pranksters have rung their huge bell and are starting up their motor to head off.

People in masses stand at the side of the bus cheering it on its way, and we stand in a huddle still in awe. It was quite a strong feeling to have witnessed this unusual almost magical scene. The Welsh wizard was now convinced that Merlin was nowhere else than sitting on the bus itself, and probably driving.

Powerful flipped out music begins to blast out from the

external speakers as the bus glides forwards and for me it feels great that tomorrow maybe should we be lucky, then we would see the whole shebang once more. Once more a chance to try and evaluate these crazy people but in a completely different environment. The day after was supposed to be at Stonehenge.

Time would tell.

Slowly the yellow from Sirius drives within feet of where we are standing and as much waving goes on inside the bus as it does outside and Ladies and Gentlemen, the Merry Pranksters pull off onto the main road and join the seven o' clock rush hour traffic for more adventure. We all, to a man, woman or child, are left beaming in their absolute positive ray. It all had lasted about an hour but that was using conventional time, that kind of thing didn't seem quite so important anymore.

So, with the bus gone it is hugs for everybody in the group and away we move to find some holy old bar in which to sink our floating feet. I tell the newcomers that they can put up their tent next to ours to a lot of initial relief but an eventual missed necessity for they never even reached the campsite that night.

So, out of a group of six, small pairs form, talking things over as introduction for some, Sparks and Myrthin, straight onto cricket as an easy inroad to the whole getting to know you, whilst the brothers talk as brothers do with a minimum of words and maximum of understanding and I chat to Lenny about what has been going on in old Vienna since my departure some weeks before.

Chat, chat, and excited gibberish, we boys had new ideas but it was still all around survival for each and everyone of us. Walking and talking we made our way back to the promenade bar and quickly moved inside. It was now a big zoom of noise full of the Friday evening crowd.

There were red skinned holiday families, hiding from the sun deep in conference. There were hapless mobs of males, loud and unabashed.
There were couples in white cotton fading into the pastel background and in the middle there was us, the latest psychedelic refugees.

Should our respective parents have been able to hawk an eye at this ragged version of their children, they would have questioned, questioned a lot. But hell, our parents were young when the original Merry Prankster bus had initially sailed forth, young and making their own specific beginnings. They were busy with families, new ideals and their early career times.

Crash!!! Thirty years on and what have they done? Well, given us the choice, the famous international choice of an upbringing, and this ability to choose is a privilege denied often by the need to work money, that famous frozen energy.

So we'd all had the choice and we'd chosen to sit and stare. Then though Myrthin and Sparks chose to go to the bar, a long, long bar, far away across the other side of the room.

This bar we knew already, we knew that it carried potions and bottles of every size, but Jesus, just give us beer, give us a break, give us a time to recover, and give us time to think for a while.
My eyes burned like mad, but somehow it mattered not, for a holiday was on and that mattered much, much more. I was now heading boldly into my thirty fourth consecutive

waking hour and my sunglasses had long since carved a home on the top of my nose.

They'd now been lodged there forever it seemed, but I knew, oh how I knew, that it would have been way too frightening to take them off. Frightening for me and for anyone else not into seeing the wild of somebody's eyes. But I was soon distracted from my distraction for a leery looking cowboy was bouncing merrily in front of where we sat.

"Hey boys! Do you like music?". He asked with a manic grin on his face.

It seemed like a strange question but before we'd had time to reply he was informing us violently of his band, that they were due to play in an hour, and that they were called the 'Flying Ostrich', or that's what it sounded like to me.

"Yeah we love music, we really we do!" Announced Fab Senior.

"But!" I interjected irrationally, "The Flying Ostrich is a hell of a funny name for a band!".

This sent the cowboy happily back on his way, he even left us a couple of flyers to study over, how's that?
"Does it say anything about ostriches?".

I ask worried about my own perspective.

"No! And it doesn't look like our kind of ticket either!" Says Lenny wearily reading the information.

"It says 'The best of the best from the Fifties, Sixties, Seventies and Eighties!!!"

That was a tall order, even if they had seen fit to leave out the Nineties, but somehow it did inspire us, it inspired us to move. Sure the movement was small but it was holy and significant. Myrthin who had just returned from the bar for the thirtieth time that day caught the end of the conversation, if conversation is what it was.

His solution was simple.

"Okay, let's drop some acid!." He says casually, as if talking about the weather or a cup of tea.

Internally I gulped and feared for my health, for yet another chemical evening was approaching, and I wasn't quite sure if the previous one had finished or not. These forever long-drawn-out days running into nights and further days as one continuous moment were becoming challenging.

"It's only weak laughing acid." Our Welsh guru adds convincing not one of us, probably not even himself. Come what may, there before us on the table was a small square the size of a large postage stamp, the 'weak laughing acid'. Around me the silence was deafening. It struck me that even Myrthin must have also been feeling the strain for he dives into drugs as a cure for tiredness as readily as most people dive into bed.

He looked around expectantly, almost desperately and it was Lenny that was first to speak. He talked of a headache and of feeling tired, but no matter, which was a timid excuse for the mad Welshman.

"Just a half, you won't even notice.."

Sparks however seemed indifferent to the whole situation, I knew he didn't really rate the drug and that he had never experienced anything, with the pseudo-LSD he'd been unfortunate enough to purchase in the past.

It was only the Fab brothers that seemed to be interested, they were interested enough to stop their lengthy soccer discussion, just for a while. I watched Junior carefully. I knew him vaguely and had ascertained quickly that there was more to him than met the eyes. He had already lived for a year in Namibia chasing wildlife with a camera. His boyish good looks betrayed a big explorers heart within.

It appeared that to him the acid was easy meat, and he quickly told us how he had already smoked dope with crocodiles, on some riverbank, in some jungle, presumably in some other life. Fab Senior giggled along with his brother. He himself was completely and utterly into doing the drug.

It was as if he would have been disappointed not to. After all he had just finished reading the 'Electric Kool Aid Acid Test' and was thirsty for some form of psychedelic experience.

I felt like it was only I, that had any true doubts about the wisdom of this proposed move. I kind of dreamt of peace and tranquillity but the reality was Myrthin in front of me, and that meant that there was no escape. I resigned myself to the idea and really trusted that my spirit would hold through and that at some point sleep would eventually return from the hills.

Anyhow we drank some more and soon we had swallowed the tiny pieces of paper, then we just sat and waited. In truth I feared little from the drug, it was unlikely that the swirling colors already loose in my head could be really tainted too far out. And for a while there was no noticeable effect as the drug lay latent in some far reaches of our minds and just dripped, dripped, dripped tiny amounts of confusion onto the already very confused scene.

A nasty noise was all that it took to kick the drug into action.

On the way from one bar to another a stranger took an illogical disliking to Sparks and accused him of being gay. Which of course he isn't, but which of course Lenny is. This made the noise all the more distasteful. The stranger, a young hood on the prowl for kicks was finally persuaded away when he saw that our number was six, and that none of us had the slightest interest in some mindless Friday night street brawl.

I remember that he'd called us all various insults and finally left to find another victim. Yet what he had succeeded in doing though was getting the adrenaline to free the drug and its power took us beneath an ivy covered arch and into a bar that reminded me of a bleak Scottish village.

Inside there were rough stone walls that jutted out at awkward angles and scared me a little. Mainly because they'd seemed to be pulsating, just ever so slightly, but enough. Worse still there were evil paintings of strange sailing boats that hung off kilter, as they had done for many a year!

But what was worse, much worse, was that the place was filled with ordinary people.

In our discomfort we all looked around dumbly then finally

sat down around a huge slab of breathing oak.

Of course, no one had wanted to go to the bar, not alone anyhow, so in the end it was Lenny and I, hanging onto the bar and swaying gently from side to side.

In the next few hours we slipped further and further under the influence, and we'd been laughing a little too much in my opinion but nobody else had minded. As always with LSD you feel what you are doing is mightily weirder than it actually is.

Mind you we had taped a half an hour of our rambling talk on Lenny's new 'Sony' recording device. We'd planned to listen to it a lot later and see what we had said. All these years later, we still haven't got around to checking the state of our heads that Friday, and who knows, maybe we never will.

Anyhow back then we lived in a world of enormous confusion and we knew that we needed a change. This widespread of male energy of ours was not satisfied with a gentle pub ambience, all of us needed something more inspiring. That our ages spread across a difference of almost eighteen years meant that each of us were after different things that acid evening, but somehow the group dynamic was working strongly.

Once more it was Myrthin who made the move, he was eager to hit the clubs. It must have been that time in the night when, it is away with the sitting and on with the dancing.
So slowly and with no real purpose whatsoever we left the bar in a gentle huddle.
Little did we know that our safety, our lives and our freedom was about to be put to a real test.

There were people only two steps down the road just waiting for people like us.
Blindly we fell out into the night.

"Is he all, right?"

It was a bouncer, and he was looking straight at Fab Junior who had dipped quite considerably on the walk from the pub to the club.

Somehow, we had ended up outside a club advertising a 'hot' DJ night. We were there mainly because it seemed like the place to be, also because the queue was already about fifty people deep. It was Myrthin who had been inspired by the quality of being at the right place at the right time, so patiently we'd started to queue.

In truth though we were in absolutely no state to stand in the gentle rain under weak lighting. The tension surrounding us just built and built and there was no way I could forget about the remaining five wraps of amphetamine in my pocket.

Myrthin himself was probably busy thinking about the remaining acid in his wallet and the others, well the others just looked plainly uncomfortable.

I mean, you know if there is something you really want to see or hear, then you don't mind waiting a while, but when it is merely an illogical acid shot in the dark, then the waiting seems ridiculous. It was though already too late for turning back, for we were approaching the entrance, and there it was, here was a security man asking about the welfare of the dazed Fab Junior.

"Is he all, right?"

"Yeah, he's fine!" Someone mumbles

No one seemed convinced and least of all old Junior himself, poor guy. His look was one which said leave me alone, I am having difficulties.

Nevertheless we shuffled forwards still unsure and still moving like an invisibly linked turtle. It was then that I saw a sign stating the club's nightmare door policy.

In the next ten minutes Myrthin had been frisked and had his acid taken. I'd bolted and hidden my plastic bag of amphetamine under a strategic pebble.

The others they had duly been lengthily harangued by a pompous security woman. A while after, the police had arrived completely independently and more, what's more, we'd all still managed to get in the damn club, even the disintegrating brothers.

That none of us had really even wanted to be in the place meant that the first moments in there were scowling dissatisfaction. We were angry with the way we'd just been treated but do you know what? Even then I realized that if you move into these places you have to play by their rules. Jesus it was obvious truth.

We had all been too high to make it easily through the doors. If we had been more aware Myrthin would have surely hidden his drugs, Fab Junior wouldn't have looked like a shell and even Lenny would have been able to stop his manic giggling. But we hadn't and we'd paid the price, so I decided to just get on with the whole shebang.

Hey, the music in there was actually brilliant, really, really hypnotic. Soon we'd all split up into various different areas of the huge room and were on our own for the first time in eight hours.

I even began to dance, and dance quite easily which did amaze me considering I'd been up for two days. It wasn't quite as exhilarating as the night before but pretty damn inspiring all the same. Every so often I would spot one of the others making their own waves in and out of different shades of light, but mostly it was yet another solo trip in amongst the masses.

Three hours later it was all over.

I could feel our Brighton stay coming to an end.

Earlier, I'd managed to retrieve the speed after some ten minutes of turning over the wrong pebbles, and lo and behold it was damp. The plastic seal had given way to the salt. But no panic, I was certain it was still functional magic powder.

What was more worrying though was that Myrthin had been missing for most of the time in the club. We the remaining five walked back to the Fab car, caught with a slight air of 'Oh my god! What happened to Myrthin?' running the show.

But no matter, for we were all still crazy on the drug and couldn't really feel too concerned about anything other than the state of our own heads. Junior still looked wiped out from the whole affair. By the time we'd reached the car I was quite happy to be off loading some good people and narrowing the scene down to just Sparks and I.

Oh yeah, and Myrthin should he ever return.

"We're going to catch some sleep in the car?". Announced the brothers in chorus suddenly.

"Really!" Say I in response.

I couldn't say that I envied their position, but it is a free world and that was their decision. They were going to stay in Brighton until one of them felt fit enough to drive back to London.

So, in that early morning drizzle, I guess it must have been close to four in the morning, we all said our farewells and moved off towards our own specific wheels.

It was Lenny that I really felt a pang of pity for. I could see the doubts light up in his eyes. He just wanted a bed, or to be home. I think the last place he wanted to be was in a cramped Volkswagen Golf with the wacky Fab brothers who would doubtless be discussing ten years of soccer for hours on end. But there was nothing I could do, we had other fish to fly.

We desperately needed a taxi and at some time just before the dawn, just before that tiny line of purple begins to rise in the eastern skies, Sparks and I hailed down a cab. We jumped in with what little energy we had left. And do you know what the driver insisted that we talked about? Yeah, soccer of course. Sometimes it seems that there is only one thing left to talk about.

Some forty minutes later we were snuggled up in our sleeping bags listening to tiny drops of rain tease the walls of our tent. It felt warm and womb-like and I sensed my eyelids were about to close. It was now approaching five o clock and suddenly as if on command, up sprang the 'Dawn Chorus' and a thousand tuned up birds started screeching for all their worth.

I felt a shiver run down my spine as the possibility of yet another non-sleeping night tickled away at my consciousness. I needn't have worried, ten minutes later, who comes swishing and giggling his way into the tent, Myrthin of course!

"Been at the fairground, amusement palace, on a roundabout!".

He tells us, and a hundred others of the camping sort. He spoke loudly and with mad excitement, proceeding to recount how he'd had his acid confiscated, swallowed some hash and even managed to slurp back one extra tab of acid that he'd got in his mouth in very short time. All in all, the man was flying off the edge of rationality.

The two man tent bulged with its three man load and slowly but surely even Myrthin got quiet, especially after being screamed at by some guy in a nearby tent. First it was Sparks who started snoring, then Myrthin went eerily silent and then it was only me and the birds. Though if you listened really carefully, it was possible, just possible to make out the distant pleading of the sea.

"Go to sleep! Go to sleep! Go to sleep!"

And do you know what?

Eventually I did, a soft lazy slumbering brushed the hair over my eyes and sent me spinning into a deep, dark slumber.

And do you know what? In two short hours I was awake again.

STONEHENGE AND KESEY.

Outside there was a devil sun in the sky and the walls of the tent seemed to be bubbling like old, blistered paint. It was approaching a sauna heat in there. There was no way I was going back to sleep, so at seven thirty in the morning I was up and come to think of it so were the others.

At nine thirty in the morning, we were parked up in a petrol station buying chewing gum. We'd left Brighton behind because that is how quickly it can go on the road. We were heading onwards towards Stonehenge. We were not actually heading there out of any real mystical, stones calling vibe. No, it was just that the Merry Pranksters were due there at some point, that Saturday long gone ago, way back before Kesey died.

Now of course we had no idea when they would be there but we certainly knew why. Merlin himself was quite likely to be hanging around those ancient stones, probably sipping tea and frightening the tourists.

Yeah we were heading out towards Salisbury and planning to catch up with the bus at some point later.

Should God be willing.

At the garage we'd all bought large and threw some petrol into the car for good measure. Soon we were off down a winding country road.

Trees bent down to wish us well and through the leaves you could see the blue tips of a famous English summer sky. Inside the car the mood was submerged in howling music and vivid self reflection.

If I am brutally honest it was probably the chance to get out into the countryside that really had us buoyant. I personally had had enough of the city for a while and it was the idea of sleeping on plush grass, in our castle of a tent. That had me really frothing at the mouth.

I was beginning to feel slight tinges of mania prodding at the outsides of my brain. Tossing tiny white jagged flying lines across my eyesight.

Now it wasn't scary, I'd had that kind of thing before. It is caused by a lack of sleep and too much happening in one brain at any one time. In fact, there was no cause for real panic but deep down I was desperate to camp out near a river and to sleep for a day.

There was only one thing that really scared me, the car. Yet again the engine was once more playing the fool and doing its best to shatter the situation. It was buzzing itself with the classic 'cutting the revs' game.

On the back of only two hours sleep in two days this was

understandably annoying the hell out of my ankles. Worse still, I couldn't really tell, I didn't know for certain, but it seemed to me that the engine's ailment was getting worse.

That I didn't pass this fear on to the others was probably because I was being swamped by an over imaginative mind. I was being challenged by automobile paranoia, so silent I stayed.

Silent as Sparks busied himself with a newspaper and Myrthin continued rolling joints. We were all absolutely shot down by the previous evenings but totally intuitive. We were learning to ignore a really heavy load.

The miles rode by and we really failed to notice anything except the times when we actually came to a standstill. It was never any good when we stopped moving. It was as if our minds would propel themselves through the windscreen to leave us and the car behind.

Each time we stopped was when I would have to begin my increasingly annoying routine of dancing. Off the clutch onto the brake whilst all the time keeping the foot down on the gas. I needed three feet to keep the revs high enough to keep the engine alive.

Yet by dancing I managed but this was a devilishly dangerous business because as you may remember, the chances of restarting the car named Norm were remote. The game was turning into a challenge, me against the truly most irritating stubborn creature on four wheels. But hey, calm, calm! I gave the engine a lot of free space and trusted in the unknown.

Whenever it was needed, I'd calmly start dancing!

That Saturday on a sunny August afternoon we slowly fought our faltering way into sleepy old Salisbury. Salisbury is a wealthy English market town. A place where people still proudly allowed their wet washing to dance on bowed washing lines. A place where people were polite and talked in whispers in public.
They didn't want us there, I could tell!

You could see it in their eyes! They would take three steps backwards as our booming, backfiring, bloody mess rounded every corner.

On hearing our approach parents would scoop up their kids and take one step back into the hedgerow. Others would run for cover under ancient oaks!

Well not really! It was just they way I felt.

We are all unkempt, unswept, unshaven and our mad music spat its fury out through the car's open windows. Unconventionally dangerous we were, me with my arms bare to the wind flying out of my waistcoat like icy forks of lightning.

The other two hardly cut a better picture. Sparks sat with his face and his blond mane pasted against the side window. He was helplessly eyeing the day fly by. Whilst Myrthin with his absolute pale out of place visage just looked fiendishly unhealthy.

He would look out to the world defiantly, always with a marijuana smoke bomb hanging from between his thin gray lips. A pretty site I guarantee we weren't, but an ancient site is where we were heading.

Behind or in front of us, there was a bus. A great, hulking, vibrating, colorful bus blasting with noise and complete with many freaks hanging off every angle of its bodywork. It was indeed a day for the weird, or the wired, or both, and we were well and truly both.

Both ways up, from top to bottom!

And from the bottom to the top was our first true post acid test. There before us a huge, multi level car park rose up from picturesque old Salisbury like a misplaced furnace. It stood in our way and with admirable determination we took it on and with admirable resistance it nearly killed us, well nearly killed me at least.

Upwards and onwards, we kept on moving around nasty, tight rising inclines as I trampled on the collapsing motor, dancing like never before on the pedals down low. Behind us there was a stream of shopping cars, and I knew should we stall, I, we, would have to abandon ship and scatter into the building like fleeing rats.

The place was bursting with cars and they would have lynched us alive these drivers surrounding us. By the time we had eventually reached the top floor, which was level nine, I was lathered in sweat and about to murder somebody. Wisely, we simply parked up, turned off and this is what it looked.

Short term, none of us wanted to be stranded in Salisbury under any circumstance. It would be like a week in purgatory.
Long term we were still seven hundred miles from the end of the journey and still two hundred miles from Cornwall.

That it didn't look good I have to report to no one, it was obviously a sinking ship that I was steering. That we actually made it, remains one of the greatest surprises I have ever known.

But enough leaping forward in time. Salisbury offered us fish and chips, some alcoholic refreshment, and a set of batteries for my cassette radio.

In two hours, we were gone.

In two hours and five minutes we were lost, completely stranded on the tiniest road in Southern England.

Myrthin had got us into the predicament by not knowing his way out of the town, actually none of us had!

Still, Stonehenge had been grandiose in the same sacred place for over four thousand years! I figured it would still be there long after our diversion.

That the car was still absolutely wrecked had become almost matter of fact. Actually we were all getting very used to living inside a world of irregular vibrations.
Outside, the view was amazingly pretty. There were thatched cottages which stood beaming proudly in the sun on that idyllic road. I took to daydreaming and dreamt to myself of one day being back, back as a merry resident of that leafy little oasis.

It was I suppose only a vague way of coping. Coping with the knowledge that very, very soon, strange things might well start happening to my eyes. Then to my ears! Then to my hands! Onwards until the whole world would became a negative Disney Empire.

No, I was in no mood to deal with Mickey Mouse or even Pluto! I already had other cartoon visions in my head and one of them was that we would at some point get off this interminable road.

ROAD, WHAT ROAD?

Yeah, that is a road and yes that it is you driving!

I shook my head and bit my lip and tried not to let the others know that I was fighting a battle of perception. I'd nearly driven us all straight into a wall.

My concentration was slipping, and it was lucky that this was only happening at a slow speed. It was though kind of daunting that I was still expected to crash a few more counties, that bleary old hallucinated day.
Finally and at the speed of reverse light we came to a junction and there before us, just above a hedgerow, was a tiny sign that initially read 'So Tinged 133'!

It made no sense but then on closer inspection, I'd literally had to place my nose up against the pole, it actually lettered out that Stonehenge was only three miles away.

So how was that? We were back on track, and the track was large, two lanes even, it must have been correct. We moved off down a swinging dip towards where that old stone circle stood awaiting us. Norm coughed his way up into fifth gear as we lazily trailed a dozen continental license plates.

"We must be right! I remember the landscape!"

Is what I would have liked to say but instead I just sat there tight lipped and fearful.

Strange things were happening to my system again. Now

long shafts of thin yellow light were forming dances in the periphery of my vision, no one else could see them I was sure! Mystical it was not, it was just my brain collapsing.

Prudently I slowed down back into fourth gear and all in all it was a rich form of desolation in the car, just plain energy-free central. I figured that we were probably three days ahead of our energies and that at some point we would have to sleep for a week.

That we never ever did remains a mystery, but that from that week on we found ourselves permanently awake, or at least more awake than ever before, lays claim to the power of the ways of the road.

Not then though, not at that point, no, then the almighty dip in energy was immense. Blindly we just followed the road with indifference as to whether Stonehenge was to our left, to our right, or even hovering above the ground, it didn't matter to us. Which is of course a shame, for it is not every day that you get your life thrown completely on its head by a remarkable coincidence.

It went something like this.

We had dipped and risen a dozen times, the landscape on Salisbury Plains is just like that, but the mood in the car seemed to be growing in expectation, a touch at least. Each of us in our delirium indeed needed to see the stones as proof of something solid.

Somehow though the very three miles that we'd been promised, the very tiny journey we'd been offered, was taking an age and a day. Had they meant thirteen on the sign we all wondered aloud?

"Or even three hundred!" Ventures Sparks.

No, there was no sign of anything vaguely Neolithic anywhere, apart from the rings beneath our eyes, and even they were safely hidden by sunglasses. No, there was not a clue. Then suddenly out of the blue, there on the right, glittering in the sunlight, behold the unmistakable formation of stones that are Stonehenge.

"LOOOOOOOOOOOOOOK!"

"Jesus at last!"

"No LOOOOOOOOOOOOOOOOOOOOOOOK!".

"What?"

"LOOOOOOOOOOOOOOOOOOOOOOOOOOOOOOOK!"

Myrthin was screaming and pointing, but strangely not at the world famous ancient site to our right, no he was pointing directly out of the car windscreen.

The confusion was immense and Sparks was now literally pressed between the two of us. Finally after an unfocused eternity I saw what he'd seen and so did Sparks.

There coming down the hill on the opposite side of the vale was the just as unmistakable shape of 'Further', the Merry Prankster's almost equally legendary bus!

None of us could actually fathom what was going on, the least of all me. For there on the screen, like a surreal cinema production, for ten seconds of time, we were looking at Stonehenge to one side and The Merry Pranksters directly ahead.

A collective shiver ran across our seats, and one could hear the logic cogs whirring out of control in our hollow heads. Each of us trying desperately to come to terms with one of the most amazing coincidences in all of our lives.

We started to shout, then scream, then holler and then whoop out joyful praise. It was as if our journey had at last been vindicated by some form of higher power. As if our instincts had been proved to be correct. A minute later the bus pulled into the car park, and we pulled in right behind it.

It was all quite dumbfounding, both vehicles had made the same journey, on probably completely different routes, and certainly at different times, just to arrive at EXACTLY the same moment!

In one fell swoop it proved to me, to probably all of us, a 'thing' which I had long since suspected, that we may well all be indeed on the same wavelength as the heroic Merry Pranksters.

Only that normally we are too blinded by convention to see what they are telling us, or even not telling us. It was about being 'On the bus', or in time with the bus. I felt immediately ecstatic and no longer jaded in the slightest. It was one further, incredible adrenaline boost.
That boost is still on the very same upward curve some years later. I no longer see things in a cynical, bland way, no, just always alive and always in a mad possessive moment of now.

Back then, having the bus in the same screen as Stonehenge proved to me one thing, namely that the life beyond expectation is the real life of possibility away from the humdrum. Prior to that point I'd had a collage of painted weirdness on the wall of my Viennese flat, but there before me in real time lay the truth. The honesty that anything is achievable if one points one's mind towards it.

Stonehenge wasn't moving but the bus was and as we both moved into the car park it was us directly behind the bus and that was an exciting 'thing'. How could we have possibly planned such an occurrence? There was no way, this was just coincidence in its basest form, and in a way the proof that there are connections beyond the perspective that most of us believe in.

Just think!

Had we been two minutes later out of the tent and bang! We would have been late.

Had we been three minutes later out of Salisbury and bang! We would have been late.

Had we not had the collapsing motor to hold us back then bang! We would have arrived early.

Had we have not been lost, bang! We would have been early.

Had the Merry Prankster's never existed then we would have been at some other place completely!

More importantly, we would probably never have been together in the summer, Sparks, Myrthin and I.

It would have been Sparks some place.

Or it would have been Myrthin some place else.

It was the Merry Pranksters that had brought us together and as we cut out the dying engine that was called the 'Norm', so the bus called 'Further' turned off its revs to come to a halt. We were both parked in the car park that Stonehenge never ever imagined would exist and around us are a hundred other travelers.

Though we knew none of them, they were all there in that moment of time called.

'NOW!

Ten minutes later I walked past Ken Kesey on the way back from the toilet, he was obviously in need of the same and obviously only human after all. But hold on a minute, I'd walked past, actually within touching distance of, Ken Kesey, the man who had once been a mere name on a page, a name on a front page. A man who had written classic literature yet had lived the wildest of lives in a seriously wild time.

That is what I had respected so much, that he had pushed the boundaries so far out of shape. His own personal boundaries and even those more set in steel ones that governed society.

So I'd walked past the big man and what is more we'd acknowledged each other in some subliminal way.

"Congratulations for getting here on time!". Was what I thought I'd heard. But that was impossible! I was probably still in the grips of drug dementia.

So, with my hair as wild as it ever had been as it caught in warm shafts of ancient breezes whistling across Salisbury

Plains, I got back to the car.

"Did you see Kesey?." I say all kind of awe struck and totally confused. I was excited which is quite an achievement after approaching sixty hours of hardly any sleep. The others 'had' seen Kesey and they had seen everything else too.

They'd stood around in the sun just glowing with satisfaction at being at that exact position at exactly that time. I remember seeing various Merry Pranksters hopping off the great bus to stretch their limbs. There must have been up to twenty of them 'On the bus' and it was all amazingly 'normal'. There was no immediate flurry of autograph hunters to talk of. Sure the interest did begin to unwind as the television cameras came out of the back of a large white van, but no, mostly it was truly a 'routine' Stonehenge car park scene!

On the face of things.

Even us, we were bursting with a happiness of some weird sort but had no urge to go running up to the Americans and start telling them of our amazing coincidence for as Myrthin said cryptically.

"They already know! They know that kind of thing, it's their game!".

Their game was a complex game and that much was clear and as Ken Kesey walks back to the bus, I think of what I thought I'd heard.

"Congratulations for getting here on time!"

The superstitious in me put away deep in my mind.

Kesey looked really fit. He was wearing a cap against the sun and looked strong. He had a blue star spotted shirt that like the beginning of the universe. He started talking to who we recognize Ken Babbs as we stand and soak it all in. We soaked it all in and then left to get tickets for
big monument, because after all there were other magnificent distractions that holy old Saturday afternoon.

The hoary, cracked gray rocks called us over. But wait, pay for your ticket and get it stamped, and then you walk underneath the road, yep, underneath the road to come out in the field of stones.

So this is what we did thus leaving the main body of Merry Pranksters to dealing with the cameras, though others off the bus were already making their way to the site too.

And how hot was it? It was scorching, the sky was just one of those perfect deep blues with a couple of ice cream vanilla clouds thrown in for effect.

In the heat we three, the road tormented heroes pulled away, talked and then walked directly from the stones. Somehow I've always believed that they, the old man stones look better from a distance.

Mainly because there were approximately a thousand other people mulling around the spinning energy down there close to the huge megaliths. So with my sleeveless waistcoat as timid protection and Myrthin with his lumberjack shirt as over protection, we strolled up the soft meadow.

Sparks walked slowest, he was wearing a light, blue "Star wars" T shirt. An Australian blown away by a myriad of ancient powers sits down away from the masses and asks me to switch on the radio.

I'd brought the radio with me to give the stones a musical treat! Rational I was not. We sat sown in the grass under a shining sky, though one of us didn't stay sitting for long. Within minutes Sparks had once more become the 'Roving reporter'.

He was like one of those war correspondents that hang around battlefields and was from that moment on, for one week only, our supplier of news. Our contact with the plans, schemes and words of wisdom of the Merry Pranksters and Kesey in particular.

"Off I go out into the melee in search of the vital information, the stuff we need to know!" He says like Hunter S. Thompson and away he disappeared.

He would then later repeat this process countless times that crazy week. It was the 'Roving Reporter' that could be relied on for any crucial tip, any significant nod of the head or essential 'where next?' type of messaging.

We two, Myrthin and I, were infinitely grateful. It was a harrowing job but Jesus, somebody had to do it and Sparks was perfect for the case.

I guess the two of us with our somewhat more reserved Welsh nature were too polite to run the risk. But hey what risk? The Merry Pranksters were not in the least way into being polite, so of course the Pranksters and the 'Roving Reporter' were made for each other.

Maybe it was just our first night in Brighton pressing us down, but the Welsh contingent, namely us, seemed happy just to lie on the grass. We lay with straw or joints between our teeth and wait eagerly for Sparks' every return. Within minutes he was bustling his way back up the slope.

"They're here, all of them and the television crew and they are doing an interview, so I better get back!."

With which he was excitedly gone once more. And of course we got excited too for excitement is contagious and that afternoon their was plenty to get excited about, least of which was the radio. We were tuned in to a sports channel which was dreamily building up to a point of fever pitch about the new English soccer season.

Under normal circumstances this would have been of mild interest to both Myrthin and I. Not that Saturday, we merely brushed away the reports with a sweep of the hand, like double indifference. We were keener to keep up with our own news service, and there he was!

His unmistakable 'Star wars' shirt pushing and shoving, deep in the melee some fifty meters from where we sat. It was a curious sight to be sure, for the television guys had a long shaft that held the microphone, into which Ken Kesey was speaking. Under this, and in constant danger of being decapitated was our own Sparks, literally on Kesey's elbow.

I think deep down both of us trapped in the meadow envied his zest but in our laconic state of disrepair it was better to watch than to bustle. After all, it was both Prankster and big business ideology, that each member of a group should play to their strengths and that is in fact what we were doing.

I'd long since become the 'Dancing Driver' in reference to my constant battle with the Norm, the constant battle with the engine. That was my role in the week's theatrical performance, to get us to where we should get and on time. Easy! Just let it go and hey presto! We get to the correct place.

Myrthin, well typical Myrthin, he'd been loosely nicknamed some five years earlier on a trip to Prague, he'd then been the 'Hassler'. He was always on the look out for this or that and always watching and surveying for the next deal. Steve Lambrecht had been the original 'Hassler' back in 1964, a real true to the bone Merry Prankster of the first generation, so Myrthin was indeed, the 'New Hassler' for the week of searching.

Of course as with any name change scenario, it took a bit of time to get used to the names, and more often than not, it was still, Myrthin, Sparks, and I. However each of us knew our specific roles and thereby the appropriate name. And look out 'New Hassler', here comes the 'Roving Reporter' with vital information.

Almost breathless by the time he reaches us, but the news is, "Kesey's talking about a 'thing' and how everything is actually a 'thing', either a good 'thing' or a bad 'thing' or even a 'thing' in the middle. Its about magic and Stonehenge and how you can feel this 'thing' very strongly in some places and that this place is one of those place with the 'thing'."

Sparks was flying and loving every minute of his new role so with a long and whistled, "Amazing.", he was off once more.

Bursting down the hill like a child running from school, except that he was in fact heading towards a teacher and that much became very clear, very quickly. Ken Kesey was in the British Isles to pass on a message and that made all of us feel very privileged indeed.

Back on the slope under a cloud of smoke Myrthin and I talked of later.

"Maybe we should go to Avebury, you know that village surrounded by stones. It's probably got a camping site!"
"But isn't that doubling back and going the wrong way? The Essential festival is on the way isn't it, somewhere in Devon, in the North!."

"Yeah but I've heard it costs a fortune to get in."

"True, we have to find a camp site, doesn't really matter where, and the Pranksters where are they tomorrow?"

Now that was a good question, so I fished out my totally crumpled piece of paper which had the whole of the Kesey's "Wheremerlin?" agenda written down and tomorrow, which was a Sunday, was blank.

"No idea man, it says nothing here! Strange. Ah well the Roving Reporter will probably reveal all."

There was quite storm now brewing down by the stones, a crowd had gathered around the Pranksters and namely Kesey. The whole gathering was circumnavigating the stones, a thing that is bound to induce a dizzy sensation.

Still, Sparks was there fighting to maintain his position of access, ducking and weaving between the now hundreds of interested faces. He was doing a fine job, and so was the New Hassler. He was busying himself with counting the clouds, between stroking another joint into action.

As for me, it was just a time to ponder on the whole weird and wild world, I mean the world of placing yourself on the edge in the search for something. Something that is indefinable but permanently tangible. Is it excitement, or sensation or just purity?

Whatever it is, back then under that summer sky I felt as alive as it is possible for me to feel. You know how it hits you, when you're in the midst of an electric storm and at home, safe and still excited!

Well, at that point at Stonehenge we were bare, absolutely at the whim of our specific destinies. And if all that sounds confusing, as I might have said once already in this winding tale, it was because I was confused. This close proximity to people of such unusual status was something new. That their accessibility was their ethos had never really struck me before but it was a growing understanding and the future was easy to see.

Basically it was just a supreme self confidence within these people, there was within them no fear of not fitting in.

There was a subtle understanding of the power of the individual, especially in the midst of a group. And only time stops me spinning off and claiming that this is an acid thing, a doors of perception offshoot, but I think deep down it is possibly true.

No matter what present day thinking might say, or what that might make me try and deny, acid is some kind of key and it makes then shakes the god like within you.

I saw in front of me these people as true to their specific 'thing' as they had been some thirty years earlier. They were communing with anyone that was interested and communing their simple message of, well wait, I'm overlapping myself, Stonehenge was still early times.

"Kesey said!", Sparks runs up to us then stops to gather some breath, "Kesey says that the Germans should have tried to bomb Stonehenge, and that under the ground there are tunnels! The British had their headquarters under the monument".

Tunnels, bombs, and the second world war, now there's real Prankster world view for you, and this was straight directly from the chief's mouth, or well the Roving Reporter's at least.

It was like hearing lost lines from 'The Cuckoo's Nest' or from the 'Electric Kool Aid Acid Test', but no, this was real time! On line talking and all taking place a mere fifty meters from where we sat, and a hair's breadth away from our holy reporter's ears.

As Sparks the cricket player might say, 'How was that?'.

Pretty damn fantastic is how I would reply.
I quickly saw that we were living a daydream that had come true in real life hallucination wonderland.

Had we been told what we were to experience some years before then we would have all laughed merrily. In fact the Merry Pranksters themselves had been kind of dormant for quite a while, quite a long time and only with the onset of the Internet and quite probably Kesey's desire to spread a message did the need to go public become priority once more.

It was as if there had been a signal of old mortality from the world beyond and how had the Merry Pranksters reacted?

Well by going on the strenuous tour of Great Britain is how. And as sixty year old prophets always probably should do, they went into the people with their message still glowing strongly after all those years.

The total eclipse had obviously caught their imagination as had the combination of timing, the eleventh at eleven minutes past eleven. It must have been all too much to ignore for these purveyors of inner space exploration.

Subsequently it had been with determination and precision that they had planned all this, and there they were in one big jolly gang moving around the stones. And I remember thinking at the time that it would be great if they actually attacked the old gray warriors with colorful paint and really cause a stir on their first day in the British Isles. Reclaim Stonehenge, which would certainly make the headlines and up the ante on this 'Wheresmerlin?'Tour.

The old monster of public outrage would be back on board once more and of course so too the attention of the law enforcement boys.

Was that the Pranksters' plan? Sensational attacks on traditional values? Just like in the Nineteen Sixties when rumor had it that they'd planned to plaster liquid LSD, all over the San Francisco Winterland arena on Halloween. Acid on the banisters, acid on the door handles, acid in the water, acid on the seats, acid on the bars, acid everywhere. And why? Well, the day after the Pranksters, the Californian Democratic Party were due to hold a huge rally in support of one Governor Brown in the very same location. A rally for who? Governor Brown!

It doesn't really matter who but a whole conference of straight thinkers could have been dosed to the eyeballs and left the building psychedelically aware. Could you imagine that one for an outrage? It would have raised the world stakes as well as the awareness.

It would have also at the time put Kesey and the Pranksters up there as public enemies number one. No doubt they would have been hunted down and made to pay. Yet their crime would have been of such a Prankster nature that no law book in the country would have had a sabotage rule to suit the charges.
Anyhow it turns out that they didn't do it or at least they claimed they didn't and I always regard that as a shame somehow.

Ronnie Reagan actually defeated Governor Brown then went mad a couple of years later. Maybe just maybe a little acid might have actually done him some good in the long run, but Nancy, well Nancy just always said 'no'.

In 1999 there were no paint brushes at Stonehenge, there was to be no blitz on the four thousand year old monument, no it was a different from of attack, almost as if all the years experience had brought about a more measured approach to changing the world. Talking was now the medium, and Sparks was still rolling his 'thing' around his head.

Later we sat and skinned up the drugs that we had with us and saw how the bus had left the car park and was now way across the moor land watching the whole scene. Kesey had carefully aligned the bus with the stones as if to energize it and the whole gang for the forthcoming tour.

And the sun burnt down strongly, so strongly that I feared

for my arms. I borrowed Myrthin jacket to hide under and regretted not having a shirt of my own, but it felt good and warm.

It was at that point that Carolyn Adams came to spook us out in her own 'Mountain Girl' type of way. She appeared from nowhere standing about three yards away and telling us in a hawking American accent.

"The bus wouldn't go without me! Those guys wouldn't dare!"

"They're going to ring the bell!"

All in all we sat their mildly in awe and totally phased.

This was Mountain Girl, who was now a woman in her late fifties. Mountain Girl was a key Prankster. Ever since she had arrived on the scene in 1964, she had been very influential on the whole scene. She comes across in the Tom Wolfe book as being way larger than life and fearless, even traveling down to Mexico on the bus whilst being eight months pregnant. She was famous for being involved in Kesey's marijuana bust in 1966, keeping the Hell's Angels under control and for her booming laugh. And hold on, there it is right before our eyes, that same crazy laugh.

We the people, we do not giggle up, or cramp her space, no we just laugh and smile farewell when she leaves.

We all watch her descend the slope to where the Pranksters are assembling, whilst we suddenly see something important. We see that we are not intended to spend the week chasing the bus after all. No, we decided then and there to let things just come together when they were supposed to.

We immediately knew that there was no point in worrying about anything and with which, we instantly relaxed and lay back in the sun. More had happened in the space of two days than we could possibly have imagined, and this, the latest thing, Mountain Girl coming up and chatting was just a charming buzz.

The truly weird 'thing' though was that she'd been talking to us about bus ethics, like how the bus wouldn't leave without her, without even knowing that we had any idea of the bus, Kesey or anything. So that had kind of made us feel involved in another way, for it was obvious to her that we were on the tour too in our own way.

"Congratulations for getting here on time!".

That was Stonehenge that Saturday afternoon. Some minutes later we watched the bus pull away with music blasting and wild people hooting, and it didn't feel sad, not in the slightest, for we all knew that this stuff was mere introduction. We knew that the other real stuff would happen later, at the total eclipse at the latest, if not before.

So, thanks Mountain Girl anyway, thanks for passing on the first lesson.
We had been taught how to move independently and that lesson would never be too far away on that week. Whatever we were to do, it was to be coincidence, the correct maneuver and would ultimately always be to our advantage.

So as the radio told us that the new soccer season had just kicked off and as the bus disappeared into the orange glow, we decided to roll a joint for the journey.
Then quietly, calmly we walked a couple of private laps

around the vibrating stones, just the three of us.

PEACE AT LAST.

Some two hours later we were deep into the next stage of the journey and jumping with glee that Taunton, Devon was going to be our resting place that night.

It had sounded suitably rural and the fact that it had literally leapt off a passing sign and told us to come, was just coincidental. The mood in the car was buoyant, we had begun to understand the Prankster logic and we were now playing happily along.

It didn't even bother us that old Norm was behaving like a truly gone out ghost for somehow we were getting acquainted to the power of life under the colored umbrella of diversity.

We pulled off the motorway and drove into tiny Taunton and just managed to catch a closing superstore. At that place we were positively inspired. The New Hassler had decided that it should be an expensive bottle of wine each for the evening and along with that we bought bread, cheese, a corkscrew.

I even managed to free a restaurant of three of its knives for using with the cheese. We were set for the evening as true rural squires should be and as we squealed out of the car park along the southern road, we found ourselves an idyllic camping site.

This was a perfect place in which to focus our pretty elaborately wasted energies. It was a farm in fact, one with a crumbling aura about it! See the three dilapidated tractors that sit in the front garden and watch the chickens scraggily pecking at the flowers. The old farmer came merrily to the gate, dressed in faded tweeds, and offered us eggs and tokens for the shower block. We took the tokens and passed on the eggs.

Myrthin then proceeded to nearly mow down a family of our fellow campers by losing his temper on the drive from the farmhouse to the field!

It was mainly Norm's fault, Myrthin on the fifty-meter journey lost his patience with the stuttering engine which was longing for rest and sped across the field like a maniac. But soon in the early evening sun and with us camped by a tiny river we were home for the night. Two tents, a car and our meal placed gently under the heavens.

Our radio played along as we sat and whiled away the time, Sparks ambled off to the showers.

"My hair is like sand! I need new clothes! And a shower!"

And with that away went the Roving reporter.

"I'm waiting 'til the morning!" Announced Myrthin rather ominously.

"Me too!" I lied. I intended no such thing. I was waiting for the Cornish ocean to cleanse my body and soul, for nothing else would do. This was despite an increasing protest from the other two. They began to take offence to my psychedelically tinged sandals.
"I'll wash my sandals instead!." I said as a compromise.

I was getting very 'skin to the wind' by this point of the trek. My favored costume was my hunting waistcoat on bare skin, long sports shorts and sandals. I was enjoying immensely the ability to feel free!

"Deal the cards! I'll tell your fortune!" I say between raking off a piece of bread and cheese.

"Red for yes! Black for no! Go on, go on, the cards never lie! Any question, yes or no, anything!"

My amateur fortune telling was infamous amongst our circle and was a sure-fire chance to wind the world around a bit. Myrthin though preferred gambling so soon we were playing poker until Sparks came back. The Roving Reporter on his return told us of the showers.

"Refreshing, and hot! Mind the huge spiders though!"

On which he produced a size-able basket of plastic flowers. This was the first of our religious icons that we would collect on our travels. Yes, we were learning, learning quickly. By the end of the stay at the campsite, namely thirteen hours later, we had acquired, a license plate from a minor unrelated accident, a large sign saying 'gentlemen' taken from the toilet block and the large silver shell from a discarded car headlight.

These tokens of success we then hung on Norm and thereby ensured our safe progress onwards and further.

But back to the evening. I remember a lot of talk about the next day and whether there would be the huge threatened roadblocks.

There had been much newspaper talk that the whole country would be on the move. A doomsday scenario of petrol fumes and traffic jams. I remember playing guitar and thinking I had reached some higher plane of music.

I even remember the point when Myrthin decreed that we should have the last of his acid which he had somehow retrieved from some secret Location.

And I most surely remember being immensely relieved that it was to be only one tab between the three of us, and therefore a minor, almost inconsequential LSD hit if there was such a 'thing'.

The acid was soon gone and the wine was going, as was the sunshine. It was getting dark out in the field, but not cold, no it was positively humid that Saturday night in August.

We'd smoked several joints and laughed and talked. It was a blissfully static pace by the side of the river. Funnily enough we seemed to be the only ones on the camp site, I mean there were other tents, maybe five in total, but apart from a couple of ball playing kids, there was no one else with which we could commune. That might well have explained how easy it was to just be, just to be yourself.

Remember we were all now into the third day of the trip,

with two hours sleep each. Drunk, high and exhausted. In the field we felt at home, so it was no surprise that the New Hassler it was who insisted we hunted down a pub.

"We need some action!" He shouted.

"Oh my god!". Whispered Sparks.

An hour later we were in the tumult of a heaving wall to wall Saturday night madness. The bar was enormous, a wealthy stopover for rich trailer park holiday makers. It was madness inside and even the carpet scared us a little.

We had walked in timidly then managed to find a spare set of seats, close to a large window just in case we needed to escape. The place was alive with the noise of popular music and shouted conversation. Around us moved a melee of fathers and mothers and brothers and sisters and friends and girlfriends.

It wasn't the calm of the field and that much was certain. Of course, the acid had boiled up immediately on walking into the place. The wine had swum home too, and even the spliffs had sent us spinning. We hadn't realized, we hadn't realized at all! We were absolutely spaced; of course we were!!!

Yet the human mind is good at adapting and soon we were getting familiar with this unholy gathering, I'd dived into Guinness stout for health reasons and the other two were busy crashing down glittering German beer. It all suddenly tasted good, really good. We happily smiled at each other and shouted across the enormous noise.

"We should ask them to put the Merry Prankster program on!".

Channel four of British National television were that night airing an hour long documentary about Kesey and the gang. In truth none of us really wanted to phase out in front of a television, as our eyes were hardly working anyhow.

Instead we started talking to a nearby family, really amicably, really coherently. Then Myrthin goes mad, gets one of the children's wooden, cricket bats and starts spinning it around his head. Whizzing it inches from various delicately balanced heads and limbs.

The family didn't have the faintest idea what to do and neither did we. Myrthin then played a few cricket strokes and returned the bat as if nothing had happened. The family shouted something vaguely threatening at us, probably having our wildness down to too many beers. But no, oh no, if they only knew what a dangerous heavy load, they had sitting next to them! If they'd only known. They didn't so it was of no concern. And anyhow within minutes a young red headed, plump bar guy came around with news of 'last orders.' So, we shuffled off to the bar and bought in the last beer of the day then returned to sit glassy eyed and calm to wait for sleep.

You could almost tangibly see it heading around the corner like a heavy velvet drape. There was no escape, there was no escape from tiredness that night.
Sleep was a coming.

It's coming!

Sleep was a parachute descending from high, a menthol warmth that was about to suffocate we three into defeat, only temporary defeat but as we left the building and escaped into the midnight air, it was to collapse we were heading.

On the wobbling journey back, we stumbled down a gentle brook. We'd decided to walk the darkened, unlit way home, it was our last challenge of the day.

The sound of a gurgling rush of water possessed the kind of energy we had no use for. We had been long since driving into the ocean, salted and ready to jump back into the sky as clouds. Deep down I hoped that the morning would bring us back as a waterfall but somehow, I had my doubts.

I knew that we were way behind with the sleeping and it would probably take more than a dead ten hours to bring us back to sparkle, or not?

The last thing I remember was being curled up in a sleeping bag listening to music pulsing gently out of Sparks'. tent, snoring from Myrthin's side and a swooping feeling of falling through clouds, then gone, gone, gone.

Dead to the world.
Dead to the outside and barely alive, barely breathing.
Just sweet, sweet refreshing slumber.

Aloof and lost in the world of darkened angels and angles direct to the sky.

In the Taunton night there was only the owls on the wing and the sounds of the hunt, nothing else, there was nothing.

Probably wild dreams too, but if I am honest, then I remember nothing.

Until suddenly in the morning, at a time unknown, the shrill of a cockerel claiming the day gets me woozy to my senses and I look around.

I see the wall of the tent on fire with light. The sun seems to be full, and I come to full consciousness feeling well with the day. Myrthin is still sleeping to my side but the Roving Reporter, I know will be awake, for he does not sleep long, ever. Quietly I free myself of the womb and slide out into the day. I put my shades in place and outside there is Sparks sitting in the sun taking in the morning.

Around me there are other campers, some frying sausages, some flinging flying games to the sky and others leaning in deck chairs engrossed in the enormous newspapers of a British Sunday. I also notice a damp dew that tickles away at my toes.

"Sleep well Sparks?" I ask softly.

He nods and seems to be immensely calm after his one night deep in the countryside.

"Today it is to Cornwall we are going!". I say with an air of pride.

The day had begun.

And as the day continued it was another hundred and fifty miles that stared us in the face. But first we had other things on our mind. That became obvious about an hour later, after Myrthin had sluggishly surfaced.

We turned the car key, and the engine was dead, d-e-a-d, dead. From beneath the hood, there was not so much as a shimmer of a spark, nothing, one pummeled motor was all that we had.

"Ring the breakdown service!" Someone said.
"It'll take a miracle to get this thing going!" Someone replied.

"I'm going to the shop to get some breakfast!" Announced Myrthin.

It looked grim, each twist of the key invoked silence, a sickly silence, yet the clock was still ticking, so the battery must have been still working.

It looked like us stranded at the campsite for Sunday at least. But do you know what? Somehow that was fine, Jesus, we had our tents in position, we had a bar within walking distance, we could survive the Taunton trap for as long as it held us.

Yet in reality that was not the point! It was to Cornwall we wanted to go, so it was the Emergency Services I was ringing.

"Yeah, a red Ford! We're on a campsite in Taunton! Which part, I've no idea, it's near a river and there's a bar called................"

I was getting nowhere fast and the person on the other end of the phone was quickly losing her patience.

"Is the engine turning over?" She asks desperate for a hook of common sense.
"No nothing! The engine's completely dead, it's been playing up for the last five hundred miles!".
My voice trailed off down into the phone line, spinning

away back on itself, then making figure eight's off into the distance.

Five hundred miles, which hit me like a hammer blow. It was just such a distance that we'd travelled fast and stoned right across Britain. It was a crazy thing to acknowledge considering our means of travel had been fighting all the way.

"It's the Star Room Camp site!" Announced the huffing, puffing Roving Reporter who had had the wherewithal to go and ask the farmer.

The name sounded surreal but it worked and the woman said that the emergency services would be with us within an hour. Great! An hour sat in a farmyard, watching the chickens watching us. It was no big deal though! Soon, there was music playing out of the speakers and Sparks and I hung onto the car doors making polite conversation with our passing fellow campers.

"Yeah, it won't start!"

No-one offered their services, no-one dived under the bonnet, but there was an air of genuine sympathy exuding from their faces and I felt that very sweet somehow. Though hold on, its only been ten minutes, and hold on here comes the New Hassler armed with our breakfast.
He was laden with essentials, newspapers, drinks, even sandwiches my god.

"Hey let's just breakfast in the open air."

So that was what we did, we ate in absolute silence amongst the farmyard animals. Only the sound of mild satisfaction borne out of a huge hunger filled the air. For the journey so far, it was as if we had been completely dismissive of the role of food in our lives, almost downgrading it as an unnecessary evil.

Which if you think about it has been a fundamental technique used by seekers over thousands and thousands of years. We though, were not quite that clever, we just kept forgetting to eat. But still the effect of fasting was totally cleansing and in fact made even the most meager of meals take on the taste of a banquet.

In the latest feast, the newspapers we read were full of the eclipse, pages and pages of the stuff. The countdown was well and truly running and still they talked of the expected chaos in Cornwall. This made me laugh for it was there we were supposed to be heading. I looked at the shell of our car and swallowed a large chunk of sandwich.

It was quite a dull day this Sunday of ours, overcast and bedded in with the threat of rain. That made the arrival of a virtually neon yellow truck all the more noticeable. It gleamed past the dark green hedges and kicked color into the spitting gray gravel track leading to the farm. It was the automobile rescue services and they were coming to rescue our mission.

They're coming!

We immediately christened the guy in the truck "Saint Yellow!"

Saint Yellow screeched to a stop next to us and was soon out into the melee.

"What's the problem? A flat battery?" The man was a tiny compact mustachioed hero of the modern age.

"Probably the dew!" He continued. "Got into it overnight! Indeed, indeed, probably the dew, probably the dew!." He was speaking mainly to himself.

I wondered whether to shake the man's hand, or at least introduce myself but he was working quicker! He'd already read the license plate and seen our inappropriate picnic. He then asked me to open the bonnet and within minutes he was into it.

"Fire the engine!" He shouted from somewhere deep.

I turned the key to once again no response. He rushed over to the truck and slid open a side panel to reveal a conglomerate of instruments and I remember suddenly feeling very confident with our Saint Yellow. He connected something to something else and was gone once more into the oil.

"Okay turn it over!."

I turned the key and the engine burst into life, a kind of sickly form of health, a coughing consumptive form of life.

"The timing's shot!" He shouted from over the noise. "Has it been like this all the time!".

To which all three of us responded with a hearty

"You bet!".

The Saint shook his head ruefully and soon tinkered and touched then pinged and pronged and in ten minutes the engine was running like a virtual Ferrari. Good god he'd even formed a rustic tiny instrument with which we were supposed to tune the timing ourselves should we have any further problems.

"Just in case hey!."

Two minutes later he was gone, like a specter.

He'd left us and the car totally tuned in and that meant one thing! It was time to go to Cornwall. So, to Cornwall we went.
I remember the journey now as one of following the sun.
We headed west and the sun lay tempting us onwards. Sometimes it was bordered by clouds, but always, always there. In my head I had a virtual aerial vision of our route towards the tip of England's long and pointed nose.

The jutting land feature is so familiar that one could almost see a red dot travelling along a map. That was us. The road itself was fine, a large modern stretch of freeway and I kid you not, for we have photographs to prove it, we were at times the only car in sight.

There was no huge snarling mass of traffic fighting their way for the best view of the eclipse. Whole stretches of the road were eerily empty and somehow it seemed as if the newspapers had frightened away the whole mad rush to the eclipse. As the week went on and we heard that version of events more and more often, it appeared to be the truth. We though cared little, for we were eighty miles an hour and flying through counties.

Inside our Norm the mood was incredibly upbeat, we continued to marijuana the day away to little noticeable effect, and we continued to play the Roving Reporter's music louder than the world of God.

And we drove on and on and on.
And we drove on and on and on.

The car was suddenly such a pleasure to drive, there was absolutely no need whatsoever for any of the clutch tap dancing of the earlier journeys. Our wonderful Saint Yellow had made the impossible come true and we were soon leaving Devon and entering the magical kingdom of King Arthur and Merlin.

Strangely enough back in very old Ruthin, North Wales, outside a bank, there is a huge stone on which King Arthur is supposed to have beheaded some unfaithful warlord or other. Arthur was in fact King of all Britain! His name turns up in many unlikely places around the British Isles. Just like Robin Hood.

Anyhow it was Merlin we were looking for! There were cheers in the car as we flew past a signpost welcoming us into Cornwall and we were there, we had made it.

There were no immediate thatched cottages on view, but the signposts started losing names as we continued our journey, and soon we were down to just one name, Penzance, and that was where we were heading.

I'd never been to Penzance before but it had that market town vibe in its name, and as it was Sunday and as we had the whole county seemingly to ourselves, then a market town was where to be.

I remember the last leg of the journey now as a race into the sun, for as we closed in on the Western most part of Britain it was the sun that led us on, bright and burning in a now clear blue light ink sky. And we laughed and we thought and we sang and all of a sudden we were parking on the edge of a harbor in Penzance itself.

We tumbled out into a highly excited summer seaside atmosphere. The smell of salt stung in the air whilst tiny fishing boats bobbed merrily in the timid waves.

There were nets strewn across walls and brightly colored buoys hanging down rusty iron staircases to the sea. People of course too, oh yes there were hundreds of people.

Somehow it felt like a gathered tribe, not in any new age mystical way, no, but in the way that all of us had defied the warnings and here we were already in place for the eclipse some three days later. That was quite a feeling to have actually made it and in Penzance that mid afternoon, it was fact high and above the water, we were safely in place.

"Okay let's find a bar! It's Everton against Manchester United at four!." I said out of the blue suggesting a touch of normality. With which the New Hassler, the Roving Reporter and I headed away from the sea and up a slight incline to where the main street loomed large.

"And something to eat!." Someone else said as we went off in search of a blast of normality. Soccer or football is one base pleasure that quite denies any search for Merlin magic, so it was a kind break from the ride. In thirty minutes we were surrounded in a pub, one with a suitably huge television screen dangling precariously off a far away wall. It was a room full of what can only be best described as holiday mayhem.

Families of four pondered the menu whilst groups of guys raced down their beers. Couples talked softly and we, the neo Pranksters just soaked it all in, without hardly a word spoken, for a while at least. But soon we were ordering and chatting the waiter and then into the locals with queries.

"Camp sites? Are there any around here?". I ask.

"All booked up boys!", a hoary beer tainted voice informs us, "Its the eclipse you see!."

It took a lot to scare us by that time and in a county full of fields and beaches we were certain we would find somewhere to steal a spot for our tents.

"Only playing with you!." Says the guy, a gray bearded local fella of ruddy complexion and sparkling eyes. "There's plenty of room, everywhere!".

"I know, there was nobody on the motorway, empty, we couldn't believe it!". I say with so much excitement it seemed out of place.

"Its those buggers at the newspapers!." He says, frowning, "Scared every poor bastard away! The town's half empty, busier than this last' week! Buggers!" We all shook our heads at the stupidity of panic and supped a sip each in an unspoken toast to those who had ventured.

"We've come all the way from Brighton, well actually Wales!". Says the New Hassler with a touch of pride in his confusion,

"Off to the Minack theatre in Porthcurno, the Merry Pranksters are doing a theatre thing there!"

"Aye I've heard about that, some Americans, I believe!".

And to our credit not one of us began trying to explain the Merry Pranksters or the bus or anything to this gentleman. We simply nodded and watched as our meals arrived. Cornish Pasties of course.

Now one thing that has been overlooked in this tale so far is that by this point, our financial stocks had been savaged, mainly by Brighton I will admit, but whatever, we were running pretty low on the financial frozen energy.

Why frozen energy?

Well frozen because it has no life of its own until it is exchanged and therefore is constantly in a state of freeze until it comes temporarily valid.

Some old Acid guzzler once told me that in exchange for a substantial amount of small change. Anyhow, we were soon going to be running short of money and that was mightily uncomfortable. I couldn't really see any way of getting my own private frozen energy to flow.

My pay in Vienna was due in on the eleventh of August, but I had no way of getting to it. I had no plastic, no checks, so it was something worthy of consideration. Myrthin was in a worse position. It didn't matter though for we were on a life fulfilling trip and things tend to have a way of sorting themselves out in the midst of such potency. So, the food tasted great and not one of us worried about where the next meal was coming from.

Not one of us knew where we were going!
Not one of cared!

It was a hand to mouth existence and by that point in Cornwall the traditional form of existence had been replaced with a far easier version.

We were free and mad in our heads.

The afternoon handed me a handful of beers and a real fuzzy head once more. There was also a deep, glowing feeling behind my eyes. By five o clock we were driving along the smallest imaginable track searching for a campsite. This was a search for a 'cool place', and we had already driven past a dozen makeshift camping areas. It seemed as if all the farmers eager to cash in on the eclipse had seen fit to offer valuable fields to the thousands of potential campers.

All in all though there seemed to be no great rush to take up their kindness. Sure in some fields there were a scattered couple of orange dome tents, maybe ten in an area the size of a football field. Orange bubbles casting shadows on deep green meadows looking for all like inappropriate fungi. Though nature still reigned supreme, in reality there were free places everywhere. We the wandering threesome had decided earlier on that we wanted to hear the sea from our resting place that evening.

Relentlessly onwards we drove.

As the driver, with my bubbling alcohol head making me feel mildly disorientated, I really understood our general need for a picturesque solution. However I also wanted to finally steer Norm home and to begin using my legs once more. In short I 'd had more than enough driving for one day.

When we finally came to a stop we were in a field close to a tiny three house village called St Just. In fact, we were just outside St. Just and that was that for the Sunday driving.

The field we had chosen was owned by a hippie farmer, who was already doing huge business with a total of maybe five other tents. He wasn't happy, he'd expected more from this god given opportunity to make cash.

"Its the newspapers! Scare stories boys! Don't you listen to the lies they spread!"

It cost us next to nothing this place, it was cheap. The tiny block of toilets was over there!!!!

There was a caravan selling tea at the opposite side of the field!!!

Most importantly, the sea was just a half a mile away, if you held a touch of silence it was possible to make out its deep subterranean roar. We were home for the day and had made it from Taunton to Cornwall.

A strong feeling of accomplishment pervaded the moment, and the tents were soon standing in the territory that we'd temporarily marked out as home. Then some while later the sun dips in front of us, moving ever so slowly down towards razor edged horizon. We three sat on the soft meadow sipping on warm bottled beers that we'd bought at a garage sometime earlier. After some minutes our discussion moves swiftly to talk of our imminent walk to the ocean.

We were trying to decide whether we should take the path or to cut across the corn fields.

"Field mice!." I said "The size of cows!."

"And the cows?." Asked Sparks.

"The size of field mice of course!." Giggles Myrthin.

"Right!" I say gradually taking a coin out of my wallet. "Heads the path, tails the field mice!!".

We never found out! Half way during the arc of the coin's flight we were interrupted. We were interrupted by the first of the obvious 'eclipse freaks'.

These were men and women that were living in a state of heightened anxiety. Living in the shadow of the eclipse already, awestruck by what was going to happen to the point of being obsessed.

The guy was in his late thirties. He bounced in front of with a finely dangerous energy. He had a very familiar look. He was balding, had a long ponytail, his skin burnt brown by the southern summer and his face was framed with a scraggly beard. He was thin, unhealthily thin and his thinness was after us brandishing a piece of darkened glass.

"Really, really, these are the things. The only safe way. My god those things you get elsewhere, no nothing to compare. This is the only way!"

He spoke in bursts with an immense passion whilst dangerously waving the darkened glass over our heads.

We glanced at him without fear, being very friendly but we were ever so vaguely confused.
"Absolutely professional!" He screeched whilst thump
ing his fist on the glass.

"It's what the welders use and will not let anything through. No damage to your eyes, brilliant, brilliant, safe!!".

God, it seemed like this Cornish salesman of the unlikely had been waiting for this moment for the whole of his life.

His powerful delivery, with flying words and arms and legs and his hand constantly swinging the glass.

That none of us were interested would be putting things too simply. We were indeed fascinated by this crazy performance. Myrthin spoke as the guy built himself up to a point of explosion. I stared at his eyes as they darted from left to right then finished sucking on my latest space cigarette. Slowly and deliberately, I asked the obvious question.

"How much does it cost mate?"

"How much mate?"

The guy seemed shocked, "How much mate! Priceless these are, absolutely priceless! How much is your eyesight worth to you man?"

Somehow all these statements of physical fear mongering had me thinking along with him. I wondered how much my eyes were actually worth?
I wondered too how anything tangible could be priceless.
"TEN POUNDS A SET!! TO YOU GOOD GUYS TEN QUID!"

That was how much the eclipse freak deemed to be priceless.

"Yours for ten pounds a set!"

It took us only a second to realize we were being shuffled by this new age business pusher. His ten pounds price tag was for us too expensive and our eyesight would have to survive by itself.

"Sorry mister. It likes good merchandise, they look great but too expensive." Said the smiling Myrthin.

"A little too expensive!".

"Too bad, too bad. And you guys what about you?"
He continued whilst turning to look at Sparks and myself.. We shook our heads solemnly.

"Your choice my dears, your choice!." He reluctantly admitted before immediately fizzing off to the next tent and the next sales pitch.

He was gone as quickly as he had arrived but what he had left behind was the first encounter we'd had with a specific type of 'eclipse' character. These unusual types that would throw their trip in your face kept cropping up that week.
"Over the fields!." Commanded Myrthin.

The three of us giggled and slurped and then decided it was time to take an amphetamine walk to the sea.
Why an amphetamine walk? Well because we still had it to finish off.

Mainly though it was because of the vast difference between Brighton and this tiny corner of rural Cornwall. It wasn't specifically a drug decision, it was about enhancing a situation. By that point in the trip I had taken to believing that we were getting almost immune to any form of narcotic. Quite probably in such a consistently heightened state that nothing mattered any longer.

Whatever!!! It was speed we said that we needed!

Sneakily and with little fuss we disposed of more of the disgusting white powder and made our way out into the wilderness. It was a true wilderness out there.

A range of fields travelled down golden and rippled to where one could see the ocean. Huge white seabirds circled overhead casting traces against a poisoned blue sky. Long since abandoned clay mines stood out like cracked soldiers defending the sea.

I marveled at the idea that people would have walked this way to their workplace. A hundred years ago.
By this point it was approaching dusk and although there was still a vast amount of light to guide our way, there was a faint mysterious dazzle in the air.

There was a faint mysterious dazzle in our veins too and as we leapt one by one off a cracked stone wall five feet up in the air, it was mild amphetamine that was once more driving us on. It started to shiver its strange logic across proceedings and nature came alive as we walked through a waist high field of corn.

The Roving Reporter was busy taking photographs as we waded through this ocean, a dry ocean. I was busy wondering about the enormous field mice and other such wonderfully scary creatures.

It didn't matter for we were floating on that rippling corn ocean, floating out to where the real waves could be heard crashing against the cliff side. We slowly then proceeded to split up into three separate journeys linked by a common thread. The so-called New Hassler was ahead, his lanky frame pulsing its way into soft thoughtfulness.

Next was I, still sensing the ground's undulations beneath my feet, gripped by the moment, this beautiful calm moment. Finally came the Reporter, carefully investigating this and that and then capturing something on film.

All in all, I think that we'd reached a significant position of respect. We were surrounded by a triumphant feeling of powerful nature. This natural haven seemed to know that we had made it to where had quite often in the trip seemed almost impossible.

The place we had reached was a state of mind, a state of confidence. Sure, the Merry Pranksters were nowhere to be seen in this new-found idyll, but somehow, they were everywhere too. All pervading. It was as if we all had reached a new understanding of our own natural ability, that all the risks seemed to be behind us.

They weren't of course they were in fact to be ever present during that week. It was just a feeling of being in the most appropriate place we could have been, perfectly in place in the greater scheme of things.

Or were we just high?

It didn't matter, it was an overwhelming feeling and as we left the field and came to the tops of the craggy cliff coastline. There below us was the slate gray sea, the Atlantic Ocean.

We were looking out across the vast stretch of water that weaves and rises all the way to the United States of America. One by one the three of us each took up a separate position on a rocky outcrop to stare out, out into the absolute unending freedom that the sea can invoke.
There was me, doodling scattered amphetamine notes into a notebook I'd brought along as an essential. I was writing down flashes from the journey and feelings too.

Over there was Sparks busy photographing the sunset trying to capture on film the mood of the moment. Myrthin sat staring out to sea sipping on a warm beer and lost in reflections of his own mind.

We stayed in these positions right until after the sun had disintegrated behind the far horizon. It had left us with a vivid explosion of purple lightning in the west. Each of us had been lost in our thoughts, lost in our hopes and dreams and only fear was a stranger that evening.

We were looking at a bright future whilst saying farewell to the sun. The same sun that had provided us with a solid platform for moving stealthily across Cornwall that afternoon.

Languidly we came together once more and walked the cliff path past gorse and bramble. We walked past old, dark, ghostly buildings. We walked past dappled horses standing in pairs looking over hedges then bolting on hearing us approach.

We finally came to a break in a hedge .and to a place where a tiny path led us back inland. Indeed led us to what turned out to be the most quaint Cornish village imaginable. There we found a pub and an outside table and promptly sat ourselves down with ales. It was pleasant to soak in the descent of darkness mildly high and totally relaxed. Soon we were talking to an old lady laughing as her dog ran up and down the village. She told us how great it was to live in such peace.

She was a retired teacher and she spoke fondly of her days living in London before telling us she would never give up her life of retirement in Cornwall.

"It's so mild, we have a great climate!". She claimed with pride.

We were in no position to disagree with her, and we told her that we would all move there to live in an instant. In that instant at least. Her dog was still busily sniffing roadside flowers up and down the lane that ran by the pub.

"Come here Henry! Come and meet these nice gentlemen!."

Of course we all wanted the dog to share in the moment too. It was that kind of mood, just happy with everything and happy to talk for hours with this most traditional of old ladies.

We were indeed 'nice gentlemen', no matter which drug was sliding through our system. There were other people around the pub too, of course there were.

The place was just the perfect ivy covered, stone walled, centuries old hostelry it should have been. Inside when I went for more beer I found there were affluent sailing types with sun chapped skin.

"Hello. How are you?"

There were a couple of old Cornish fishermen with frosted beards.

"Hello. How are you?"

There were young couples lost in romance. I decided not to intrude on their privacy but each time one of us would go into the bar, it would be with warmth and laughter that we were confronted, and that made the whole situation perfect.

That Sunday night we were welcomed by the local Cornish

settlers. We fitted in, which is quite a thing when your head is running fast with high powered amphetamine.

"Take care, see you again sometime!". We finally shouted as the old lady and her dog went off to prepare a supper of scones and tea. We had been glad of the normal company in the midst of this blitz on the road.

An hour later we were off down a darkened lane heading instinctively to where our tents were waiting. It must have been about eleven o clock in the real world, but for us, well even the amphetamine was fading. A monstrous rousing need for sleep had once more submerged us all. Whether it was the fresh air, approaching middle age or just the road life pulling us back, we cared not.

Soft meadows were waiting for our frames and in a group of three we penetrated the night and surged gratefully towards our sleeping bags. In a matter of minutes there we three lay. Sparks in his tent and

Myrthin and I in our now familiar sleeping positions.

Suddenly Sparks puts music on the cassette player and suddenly I find myself drifting into a trance like state. This blends with the music so carefully that at once I am aware of the countryside outside, the walls of the tent, the pictures at the back of my eyelids and most of all these persistently beautiful tunes that rage above everything else.

First there was Blur, an English band with a song called 'Tender'. I was familiar with the tune, I even liked it, but that night for three minutes of time I lived it.

What it talked of with its painful pleading melody was that 'Tender is the night', which it most certainly was. One year

later when I truly fell deeply in love, this song by Blur was prominent in the first fantastic phase of acquaintance with my now wife. That this song was so inspiring to both of us was more by chance more than design, but somehow it seems quite surreal that in the tent that night in Cornwall I was almost foreseeing the importance of what was to come.
"Lord I need to find, someone who can hear my mind!".

Then came a song by the unlikely pairing of Nancy Sinatra and an unknown crooner who went by the name of Lee Hazelwood. The song was called 'Summer Wine" and it carried on where Blur had left off. It was quite the most beautiful thing I'd ever heard. It was new to me this piece of music, and in high melody Sinatra sang of dealing a wandering cowboy a potent dose of summer wine. Then having doped the innocent rustler the song sees her running off with all his worldly goods. He wakes up, all shy and battered, then replies to cruel fate in a regretful bass mourning towards his loss.

His loss being both a vision of beauty and his gold. I remember listening intently to the unwinding story with tears in my eyes and a thumping in my heart and I knew not why.

No-one spoke, for the world was completely focused in on the tiny music at the edge of the field. "Summer Wine" at that moment in time was the most perfect piece of music I'd ever heard. It even reminded me that as a kid I would stomp around the house in Wellington boots to Nancy's other epic "These boots are made for walking".
For a while the seven year old me was by my side and we both listened carefully to what Nancy was telling us. It was all quite stunning.

Tiredness had taken on a new form. It was as if we were all dreaming whilst still in some way conscious. There was now no need to yawn or to think, it was just a free fall into the most dramatic cloud formation ever.

And just as sleep began to stroke us down in came a German band from the early Seventies called Ash Ra Tempel and they promptly obliterated the quiet.

Their dumbfounding explosion of noise which goes by the name of 'Ambos' was the reason. This piece, an instrumental, is a riot of the senses, so much so that it had been banned during the car journey up to that point.

We'd banned it as being too compelling for sensible travel, but there in the tent it came on and took its revenge. It took me to a Tolkienesque pre sleep landscape and had me spinning at speed across the heavens. It was almost impossible to handle, what with the speeding, wailing guitars and the tiny, quiet passages that reach out for your attention. In the end

I think I gave up and watched my soul shrink into sleep. It was all intrusive this late night concerto and I took refuge in slumber. We all slept, me, the birds, the worms and the trees. Even the two other wanderers slept. Deeply I rested and rich were my dreams.
The day after was a Monday.
I'd just left behind quite a Sunday.
I floated out over Cornwall and watched the world from a great height.

ONLY ONE WAY BACK!

The sticky toast dripped butter onto my fingers, and it was morning.

Our breakfast came out of an old caravan and for showers there was no time. It didn't matter for we were moving again. We were refreshed, reborn and about to move somewhere new.

Somewhere even closer to our hearts for the Monday morning meant a new week.

The eclipse countdown was booming all around us and we chatted to the handful of others on the campsite about the eclipse hype, the weather and the sea. It was a normal beginning to an unusual camping week that lay ahead of us.

By that point in proceedings I was sporting a four day beard and my face was tanned brown by the whole swathe of outdoor life. I was still in my ever faithful waistcoat and still running around in my ten year old Adidas shorts.

My faithful battered sandals still lived on my feet. It was my road gear and we were gearing up for the road once more. In quick time we'd packed up the still damp tents and bundled them into any free space we could find in the car.

Norm the motor had taken leave of his duties and enjoyed a well-earned rest but now the dozing was over. It was a new day and we all merrily piled into our usual traveling positions.

Sat comfortably in position it dawned on us quickly that we actually had no idea where in fact we were going.

Sure we had vague plans of checking out the Minack theatre for tickets for the eclipse show, and we had other vague inclinations to get to a bank.

"Where are we going?" Myrthin asks me.

I pondered it awhile.

This ease with such a lack of direction felt good, somehow it was proof of just how deep into the whole experience we already were. It was pure freedom to be able to come and go as we pleased without ever a disagreement amongst us.

We were all totally focused on the undefined aim of learning some inexplicable something from someone. We were all using and acting upon our basic animal instinct. The old car called Norm was not though in the same high spirits.

For the next half an hour we'd tried to get his engine going but somehow the damp field had killed into his system, again. His timid spark had been lamed by nature once more.

Again, a couple of helpful fellow campers came by to offer us advice as we tried the ignition. Though somehow, we were by then totally familiar with the temperamental motor. We knew that patience and trust was the deal.

We knew it was just a matter of sitting tight until the engine finally worked, however long it took. We were in no rush and told anyone who was interested that we knew the value of time.

"No panic, he's always like this!". We explained to two strangers who wondered a little then said no more.

"We are at the hands of bigger powers. They are in control!"

Soon, the big women in the sky ordered the engine into life. Then it was my crucial task to try and make sure that the engine stayed alive. I would once more begin my pedal dancing and off we glided noisily across the field.

We moved out into Cornwall like an injured whale, we were not embarrassed though. We waved happily to our fellow holiday campers. Within minutes we were away. Me busy keeping the engine over revved and when we were stopped by sheep a couple of minutes later then I'd busily jumped onto the clutch and accelerator simultaneously.

It was getting easier this driving the impossible . In truth for although we knew we would never break the stubborn creature in, it was comforting to know its idiosyncrasies. I knew it was just playing with us.

"Let's hit Lands End!" Says Myrthin excitedly, "I've never

been there!"

It was a good idea so that's just where we went.
We drove with abandon along tiny narrow lanes to where the final pointed nose of Cornish rock juts out into the sea.

As it was only ten o clock in the morning we were three of only a handful who were already keen for simple tourist activity.

We were there before the clock had had time to move, us parked in a relatively empty car park, which looked like a huge concrete stain on the verdant countryside. I seem to remember that one had to pay an entrance fee, which made little sense to any of us. I mean paying to see land is like paying to unlock your own front door.

Anyhow there was no real point in complaining, so out we went. Out with the brisk wind breezing through our hair. We had paid to watch the seagulls calling our names out loud high above our heads.

It was at this point that I was disturbed to recognize a faint air of what seemed like melancholy in Myrthin's movements. He wasn't saying much, just silently plodding along in front of us, and a far cry from the wild rebellious version he'd packed together so far on the trip.

I didn't really feel like quizzing him on his troubles and neither did the Roving Reporter so instead we just headed on with the other families, on towards where the cliffs dropped dramatically into the crashing waves.

Lord knows what was on my friend's mind but the good news was that it came and went as quickly as it had arrived. Noteworthy it was though, for it was a sign of an underlying something that the man was obviously feeling but not relating.

I recall that I put it down to tiredness or money worries, at that time we were beginning to run the cash really bare, all three of us.

"Look! Look!" I shouted pointing down to a dark shape on a tiny rugged rock some hundred yards below us.

"It's a seal, they often hang around here! It's the landscape!"

"No way!" Says Sparks. "It's a rock!"

The rock then twitched his head and even the doubting Australian was convinced. We all enjoyed watching the curious animal for a while, envious maybe of its easy plight of just sitting and watching and swimming and feasting.

But in its own way I'm sure he was watching us too, jealously eyeing our ability to leap freely from stone to stone with loose cigarettes hanging from our mouths. Or would a seal ever understand our crazy ways. I imagine it would all seem a tad pointless to an animal. Anyhow we then moved over a small wire fence which supposedly acted as a means of keeping foolish ramblers away from the edge of the cliff. Not us, not us, oh no, we were already so far over the edge that flying might become second nature.

No-one shouted us back and no-one called the cops, for it was only us getting a closer look at the seal. The seal was our brother, really, that's what it began to feel like.

The sea animal looks up to rise of the cliff and sees us silhouetted against the light blue sky and wonders. It softly wonders whether we really exist or are merely figments of its imagination.

"But oh no, seal my friend!". I shouted.

"We are as real as you are and in our own way as free too. Free to come and go to risk and to travel!"

The seal stared through the sea spray up to where we stood.

"And now we go!" I sang into the wind. "And now we go!"

With which we waved him farewell and headed back towards, well back towards the 'tea shop' if you please. Clotted cream scones and cakes, teas for fifty pence, meant that we were very confused. Having just been to the very edge of the land called Cornwall, where next? What next? What could possibly rise up and continue where the musical mysticism of the night before had left off?

"I've got to ring Sandra!." Says Sparks suddenly out of the blue. "I'll ask her to check the Internet! See what's happening today!"

It was an obtuse statement.

Sandra, his girlfriend was back in Vienna, she was over one thousand miles away, that way.

So that is what we did, I went to toilet, Myrthin lounged on a rock looking out to the sea and Sparks rang Sandra.

On returning from a simple pleasure, you see it is imperative to catch toilet opportunities when you can on the road, on returning there was an increased buzz amongst the two men I had only recently left. You could tell by the determination in the Roving Reporter's voice.

"We're going to the Minack theatre to get tickets and see if we can find a closer camp site."

"Great! Good idea! How was Sandra?" I ask out of politeness.

"Oh, she's fine, she says it's thirty degrees in Vienna!".
At Land's End it was closer to thirteen degrees but whatever the weather, we went back three hundred and sixty degrees, and the trip was rolling once more.

To the Minack theatre we must go, fair weather or foul. So without tea, without clotted cream and full of increased optimism we dived back into Norm and cranked the engine up which started first time.

Myrthin busily found the tiny village of Porthcurno on our map and he directed me out of the gate along the track and away from the most Western point in England. Of course we were soon lost and busy sucking on a spliff as compensation but the music was with us once more and happy were our faces.

Porthcurno finally turned up from behind a hill and we drifted down a thin road into a tiny village banked on two sides by steep slopes. Further on was the turquoise ocean the so called Atlantic Ocean. It was a typical settlement of the area, with one shop, one bar, a bus stop and about a hundred eager day trippers making their way to and from the beach.

To the beach! Said one sign.

To the Minack Theatre! Said the other, the one we were

more concerned with.

Slowly we drove through the village past another two shops selling plastic surfboards and inflatable dinghies and the like, yet the road was wide enough for one car and one car only. Then up we went, up a steep slope that wound around on itself like a sleeping python.

It was now a hell of a gradient and all the blood rushed to the back of our heads. Up, up and up we went until we leveled out and a sign told us it was a quarter of a mile to the theatre. There below us lay a beautiful azure sea lapping into a golden sandy cove.

"Look at that!." Said the Australian who was familiar with beaches.

He should have saved his surprise, for on turning the next corner and as the hedgerow disappeared, there before us lay, well our final destination is the only way to describe it!

"YAAAAAAAAAAAAAAAAAAGH!" We all screamed.

In front of us in a field at eleven thirty that morning we saw our camp site, and not only a camp site. In the field was a large tent, about a dozen smaller ones and most importantly, glittering against the sun, was that damn Sirius, yellow painted collage covered Merry Prankster bus again.

They were already parked in place and already camped up ready for the play in two days time.

Excited babbling talk filled the car.

"We've got to get in there! It's perfect!" Optimism.

"But its probably private!" Pessimism.

"We must get in there!" Determination.

In a minute we had Norm backed up a farm track and were out at full speed to try and find someone in charge, Kesey himself if need be.

"Christ, he'd understand." Says Myrthin. "Jesus we're supposed to be on that field, it's obvious!." He said stating the pertinent in hope that it would become truth.

So off we went like a very excited load of damp dynamite, blasting inappropriately through the placid country scene. At a virtual run we came puffing around the back of the field to where the ticket office lay. 'Minack Theatre Tickets and Information,' said the sign.

We ran quickly through the door only to be confronted by a slow moving old aged guy. His glasses hung hypnotically on a chain around his neck as he turned to face us. With precise movements he looked up from his papers with resignation in his eyes. I couldn't stop myself.

"Hello, hello! We need to talk to someone about the camping!."
"Oh, the camping is nothing to do with us.." He replied with an air of supreme control.

"It is private you see! You have to see one of the Americans."

The Minack theatre was more used to respectable open-air versions of Shakespeare classics. They had little experience in dealing with old time LSD visionaries from the West

Coast.

"It's all private. Nothing to do with the theatre."

Oh, Christ private! Now that would be a test! Even so we thanked the kindly gentleman and shot out of the door.

"Go on Sparks, tell them you've come all the way from Australia! They have to let you in!." I say desperately.

"Good god we've got to get on the site!"

It was as if this was some kind of final examination of our merit. If we were to be denied the chance to hole up on the field for three days then that would mean two simple things. Firstly, the week would be spent in frustration knowing that our sacred site had been denied us and secondly that we were indeed not as tuned in as we'd hoped we might be. Yet there was no doubt that we'd pulled this whole trip off perfectly so far, so in fact nothing was actually going to stop us joining the small merry band on that field of pranksters.

Nothing, it was already fated!

We immediately caught a guy walking around close to a gate, the field itself was sealed off from the outside by fences and locks.

"Is there any chance we can put up our tents here? We've come a long way to be here." Says Sparks with a manic grin.

"A long, long way!"

To which we were told we should have a word with John,

whoever he might be, he though was apparently the man with the power to decree our fate.

"Talk to John he's organizing everything!"

So off we went in search of John, and don't forget that in front of us all the time is Further the legendary bus, quietly grazing within touching distance of where we stood. Where we stood as virtual outsiders trying to jump onto the inner space scene. Groupies though we weren't, we were more like pilgrims, yes, desperate pilgrims.

John took some hunting down as there were few people if any mulling around the two dozen tents set up in the pasture. In the end though it was a kindly teenager who finally directed us towards John, John the Baptist, John the prophet. Actually, John was a middle-aged man, dressed in black and carrying a clipboard.

"Go on man! It's best if you go. Say you've come from Australia!". Says I with sound logic. I figured it would be more difficult to refuse someone who'd travelled ten thousand miles. Though Myrthin and I had travelled five hundred, even though in fact I'd travelled one thousand five hundred. Good god we were wracked with nerves, confused and fearful too.

"Go on Sparks!"

And to his eternal merit off went the Roving Reporter to speak to John.

We, well we, waited some fifty yards away silent in our bundle of twisted tension.

Over by the bus Sparks and John discuss and converse and

gesticulate, whilst we, the two Welshmen, watch and hope beyond hope. They then turn to face us, us and our pent-up expectation that rises and falls.

Sparks was smiling though and in fact so was John. A thumbs up from Sparks brought us two into a huge, warm clinch and that was that.

"He's going to open the gate! We've got to bring the car round!" Shouts Sparks nonchalantly whilst probably shining inside.

Bring the car round, my god we'll bring the car round.

Myrthin and I we hugged each other like two victorious knights.

We were there, absolutely in place for the Total Eclipse and side by side with the Merry Pranksters, the unlikely catalysts for our whole journey.

We were like children let out of school early as we ran towards where we had abandoned old Norm. That was that, the Roving Reporter waited with John the head honcho from Channel Four television whilst Myrthin and I carefully jumped into the car.

The engine started easily and in three minutes we were thanking Saint John and pitching our tents in the field.

At last we could well and truly say we were finally home.

We had our place for the duration of the week, right up until Sparks was due to fly back on Friday. It was going to be us, the Merry Pranksters and a head-ful of the Total Eclipse. We were commencing the next stage in the process

210

of leaving worrying behind and concentrating on the fun in life. As we pitched our tents I noticed mine no longer had a door, the zipper had been bust in Brighton. It was a slight analogy as now we had no place to hide, we were open to the world and close to the waves.

"When the time comes it comes quickly!". I said realizing something, something important. You never really know what is ever coming around the next corner!

As we'd turned Norm off and parked him up against the fence, I'd deviled a look around the amazing field. It was a midday scenario unlike one I'd ever scene.

There was the bus all shimmering in the sun about thirty meters away, next to it a large marquee, the type they sometimes use for auspicious weddings.

Next to this were about ten small, identical red dome tents, obviously Prankster living accommodation for this Cornwall jaunt.

There was a tea tent too, a Chai tea tent to be precise. There were also a couple of portable plastic toilets, and a television control van with aerials striking out in all directions.

Also scattered around the field were a further dozen or so unofficial tents, non red, and all varying in size. There were a handful of vehicles too and last but not least there was us.
The idea that Ken Kesey was camping in this very same field sent us diving into old Norm to dig out our damp and collapsing canvas.

It was the real chance we'd been waiting for. The chance

to find out.

Soon we had already busied ourselves with poles and pegs in a deft need to claim a little part of Cornwall as our own. Soon our much-travelled Bedouin set up was once more in place.

Norm for his part was now due to take a back seat, it was over with the driving for three whole days. We had in fact travelled over six hundred miles in four days in a car that was fighting collapse over most of the journey. In our heads we had travelled much further, much further, at times at great speeds, but our heroic struggle had been vindicated. We were now only a five minute walk from the cliff theatre and absolutely in the right place for seeing the sun turn black and back again.

I recall having the initial feeling of a strange aloof need for solitude in some way. There was certainly no desire to go running up to the nearest Prankster with great bonhomie, explaining our wild and wonderful journey.

No, it was down to the village we were heading and out to get drunk in celebration. As we left the field, we all took one last look at what we'd found. It all seemed a touch surreal, a little too much to comprehend. With a slight shrug of the shoulders it was a temporary farewell to the Merry Pranksters and a welcome a huge new energy that took us to the winding road down the hill.
The walk was blissful, the air was warm and the sun was high in the sky.

"I'm a starving man!" Said Myrthin. "I've got to eat something warm!"

"Yeah! But food comes later! !". I replied to vacant but

understanding nods from the other two. "First we need hats, hats for the week.."

Neither of the others knew what I was talking about.
After ten minutes we had wound our way down the smooth serpent of a hill, scanned the golden sandy cove which lay to the right of the road and were trying to deal with a Cornish guy for two straw hats.

Sparks had insisted that he didn't need one and who were we to disagree. He was after all, the roving reporter and clear in his mind. For three pounds each Myrthin and I had acquired straw Stetsons, similar ones but not quite the same.

Perfect they were for any seaside metaphysical experience. Three pounds for the hats despite our combined financial resources being pretty depleted, but no matter for we had a plan! We would eat heartily in the local pub, get flagrant on Irish Guinness, buy wine from the local shop and wake up in the morning to ride a bus into nearby Penzance. There we would try to pull off a bank job of some sort! Simple and effective, but a plan none the less!

The local pub, the first step, was a huge barn of a place, and an empty barn at that. It was a two layered set up which in some identifiable way looked as if it had just been through a war of some kind.

Had the Merry pranksters been there?

Had the Hells Angels been there?

Or was it simply the Total Eclipse Freaks?

We never did quite find out but after ordering food, buying

beers and taking away the remnants of ten incomplete packs of cards, we headed out into the garden to enjoy the scorching early afternoon sun. It was safe now that we had our hats, we could stand anything.

Outside we nodded our greetings to the dozen or so others; we didn't recognize anyone from the massive counter culture movement of the Sixties; but no matter for we had cards. After some time, we'd sorted the various different packs into an almost complete set.

What's more Myrthin the New Hassler had acquired a colorful joker to place in his hat, it was kind of apt. I later made my own hat band out of a red and white plastic bag which looked quite dashing too and was broadcast later across the nation on the day of the eclipse, but I get ahead of myself somewhat.

Nothing of great note filed our way that afternoon in the sun, the bar got busier, and we returned to our floating first nature after feasting on Cornish Pasties once more.

At five or six we left the pub after having had an interesting chat with a local about an old pipeline that used to run all the way from tiny old Porthcurno to big old America.

"See that pump house over there! Well, that's where it started and then went out under the sea!"

"Really! That's amazing, really interesting, really, really. Mad huh!"

"Is it still used or is it empty?"

Nobody was making any real sense but it didn't matter

for once more we were communing with the local middle aged community. In truth we were interested in anything anyone had to tell us, literally anything. We were busily soaking in all the information we could, about anything at all!

Then on the way back to the tent we picked up wine from a "Selling Everything" shop, before checking the times for the morning's bus journey into Penzance. Wild and merry off we went up the winding hill once more. We were fried, happy and inspired too. Half way up the hill we exchanged greetings with

Kesey's publisher, the guy from way back on Brighton railway station. He was with another American and seemed to remember us, or at least recognize our style. We tipped hats and they went down, and we went up.

There was none of that spaniel energy of that long before amphetamine morning at the station, no desperate need for tidbits of information. No, we were so deep into the anarchic soup by that point that we were truly reveling in our own independence. That much was obvious as we rustled our way up past what was the halfway point of the strenuous climb,

This was a large guest house called the 'Seaway Hotel', or some other nautical cliche.

A "No vacancies!" sign hung from the nearest window and inside happy revelers stomped into their dinners. We, the loose, the edge heads carried on walking with our wine to the wind.

A few steps further up came a small group of younger Americans, loud and laughing, just like us, so we whooped a few hoops and they looked as us with as much confusion as we looked at them.

"Who were they?" We ask ourselves as they ask each other the same question.

"Who cares!" Says we and them too!

Good people, happy, in the best place in one of the best times.

Americans, Welsh, even Italian Australians, half the world was on top of that blustery hill. We weren't quite there yet though, it was a hard climb with our swirling balance so we stopped by a bench, a bench with a view to take in that view and it took our breath away again.

Down, way down below, there lay that beach once more, enticing us with its dance into the waves. It was a small cove with cliffs on three sides and a golden shimmering sand that turned turquoise where it met the sapphire blue ocean.

For some time we smoked space smoke and marveled at the scene, it was pure, untouched by anything mankind has thought of as wise. Good god even the pipe was well hidden as it advanced on America.

So the smoke made us slow but our hearts were beating fast. We continued the walk at a forty five degree angle. The final stretch was a similar experience to the one of the morning. We saw the field and we saw the bus and amidst all this was now mild activity and life.

Children were playing in the wide forum that the tents circled, dogs were skipping in amongst the kids and way down by the magic bus there was a bit of commotion. That's where we headed.

It was the Thunder machine that was causing all the commotion. The what? The Thunder machine I say. This was an original 1964 Ron Boise construction that had been there since the very beginning, at the Acid Tests, at the original psychedelic parties, and there it was before us on that field.

Ron Boise was a mad sculptor that had specialized in weird metallic creations, one of which was a Karma Sutra model made out of two cars.

The Thunder Machine was another, a musical instrument, a sculpture and a legend all of its own. Think of one of those roofed motorcycles you sometimes now see, then enclose it in an armor of vivid psychedelic swirl work. Place a cello with fifty strings inside and that was it, more or less.

Except that this is in plain language and the Merry Pranksters never used plain language. The Thunder Machine was all out Kesey's gang, a truly mad contraption. We arrived to join the gathered twenty or so in the crowd. It seemed as if there had been some minor damage in transit and the crazy thing, almost as if it had a life of its own, needed tuning or painting or something deep that the Pranksters themselves only knew what.
And there's Kesey commanding the show.
"Bring it down over there, slowly! Hey, watch what you're doing with the wheels!"

And there's Ken Babbs at Kesey's shoulder booming advice to the carrying helpers.

"God damn! Take it easy with the strings, man!"

And around stand Mountain Girl, Faye Kesey, Kesey's wife,

Chuck Kesey, Kesey's brother, George Walker, Mike Hagen, and other mainline Merry Pranksters of the first age.

We are suddenly not watching any kind of performance, we are now all one in this shipping of the Thunder Machine, all at hand to help with the lifting and catching.

Myrthin places his drunken strength around the back of the bulky contraption and in an instant the Thunder Machine is safely on Cornish ground. It catches the breeze and sends several psychedelic twangs of music into the salty air.

Quite freaking amazing really, us, the Merry Pranksters and at the most twenty other extra campers. A really tight community of seekers and teachers. I took time to survey the faces in the rest of the crowd.

There was a weird collection of the new age eclipse types, a handful of older Hippies who stood side by side with a dozen 'Rave Generation' teenagers next to a whole group of under tens. It was a peculiar little gathering.
And us, well I remember the Roving Reporter moving in close to the Thunder Machine and I remember standing with Myrthin, both of us somehow already changed, already for want of a better word, looser.

Certainly, looser about ourselves and certainly wiser about each other. We stood close and had no urge to go star hunting. We felt no urge whatsoever to go bursting onto these legendary figures with a sheet full of questions.

We were absolutely determined to pay respect to these people's space and avoid being unnecessarily in their faces. People are always merely people and even if you have an aspect of fame about you, and even if you are as open to the public as the Merry Pranksters are, then still there's no need to drown in unwanted attention.

It was good though to get a bearing on who we were actually living with, this small gathering of people there for a multitude of reasons, as many reasons as people themselves, were each there for their own personal process of whatever learning. Ours had been a pure instinctive reaction to the opportunity which had presented itself.

We had acted on the knowledge that special things might happen, without ever actually expecting too much. As a result we had been rewarded with a front row seat, actually no, this was no theatre this was more a family, we had been rewarded with kindness and good fortune.

That indeed was a sweet sensation to be riding with as Ken Kesey climbed aboard the Thunder Machine for a trial run out to inner space. There was much laughter in the tight circle, for this was a most private performance, anyone could watch, anyone could join in, but beware if it's attention seeking that is doing the screaming for that most certainly is not required.

"I met her in bar room in Barstow!". Kesey now singing as he twangs on the strings which then emanate as whooping Eastern cries of joy.

"Country road, West Virginia!" Strange booming from inside the machine, "They're Comin'! They're Comin!"

"They're coming all right!." Booms Babbs, standing away from the machine,

"Like Christmas and the Kentucky Derby!". He then also joins in with the refrain, "They're coming'!"

Myrthin and I had no idea who was coming, if anyone at all, but this was just superb, like a barnyard Merry Prankster good old acid test party.

And soon we were all joining in with the now hilariously doomy "They're Comin!". The Roving Reporter is close to the bus, but not that close as the bus is cordoned off, a plastic ribbon runs around the outside as some kind of barrier. We find this unusual but can certainly understand. Good god, there would be no peace in the valley without it, the bus would be under constant attack.

"They're coming!"

So there were smiles all around and familiar ease amongst the late afternoon revelations. We were excited to the point of merriment and what was greater was that we knew we were about to have three more days of this strange experience.

I looked back up to our rosy, red Norm and offered quiet thanks for his sterling efforts in getting us to where we were. In essence that godly little Ford had directed us into the most appropriate state in the world. Babbs, Kesey and the gang sang some more then moved off into the large tent smiling, vibrating and bathed in purity.

The kids, the kids, some as young as five and others as old as ten then commenced running in circles in a chasing frenzy. Entertaining it all was as we moved back the thirty meters to our own domain, we needed a corkscrew to free the spirit of the wine.

"Amazing huh!" Says Myrthin.
"Absolutely brilliant!" Say I.

"Good god!" Says the Roving Reporter.
In short we were all radiant and radiating energy.
We couldn't quite believe it all whilst at the same time it somehow seemed perfectly natural, which of course it actually all was. The wine was soon opened, and we toasted the sky and poured back the red booze. Myrthin began folding papers again.

"Need to score some hash, we're running out!." He announces whilst crumbling some powder onto the scene. "Shouldn't be hard huh?." He coughs with a twinkle in his eye.

"The drug culture is bound to be well represented in amongst our little family!."

"Represented!" I scream, "Jesus we're with the inventors of the damn thing!".

I slurped down some wine.

The Roving Reporter then fished out the cards and off we went once more. Sitting outside the tent as free as flies in a summer breeze we commenced an early evening round of, whist or poker or something easy from the world of the tame.

We played and watched and drank and smoked and laughed and listened to music. Every so often people would walk past on the road directly behind our tents, and as we had long since grown acclimatized to the unlikely situation, we hollered greetings to young and old alike. They always just always hollered back, it was just like that, there were absolutely no pretensions, just a valuable communication of any kind. A while later a ragged dog took up lying with us, a mutt with dreadlocks and the sweetest inclination.

He belonged to a group from Northern England, they were camped eight to a tent and were in their early twenties. Whether they were in the field because of the Merry Pranksters or just because it was convenient, was never made clear. Although we talked often, the question of Kesey and the Pranksters never came up.

That was how it was, everything seemed to be known and that which wasn't, was too big to be answered anyway. So we had a dog for the day, or for a couple of hours at least, and its latent energy dragged us off to join in a game of soccer, one which was taking place in what we had already christened the 'arena of the middle ground'.

One didn't need to ask or to be asked to join in these regular sporting activities for all one needed was a will and a left foot. Soon the ball was chasing the dog and the dog was chased by another dog who was followed by three cute under fives.

It was mighty enjoyable and in its own way exhausting. There was a heat around adjacent to that summer week that had us constantly lost in gentle waves of perspiration. Wisely the soccer was non competitive, merely a passing game which involved passing the ball just beyond the dogs whilst looking out for the kids. There were about eight of us altogether, all British and addicted to watching the flight of the colored sphere, the kids they loved it.

Wildly giggling they would invariably get a gentle pass from one of the big ones to which all the big ones would encourage the little kid to "shoot", "go on", "have a go!". Which they always did. Being teachers,

Myrthin and I enjoyed this responsibility free zone as a

reminder of the great side of working with kids, namely their absolute zest for everything.

The kids, or the 'elves' as we called them were a curious collection, ranging in age from four years old up to the almost robust, ten-year-old girl called Carlita. We got to know most of the kids over the course of the few days and Carlita, good god, both Myrthin and I pitied the teacher that had the job of educating that specific unexploded bomb.

Carlita was sometimes wild, sometimes gentle, quite often brutal but always a handful. She was there with a New Age Traveller pair, who were camping in an old ambulance in one corner of the field. Anyhow Carlita was the boss of the elves and that was that.

I recall her often stomping off with the ball after no one had paid her any attention for something like five minutes but someone always retrieved the thing and she would then disappear off to sulk behind the bus.
One of the elves was Caleb Kesey, Ken's grandson. During the week he developed a passion for cricket, aided and abetted by an ever eager Roving Reporter.

Caleb that evening though was too busy chasing the dog chasing the ball to be bothered with the soccer game, and soon we too collapsed in a heap somewhere on the edge of the arena of the middle ground. Out of the heap and after a shared round of refreshing red wine a game of cricket was called in the early dusk in Cornwall.

"Anyone for cricket?." Oh yes, oh yes!"

That we then spent an hour playing a game of cricket with various Pranksters watching and playing, was psychedelic in itself. These Americans were immensely interested in everything, even the fine art of cricket.

I tried to cajole one of the interested party into taking up the bat, but he claimed it was more fun to watch. Caleb Kesey though, was keen and there he suddenly was, five or six years old, swinging a cricket bat like a baseball bat, whilst Sparks, the cricket player was busy encouraging all the youngsters to improve their stance, keep their bat straight and keep their eye on the ball.

Me, well I just stood around with my wine in my hand, watching the sun over the sea, thinking a thousand lost thoughts, and wondering about all that we had been given to wonder about. Myrthin for his part was busy laughing his way to the middle of the action, it was his turn to bowl. Even Carlita returned, though still in a fog of her latest dissatisfaction.

And if you wonder why I take time to describe this typical summer scene, I will stress that it was just the overwhelming normality of it all that was so inspiring. This was like one big family of fun out in the open air, the Merry Pranksters, the campers, the kids and us, one happy holiday collective.

It struck me hard that some of these figures, these warm beings, strolling around the field were the ones that had once fascinated me and come alive in the pages of a book that had helped form the adolescent me. It was like meeting elders of a very old, familiar tribe.

But hey, what was all this really about? Hanging out with kids and grandparents was not actually the thing we had foreseen as being the lesson in psychedelic learning.

Sure, these were no ordinary grandparents, but they were 'old' you know, and as old is old, I couldn't help wondering on the why. After playing cricket, which had been fun, we spent some time drinking our wine and making acquaintance with the guy at the tea tent.

It was not only tea that bearded Californian was selling. He was in his mid twenties and saw it his position to keep the campers in touch with what they needed. None of us had an immediate need of his herbal drink but he was also selling some other less legal merchandise. So we talked it up with Jarzo, honestly, that was his name, not really needing to buy any more drugs, but just in order to find out what we could buy, in an emergency.

"M.D.A are the hot rockets, sure to blast you out of bed every time.". Says Jarzo with eyes which were those of the classic wired cat.

M.D.A., well we ordered some for the day after, which was the day before the eclipse and hoped that this ecstasy offshoot would take us into the eleventh with the right perspective, and if not then I still had one mangy gram of amphetamine powder left.

But look, it isn't the drugs, it really isn't, somehow all these substances had stopped being a narcotic, more of a conversation piece. Back in the other world these subjects were for shady corners of pubs and clubs, yet out on the field, or on the road, drugs, I am almost ashamed to admit, were a routine.

Now I am sure there are several well tutored beings out there that can master such experiences without a gut full of sizzling powders, not me though, not Myrthin, not Sparks and certainly not the tea-man, Jarzo.

Good god, grandparents and dope fiends, do they mix? Well on that field in Cornwall there were no edges, the whole scene was one big blur.

And amidst all this there is Channel Four Television and their cameras, mobile studios and microphones. I mean it all seemed to be from another kind of planet.

We walked around with wine and dope as others in other fields walked around with buckets and spades. The toilets were way over at the bottom of the field, there were no showers.

This was all in all a repeat scenario from the original Prankster days. Days when the Pranksters used to inhabit an abandoned warehouse, with no toilets, and no showers, when even the honorable, acclaimed dandy, Tom Wolfe in his white suit was forced into pissing in a nearby gas station.

Then the Pranksters had the bus parked in the warehouse, and people slept where they could. They made makeshift domiciles, they ate elsewhere and the warehouse was Prankster Central.

Thirty five years later, the same spirit is running alive in the field, exactly the same spirit. And now as well as those originals there were the original's kids, now the same age as the originals were back then, and there was us, the latest originals. We were the ones that had just felt that they should turn up and join in. So 1999 was Cornwall and 1966 had been San Francisco and everywhere between had been neither and that was a void in placement.

The total eclipse it seemed was just too big or too

insignificant to miss. That was the feeling that was rising in amidst that crazy scenario back then.

We were all in fact close to the Merry Pranksters' ethos, in fact we were all Merry Pranksters. It 'is' probably one big family, and it seems membership is open to all, well to all who actually want the membership.

There must be many for whom there is probably nothing worse than a Merry Prankster. But of those who needed no introduction to the power of latent possibility, then Camp Prankster was where it was at.

We all felt that there was no need to prove yourself or to fit into each other's perspectives of what should be, just being there was the 'thing'. Later that evening, next to the bus, a group of us are busy singing a Welsh lullaby, completely invented by Myrthin, not many of the gathering spoke Welsh, so it was Myrthin singing the Pranksters.

Then who stands and listens and even joins in with the chorus? None other than Kesey the non chief. He watches not smiling, just watching and taking things in, trying to get a hook on the singing 'thing'. He stands a little bit aback from the group, whilst other Pranksters are busy singing 'Goodnight!', and Kesey watches, aloof in a way, then joins in with a few bars, and that was that.

"Goodnight!"

We all hug each other and Myrthin is buzzing and the wine is gone. The group drifts off to the various parts of the warehouse, field, or bus and we three, its now really dark, go back with the group of raving youths to hang out in their tent and share in their vibes.

After a while I get bored of sitting cross legged and head off with Sparks to lie under the stars and ready myself for sleep, for the first night of sleep in the warehouse.

There is a gentle hush across the whole area, the whole of Cornwall probably. We were two days away from the end of the world and there was a tangible apprehension in the air. From the rave tent we could hear soft music and as we lay on the slowly melting grass, we saw Myrthin disappear as a shadow down to the Tea tent.

"Going to sort out Jarzo for tomorrow!". Says Sparks.

"There goes the New Hassler on his latest never done deal!". Say I

And that was it, way past midnight, it had been a mad day, we had managed a drug free evening but from that point on the days were about to get a lot madder.
Five hours later, sleep had been and gone, Sparks and I were off to the beach.

THE GOLDEN TICKETS.

It was just after dawn and the day before the eclipse. It didn't really make much sense being dragged out of the tent at sometime just before seven, but I wasn't fighting, it seemed like a good idea.

On the walk down the hill it was our world, there was hardly a soul awake and we had only the birds for company. Seagulls squawked their circles high above our heads, and it was a deep blue sky in which they lived.
Sparks had been right, this was a beautiful summer's day and the beach was the place to be. We walked along a path surrounded by the biggest leaves I had ever seen, like an enormous cactus but in Cornwall there was no desert. There was sand however, my god the cove was just idyllic.

Golden sand, a pale blue ocean and craggy brown cliffs on either side. The feeling was strong, it was like being sucked along by a magnet. As soon as our feet slipped onto the sand, already a heady feeling pervaded my soul for there is no sand in Austria.

Then we noticed that there were two other humans swimming the crystal waves.

Two women who were laughing their way through the spray, it was almost romantic! The two sets of strangers, the early morning, in high summer. But Christ, we wanted privacy and our own beach that morning, that is why we were there.

So, the women swam, and we idly threw pebbles into the ocean. Sparks was probably casting his mind to home town Australia, and beaches from his past, whilst I, well I was just entranced by the rhythm of the sea.

The water was clear, a beautiful topaz color and I felt the urge to dive into its soul. Soon, after the others had toweled off and made their way away, it was our turn to crash into the foamy waters. Me naked, for I was unprepared, and Sparks in costume, he'd been up first.

We then both sprinted into the waves and Jesus it was cold,

freezing cold, as cold as only British seas can be. I only managed a few strokes of manic breast stroke but Sparks he got acclimatized quickly and stayed swimming for a long time.

I was out in no time, absolutely refreshed from the experience and clean, the dust of the previous days had been laundered, it was a new me that found himself dripping back into my hunter's jacket.

A new me and the same old clothes, a comfortable combination. I shot a couple of photographs with Sparks' camera, then sat on the sand and watched the morning come around. After a while we'd had more than enough peace and our wild week continued. We walked away triumphantly, meeting one of the Pranksters on the way.

She was a woman in her fifties, we didn't know her name, but we chatted happily, just pleasantries. We talked about whether the village shop was open, about the weather, and about how cold the sea was.

Just normal, normal, normal. But friendly, friendly, friendly too. After waving goodbye on our way ahead it was to the shop, we went but we were there too early and ended up sitting on the steps waiting for nine o clock to arrive. Desperate, beautiful and pure times.

But hold on money, good god, that was our problem!

We were down to the absolute bottom dollar of our reserves and needing the bus fare into Penzance. It was only a meager breakfast that we afforded ourselves.

So, Penzance was our aim for the day, and the reason was to hit a bank. Three hours later we were on the top deck of an old Double Decker bus, heading through the narrowest of Cornish country lanes. It was an incredibly gripping trip this one, we were definitely heading towards a fateful meeting with money.

We had worked it out that I was to borrow a bunch of money from Sparks, as he had a plastic credit card. He would then get it all back as soon as I landed in Vienna.

Myrthin himself was relying on there being a branch of his local building society in the small market town. So our rumbling progress moved above the hedgerows, wild animals ran for their lives away from the huge motorized beast and we spotted a hawk flying after a rabbit and before we turned around we were in Penzance's hustle and bustle.

The streets were alive with tourists, our eyes were waylaid by a real chaos of color in the summer.

People were everywhere and it was a huge contrast from the beginning of the day. We had been in deep countryside for two days and suddenly Penzance seemed more like New York as we hopped off the bus and quickly found our banks.

We were immediately the richest men in town. So, what do rich men do? They find somewhere to spend their money. Sparks bought a couple of CDs, then both Myrthin and I bought cigarettes.

Within an hour we were in a bar playing pool with some local old men who found our long hair ridiculous. We laughed with them and drank Guinness; it was yet again entertainment with the older generation. It seemed to me that the wilder and further out one got, then the better one

got along with everyone, especially those who would have never normally occupied your time.
Now there was one major thing that was on all of our minds that sunny afternoon, one cause for concern. We had found out that the Merry Pranksters' Total eclipse spectacular, 'Wheresmerlin?', taking place only one hundred meters from our tent, was absolutely **sold out**.

Now this eventuality had not been in our non plan at all. Sure some loose Prankster had told us the previous night that we could help carrying props down to the stage and would get in for free anyhow, but that seemed a little bit on the risky side of things. It was just one man's word. But there seemed to be really no other option.

We'd already considered climbing up the cliffs but that one had always seemed unlikely, so it was shaping up as us having to offer our assistance in return for entry to the big kick.

This last resort was right in there with the Prankster ethos, but as you should 'Never trust a prankster', it was far from a given thing.

During the long journey so far, we had successfully navigated many indirect routes but missing out on the show would be a huge kick back into reality, a huge kick off the psychedelic bus so to speak.
But yes buses, and my god, we needed to get a bus

back home, to the warehouse, to the camp site, back to the Minack Theatre at least.

It was late afternoon by the time the old folks let us leave the bar and so we oozed out onto the even busier streets with a fizz in our minds and a drunken roll to our souls.

We walked down the sidewalks in dazzling sun, though we knew not where the bus was leaving from, or even the number of the service.

Yet as we were in a metropolis, it was to a liquor store we headed, for we needed fine wines for the duration of our stay. Inside the store there were crowds of people all buying what they could to help take them through the end of the world the day after.

TOMORROW THE SUN WILL DIE!

For no one knew what lay on the dirty other side of the eclipse, for not one of us had ever lived through one before, and certainly never in 1999, and absolutely never at eleven minutes past the eleventh hour on the eleventh of the month.

There was and I kid you not a real fear in the air, or if not a fear, then at least an invoked caution. I suppose looking back now, none of us actually ever thought that the world would end, but there was just that weird slight chance, and that was unnerving enough.
But wines, that was the way, wines and M.D.A. from Jarzo, that was the only way.

So, after handing over big money for seven bottles of fancy Rioja, because the name sounded so good and seven is a lucky number, we blasted back out onto the street.

The same old rural scene awaited us. It was a pleasant chaos of people running everywhere and at least a dozen bronzed guys standing behind make shift stands. They were selling 'the only safe way to watch the eclipse'.

The sea air blowing through our mind was humid, like a salty mistral spinning wild as we looked left and we looked right. Suddenly there pulling up right in front of us was a bus at a bus stop. We ran quickly to catch it not knowing where it was heading, it seemed though instinctively perfect.

"Are you going to Porthcurno?." We ask the driver in a gale of our own making.

"Certainly, are boys!". Replied the smiling gray haired bus driver.

His shirt was open to the waist revealing a cherry brown explosion of perspiration.

"Great! Three tickets please!." We say, still ever so polite.
And that was that we were on our way. It was no real surprise anymore this knack of impeccable timing of ours.

This was becoming an inbuilt ability to place ourselves exactly where we needed to be. It was becoming second nature, almost routine, albeit a supreme routine of the hidden sense.

So, once more we wound our way up to the top deck of the bus and crashed down in the only free seats, right at the front of the bus. I sat next to Sparks, whilst Myrthin, well Myrthin sat down next to one really extreme looking customer.

This guy, in his late fifties, was a no-shirt, pony-tailed, cut-off jeans classic.

A Woodstock, Glastonbury veteran without a doubt who was traveling with a cute four-year-old girl, his grandchild as it turned out.

In no time Myrthin who was rising on a wave is busy in the world of communication with the two.

He smiles and winks for the kid and knowingly nods to the grandpa. It was all very typical of the week, especially when one looked around the bus.

The rest of the passengers were sitting as straight as the day, well it seemed that way at least. Sparks and I kept quiet as the Guinness had weighed us down somewhat, but Myrthin he was having the time of his life. He was busy looking straight out of the windscreen high above Cornwall, alive and anticipatory. Anticipatory of what? Well even he didn't know at that time.

Twenty minutes later we each possessed our latest golden nuggets. We had been handed our tickets for the 'Wheresmerlin?' extravaganza and all were finally in place.

The mysterious old guy had eventually started talking and it had turned out he was going to Porthcurno to try and return his tickets for the Merry Pranksters' performance the following day.

He'd had three tickets and we couldn't believe our luck. He even insisted on selling them for face value prices. I mean how could we have refused, it was all too easy, all too ridiculous.

Mr. P. Keswick was the name on the tickets and thanks to him we were now guaranteed entrance to the cliff top eclipse. The chance of a lifetime was now guaranteed. For the eleventh time in only four days, we were once more joyously jubilant at our good fortune, our good luck and the power of coincidence.

But hold on, coincidence, the occurrence of simultaneous or apparently connected events. It just can not account for the way in which we three were now moving, it was certainly something deeper. The 'mysto' as Tom Wolfe had described it in his 1968 Prankster novel.

This 'mysto' was allowing us the gift of perfect timing and providing us with everything we needed, without us having to second guess. We had moved into a clean spot of understanding whereby we were always acting on instinct and just as the day knows its path so did we.

We were trusting our feelings for we had nothing else, and sweet Jesus, the rewards were beyond our conception. We just couldn't explain anything that was happening to us anymore. It was as if one of us would set up a challenge and the solution would appear from somewhere distant completely of its own accord.

Was this magic we were feeling?

Was it proof of a higher force?

We didn't know, but one thing was for sure, this all pervading feeling of being completely at the will of the wind, and the reward for such thinking, was absolutely the same deal as we had all read about in the 'Electric Kool Aid Acid Test'.

Without any doubt, for these stranger's tickets were the last proof. We had begun to learn the basics of the Merry Prankster's world and the next lessons were to be much more advanced.
As we got off the lumbering bus in Porthcurno and bid

the strange Gandalf figure farewell, for he was immediately returning to Penzance. My were we high with the power of being, and my were we humble and grateful too.

This was all becoming such an enormous experience, an enormous experience in the possibilities of the untouched part of our brains. The possibilities of the untouched parts of our universal understanding.

Or not!!!!!

Back at the camp site Myrthin bought us three fizzy little M.D.A tablets that looked like aspirin. Jarzo had insisted they were strong so we had taken up the challenge.

It 'was' the night before the eclipse and there 'was' a serious apprehension in the air. Even little Caleb Kesey was nervously telling us about his costume for the big day. He was to be superman, or a super hero. Indeed, who else young Caleb?

"I've made my own cape!." He told us with excitement and pride flashing in his young eyes.

Then there was a further huge game of cricket in the arena of the middle ground and afterwards we sat by our tent to begin our wine, for it was approaching dusk. Some time later a guy came and we momentarily gulped fearing unknown controversy but it was only a man claiming to be a Channel Four television employee asking for donations for the camp site.

"I mean guys." He talks in a soft Southern English accent, "Ken's put all his savings into this and we have costs and just a donation, you know good will...."

The appearance of our money stopped his well meant speech short.

We passed over thirty pounds and he was soon gone, happily moving on to the next tent. Whether the guy was authentic I couldn't tell you, but money, dirty old money, we didn't care.

We would have happily paid twice as much. Money just didn't have a place in the way we were thinking. But Jesus, if Ken's put his whole savings into this venture then it must be as significant for the Merry Pranksters as it is for us.

An hour later we had swallowed the pills and sat in front of the tent watching darkness drop a bag on the day.

It was a mistake.

It was a bad mistake.

I could feel this drug sucking away my energy, tainting the purity that we had worked so hard to achieve. My pictures became colorless, and a slow version of life crept up behind me, but it was too late. I'd known the drug was pointless, I had nothing to gain from being a chemical in a field. There was though no rationale to refuse.

I didn't need the damn thing for I was already high, higher than I'd ever been, it was silly to take it and therefore the rest of the night became a darkened version of the clean afternoon.

Some time later a dog came to join us, it just appeared from nowhere and lay down at our side, a scruffy terrier, like a guardian, or a refugee from an unseen storm. In a strange way it made me feel more at ease, a little at least.

"Do you reckon it'll be this dark tomorrow?." I ask no one in particular. "I mean at its peak it must be, it must be pitch black."

The other two pondered awhile and proceeded to give worried frowns as a reply. I felt that in some ways the eclipse had been taking a back seat rider for the week so far, but now that it was coming ever closer I could sense the weirdness begin to take over. Or was it just the drug?

The day after was undoubtedly to provide a true 'once in a lifetime' experience and that was quite a feeling to be sitting with, especially fighting on a new and dangerous drug. 'Coming up' they call it but in truth no one was coming or going anywhere, the M.D.A. was just not conducive to my state of mind. So, we slurped on some wine, then decided to leave the darkening field and the dog. Of we headed to the bar down the hill.

We were soon there and it was a busy merriment that awaited our arrival. Somehow though, I was just not truly inside the building, just not happy with the situation. I even missed the dog, I really did.

Maybe it was a dip in my energy! Maybe it was my apprehension!

Maybe, just maybe it was the non-logic in taking a dancing drug with no music to dance to.

Whatever, like Myrthin's melancholic start to the day before, it was now my turn to drift into a real quiet, almost aloof state of mind.

In the bar we sat around a large table and drank and watched the room, silently for by now the chemical had really begun to work.

I felt only marginally in control, but still I had enough perspective to know that I had to leave. For me the bar was just not the place to be, it was too conventional, it was too bright. So, after an hour we left the distorted noise to hit the camp site once more. We were restless somehow, it was difficult to relax, and the drug wasn't helping at all.
We wove our way back up the hill, it must have been close on eleven o clock by that point, twelve hours before the eclipse. We were silent, it was each of us lost in different thoughts and different frames of mind.

There was no real slump in our progress just that somehow each of us was busy preparing our heads for what was coming up. Back at the camp site we got to talking to others about the evening and how the general mood was biting.

It was biting everyone. Even the Merry Pranksters could be heard pranking up inside their large tent, busy reeling off vague, pseudo-Shakespearean couplets. They were practicing the WheresMerlin? Pageant, and obviously eclipse bitten too.

The drug seemed to be a huge, pointless disappointment and had nowhere near the kick of clarity of any of the other drug nights we'd carried out so far that week.

We talked to the other campers of mild things and were heartened by the company but then Myrthin decided to buy another pill!!

My god! It struck me as a sign of his dedication in coming

to terms with the whole of the week's events. I mean we had ridden on adrenaline for so long, that it was scary to consider that the following day was supposed to be bigger than any day before. You know that feeling that something must be made special, for it is already a special day, like New Year's eve or your birthday.

Myrthin was in fact now fighting gravity, he was flying constantly, he was now driving his soul onwards up to the Total Eclipse. Sparks and I, well we were strung out happily for a while at the Chai tea tent, talking to several strange characters.

Indeed there were many great people around there but soon after we got to know the others, unfortunately.
Jesus these were terrible types. They were only a few in number, but it was frightening to behold. It was worse on the drug, the worst.

On MDA these characters were hard to handle. These were the ones who had long since melted away their candles at both ends and were now in their early fifties and a pretty desperate breed.

These were real hippies caught adrift in the year of 1999. They had no time for thinking, and no place to be, and no respect for anything.

Always on the look out, and always hassling the next deal from under the sheets. It was the Garden of Eden gone sour! It was the same trip as ever; these were probably the ones who had chosen to drop out on Tim Leary's command and had then ceased to function in any effective way.
They were quite simply negative freaks.
There were beards from Glastonbury, a very true esoteric capital in the worst sense of the word.

There were long hairs from Cornwall itself and there were even shoeless wonders who'd travelled from all over the world.

It was these people that made it immediately obvious that the doors of perception for some should remain permanently closed.

For once I felt like Ronald Reagan or Margaret Thatcher, George Bush, father and son both, well vaguely at least.

I was still drugged up to my eyeballs, so there was a difference, but these characters brought out the worst in me. Intolerance I call it. Even though I knew that there was a nugget of gold in each and every one of those old broken-down cases, they were hard to take.

I was slowly presented with a head full of doubts, there before me, high on my seedy drug, were the failures, the tragic and the lost. Their misery was obvious in the questions that these people asked. Personal questions which invaded not only the space of the famous,

"Mountain Girl, how did Jerry Garcia die?"

And to us

"Have you got a spare smoke mate?."
"Can I have a hit on that, go on?"

Or even.

"A small sip of your tea?"

"How's your wine? Could I have a slurp?"

These characters, and it was mainly represented by the worst of the original generation of the long gone Sixties, were, as Sparks put it one day later, "A DISGRACE.". The mystic inside them had long since been replaced by the miserable.

It was such a huge shame that I quickly had had more than enough.

"I'm going back to the tent!". I say.

So off we went Sparks and I, up the field and once more to the grass in front of our tents where we shared a smoke, listened to some tunes and collapsed into our sleeping sacks anxious, dispirited and most probably just plain drug exhausted.

The day after was the big one and I for one wanted to be ready. I had no way of telling but it felt mighty late and as I lay there in a slight, white, light, electric, drug haze I almost feared for the following day.

I feared for the birds.
I feared for the waves.
I feared for the old and young.
I feared for the wise.
I was drug crazy again.

Yet by the crack of dawn, I was fine.
Recuperated and a thousand times more tolerant.

I had, I felt, exorcised a certain cynical side of me.
I felt clean once more, cleaner than ever before and that felt good.

TOTAL ECLIPSE.

So, this was it, this was the day. And how did it look? Well, it was Sparks and I, the Roving Reporter and the Dancing Driver, making our way down the field at about seven in the morning.

The day of the eclipse, the eleventh of August in the year of Nineteen Ninety Nine.

It felt like some form of success to be alive, to be there in this old world of ours on the day of such a strategic natural phenomenon.

It was their time, the Romans and their calendar, meeting with the old ways, a piece of absolutely unlikely synchronicity.

Think about it!
Our time is only two thousand years old and the eclipse has been a constant over millions of years, yet somehow in this

the last year before the big millennium change, something had managed to contrive this!

The eleven minutes after eleven on the eleventh, massive coincidence.

Was it a proof of a higher knowledge?

It seemed to be that morning. There was certainly a great coming together of some kind and though understand it we did not, we had felt it all week.

We had felt that it was possible to turn into looking at a higher picture and to strand things together that may well seem unconnected.

That morning for two minutes our world was going to be turned dark, turned dark in the summer, and in Cornwall first.

Cornwall that renowned home of the mystic. King Arthur, and a thousand ancient sites, the Celts and with Atlantis allegedly just off the coast. It was all in all an esoteric orgasm, for those with that ill defined inclination for chilling mysticism.

It was all in all, my dear friend and I strolling down towards Further the bus sharing a half finished bottle of wine. Absolutely non esoteric. It was all in all cloudy, so no sky. It was all in all really, really eerie, no question.

"Hey Sparks, pass us the bottle, let's have a slurp for the day ahead."

Myrthin was still busy sleeping off his second M.D.A. tablet and for once it was not just the two of us that were up and running at that early hour.

The atmosphere was tight, very oppressive, you could sense it in the birds' uneasy flutter.

You could sense it in the quiver in the waves and you could most of all sense it in the eyes of us there at that moment of time.

No-one knew what to expect for none of us had been through this before but there was a massive feeling of unity amongst the right minded, the crazy and the dreamers.

"Hey, pass us the bottle! Top of the morning."

We toasted the bus as we passed it, moving down to true Prankster central for by that point it was absolutely obvious that we had long since passed our own specific acid test, without even trying. Pranksters we, Pranksters you, Pranksters all. We moved amongst each other passing on nervous smiles and very little conversation. It was just a massive vibration.
And the vibration was totally unsettling in a positive kind of way.

It was a feeling of uncertainty and that was great for there is quite probably nothing more dangerous than one who is certain. The one who is convinced he knows everything.

Not one of us knew anything of what was going to happen that day. So down at the tea tent there was a mild commotion of activity.

Jarzo asks about last night's drug.

"How was the hit? Strong huh! Leaves you with cobwebs behind the eyes I always say!."

"Jarzo my man!", I respond lazily, "A new drug, but a bit of a nothing new hit!"

To which Jarzo feigned understanding which I doubted, for the meaning was even unclear to me.

"But tea we will have or at least for the Roving Reporter!" I say cheerily.

"I am happy with the fire water!." I took a sip from my never-ending wine.

This wine had been out in the night air and had refilled itself on the droplets of the morning dew that had so heavily descended on our field. No not really, I just hadn't drunk as much as I had thought the night before, but chilled it was, perfect. It was cold that cloudy long-ago morning.

"Shame huh!." Says Jarzo blinking up at the sky whilst pouring out a warm cup of tea for Sparks.

"No, there's plenty of time, and well, it'll still get mighty dark!". Says the Australian.

I fish out my notebook to catch the atmosphere and begin busily scribbling notes about the waves. I down a further sip of wine, and then more laughing but not out of fun, more nerves than anything.

Ken Kesey is in front of us busy writing on his laptop computer, he sits like a friendly bear perched on a small camping stool and smiles his greetings but is obviously deep into something very important.

A personal moment before the public turn up to watch. He is already dressed in white overalls which has been Merry Prankster work gear ever since the Nineteen Sixties.

From inside the large marquee, you can hear the strains of the still practicing other Merry Pranksters.

It is now just two and a half hours away and so it's last minute preparation time. George Walker, an original goofing Merry Prankster, appears dressed in a completely silver suit from helmet to boots, he glides past as if on air. That man always reminded me of a psychedelic mountain goat in the way he moved languidly over any object that crossed his path.

I scribble a bit more and then we walk down to the theatre car park for the first view of the ocean morning. The car park is already busy, busy with the converted trucks of modern day travelers, family saloon cats in cars, motor bikes and other people.

Staring at the sky seemed to be thing to do, there was already an anxiety that the clouds would obscure the view, but there would be no view anyway.

It was darkness that was supposed to be happening, was it not?

In the car park I hear the lilting tune of 'Greensleeves' emanating from one of the robust big wheeled tucks. It sounded so crisp and beautiful, indeed it was 'the' perfect soundtrack.

Then from the same truck I hear a woman's voice saying something very, very profound, almost ominous.

These were her words.

"It will inspire things from people. Which is good at this moment in time!"

She announces calmly to some unseen confidante.

I gulped and understood what she meant.

It seemed that riding throughout all of this trip and in fact everything that paranoid old pre-millennium change year of 1999, was this whole feeling of mortality.

It was as if you were constantly being reminded of your own inevitable ending. At least that is how it seemed to me. It was simple reality, for they were telling us constantly about how this year '2000' thing was once in a lifetime, and how you were going to be lucky enough to witness it.

What they didn't quite tell us was the underlying truth.

HEY YOU!!

You won't see another one!

You won't get into 3000 AD

You are here in this moment for one time only.
It was all just a reminder of the transient nature of our passing through this web of life.

Now some of us didn't really need too much reminding, some knew this already, the old knew it, the bereaved knew it. It was for the others that this whole thing was bringing up a new territory of self confusion.

"It will inspire things from people. Which is good at this moment in time!"

See that is what the unseen voice meant, she meant that people all over the Western world were being forced off dead center by, well, by events out of their own control.

So, what was the reaction? Well let's have a party, like it's 1999.

Amidst the fuzz about the future, as I have said previously, the arrival of the total eclipse was like some kind of devious prankster omen.

No not the Merry Pranksters, I am talking about those enormous cloud sized deities that ride the wind up on high in some other as yet untapped realm.

"It will inspire things from people. Which is good at this moment in time!"

So that was the situation, unease amongst some, blind zest amongst others, vague interest in most, but just about everyone was being challenged or tested. It was as if the big spirits on high were saying. "Look get through this eclipse thing, then ride the new numbers and see where you come out the other side."

I was scared too, for no reason really, just probably mad from the excessive week, but as I stood scribbling notes and glancing across the deathly still of the gray wave-less swell, it all seemed a little ominous.

I swigged from my wine bottle, which was still chilled, the air was almost cold that morning.

Sparks was sipping his Chai tea and lo and behold, we should wake up the sleeping Myrthin, as no one wants to sleep through the end of the world. It's back up the field we head, me glad that my coat was warm and that my jeans reached my feet. It was no time for shorts and waistcoats that cold August morning. Even Sparks, who bares his legs at the first rays of Spring sunshine, even he was wrapped up in a corduroy outfit, head to toe.

At the tent there was no action, Myrthin's boots stuck out of the edge of the tent, but that was it.

"Come on! Myrthin! Wake up. It's about eight o clock!." I shout through the gap in the curtains.

"What! Huh! Who!" Moans the sleeping mess on a sleeping bag.
"It's time to get up! It's all beginning!" Replies Sparks.

Almost involuntarily Myrthin begins to emerge from the tent, his legs first and then later his increasingly crumpled visage. He had just had two hours drugged sleep, again, but it didn't take long and no convincing.

Myrthin grabs a bottle of wine almost instinctively and soon we are back at the Chai tent. I was busy giving

Myrthin gulps of my own wine and he himself was busy giving Jarzo nasty looks, his purple heart sunglasses seemed to be changing shades.

"Not my fault man! You wanted more! Good huh! Top dollar, sweep to the wind gear! Really is!" Jarzo laughs still riding his own wave.

Slowly the Merry Pranksters begin to emerge from what must have been a run through of the play and interested theatre goers make their way up to the campsite out of curiosity. Many were surprised at what they found. The rustic camping ground, the psychedelic bus, the odd collection of breakfast takers and what surprised them most was the easy accessibility of the 'legendary' Americans stumbling across the morning.
"Accessible yeah but don't bug me for autographs because I don't think they are worth the time of day." Says someone close to the bus.

And we, we just fought for some perspective.

After standing around for a while it was our idea to go and catch the queue for the performance which was supposed to start at ten in the morning. Just after eight was probably too early but no, there before us was already a snaking collection of eclipse theatre people.

"Let's go and have some fun!." Announces Myrthin ominously as he passes me back my wine.

In the queue fun we did have. It was an unusual crowd gathered with us, unusual in the way they fidgeted in silence.

There were families in plastic ponchos.

There were local older types.

There were a couple of darkly clothed weirdoes, who we presumed to be the Edgar Allen Poe set.

There were many people of other lands and continents and there was us, the three.
We laughed a lot, we laughed especially when we were interviewed by Dutch or Swedish television.
"Where is Merlin?." We were asked by an attractive, well-dressed woman with a microphone.

"Merlin is you, me and everyone else!" I replied.

"Back over there in a tent!" Said Sparks.

"Hi I'm Myrthin!" Announces Myrthin to confused looks.

This contact with the outside world sent us spinning and they were soon gone. We were then left alone once more, us and about a hundred others. Then Chuck Kesey came past us, Chuck is Ken's brother.

"Hey Ken, it's a real pleasure to meet you!". Announces a friendly looking older man standing in the queue!

Chuck does look remarkably like his older brother, so is probably used to this kind of mix up.

"I'm Chuck!." He says with a laugh in his deep Oregonian

way.

Chuck was on the original 1964 bus trip and has been involved ever since. He knows how to deal with people and when he was asked at some point in the week about the bears in Oregon.

A strange question I do admit.

"Hey Chuck, are the bears dangerous?"
"Forget the bears!" He answers, "It's the pigs that'll kill you!"

It was the tension that was driving us and the wine and the relative cold.

Atop a chilly cliff top just beyond the dew, fried and synched in, tickets in the crumpled corner of our pockets, building it on up, building it on up.

Then after a while someone lets us all in and we make our way to the theatre, well the side of the cliff.

The Minack Theatre looks like a giant has bitten a huge mouthful out of the craggy rocks. Then a thousand years later some wise visionary decided to place an amphitheater there.

And why not?

For it is a breathtaking Location and as we bustled our way down the winding staircase towards the stage, it was pure excitement that was running through our veins.

Already in place were the odd assortments of Prankster past history. There was the Thunder Machine, a throne, several musical instruments, video cameras, cables, and the like.

I must admit I recall feeling a touch guilty that none of us had offered to assist in the carrying of all this wild equipment. Then again, we were never asked, so I suppose, it was fine on both sides because of course we would have willingly helped.

We could drink of course, which we did. Myrthin had woken up pleased that we still had other bottles of wine, we were now into our second bottle of the day, which sounds pretty desperate and I suppose it was.

Yet what alternative was there? We were by that point into the sixth day of fending off the ways of the straight world.

We were working with different forces by that time in our experience of living in immediacy. So, slurping back the wine and look, the music soon starts up.

It was Neal Cassady's son on an electric guitar, and some other guys on lutes and string instruments.

A mild jazz fills the air, the cloudy air, for there is a real heavy layering of dark, growling clouds above our heads. Unfortunately this means that there will be no spectacular view of the eclipse for us cliff edge people, but, hell, who cares!!!!!!

There's the sea, like rippled glass, gray too, but somehow shimmering and on it, at least a dozen ships and boats of various sizes, all in place for the shower of darkness.
And look, over there on the adjacent cliff tops are at least a hundred others scattered in flashes of orange and puce on the grassy green high land. It all had a feeling of being

a big 'thing', an event, and that was warm enough to deny the cold air.

I looked back up the slope, to the people gathering for the play, a curious gathering we were. Directly behind us were a family of five, wrapped up in plastic waterproofs, all busily munching on sandwiches and sipping tea, tea that came steaming out of a thermos flask.

Wholesome huh!

What they made of us didn't matter, for we were just doing what we had to do to survive.

It was approaching the start of the play, at least that is how it felt.

Zane Kesey, Ken's son was busy wandering around with a video camera, whilst little Caleb was swishing behind him in his superhero cape.

To the left of where we stood was the 'backstage' area, which was an ornate staircase away from the stage.

Back there were the main players. I could see Carloyn Adams dressed in flowing velvet robes, George Walker in his inevitable costume of silver, blowing on what looked like a silvered Alpine horn.

Chuck Kesey was there still in his civilian costume, laughing along with each and everyone whilst the young guy, John Swan was dressed up as a court jester.

We three drank, smoked and then Myrthin rolled up the first joint of the day. I remember being momentarily hungry at the sound of a packet of cookies being opened by the picnic family behind us, but that was nothing new, we were always hungry, we'd just learnt to ignore the fact.

And then I panic a little, for my bladder is telling me that I need to escape to the toilet before the whole thing starts. As the band the Clash once sang.

"Should I stay, or Should I go?"

I decided after a private battle that in fact, I should go. I should go back up the winding hill to the top and the toilets.

"Off to the toilets!" I announce to the other two before moving off at pace up to the steps.

There were now hundreds of people all around, some sitting and some still coming and going. Hundreds of us all there gathered for the end of the world.

And who is the only one fighting against the tide, moving upstream, yep, the Dancing Driver. Up, up, and onwards, complete with sunglasses and my straw hat, which meant I felt well protected. Faces, faces, all kinds of faces flew into my field of vision and faces flew away again. And I carried on upwards, ever so slightly peeved that my bladder was playing mind games with me. Ever so slightly woven by the wine and the effects of the week on the road.

I had made my way literally three quarters of the way up, battled and danced into the hill, when a face amongst the sea is a face, I know.

Coming towards me, completely unrecognized is one Ken Kesey.

Ken Kesey just on his way down to tackle the eclipse on his own terms. He was still dressed in his white overalls but somehow completely unnoticed by the masses.

Maybe they knew him not.

Maybe they failed to see.

Maybe he just wanted it that way.

Whatever, I am now just feet away, me on my way up the hill and Kesey on his way down.

Now from my own minor work with the hapless but great band, 'the good library', I am aware of this pre-gig feeling. That strange time when you try to psyche your way through to the magical high ground. It is a time, for me anyhow, when you try to focus, or rather defocus, just to tune in to something higher which is absolutely necessary if you are even going to come close to courting with magic.

The sixty-four-year-old man making his way towards me was about to take on a Total Eclipse. This was a man who had written classic literature, a man who had raised a family, a man who had run for the way of righteousness for at least thirty-five years.

Yet this too was a man who had the year before survived a stroke, a man in old age and ultimately a man who was undoubtedly aware of the mortal nature of our kind.

Whatever, I am still just feet away. I am momentarily confused.

Should I leave the man his space?
Should I make some wise crack?

Should I go and try to touch something deep?
Should I pretend I hadn't seen him?

Whatever, I am still just feet away. Somehow still guilty that we have not helped with the lifting and dragging down to the stage.

Yet suddenly we are walking past each other and our eyes have certainly caught hold, so there is nothing else for me to do other than in quiet confidential tones offer the only thing I would wish on anyone.

"Good luck!"
I meant it with all my heart, and I instinctively place my arm gently on Kesey's shoulder, as if to underline the genuinely warm emotion I am trying to pass over. Kesey smiles gently, confidently and he seems completely appreciative when he offers his thanks.

"Thank you." He says sincerely.

Yeah, as always, he was always sincere Ken Kesey.

Then we both moved on.

Me happy that my bladder had fooled me into moving into the right place at the right time. Of course, it was now completely understood as being an instinctive reading of some hidden high signals. Kesey moved onwards down to the stage.

It was getting towards eclipse time.

It was getting towards the challenge.

It was getting hotter in the cold.

It was getting clearer in the mist.

It was getting darker in the light.

It was getting lighter in the dark.

I don't remember my walk down to the other two any more than I remember if I actually visited the toilets. Things get a little hazy from the Kesey meeting point onwards.

Crowds of people, some unsettled, others just there for no obvious reason, wearing colored plastic raincoats against the cold.

Smiling children and worried elders both.

Music rose up from the stage and not many were really listening but at our seats we huddle together us, the three.

The ocean out there is calm, almost silent, no waves just gentle raised ripples like silver frost, and a lined horizon way out there is straight.

I point my finger out above the stage. Nervous gulps of red wine that stains, runs in colored droplets down the green glass of the bottle. It says Rioja on the label.

Music gets louder but still just jazz and impatience in the swollen ranks and an hour or so away from the eclipse.

Kesey now all in black, top hat, a radio microphone catching his words as he stands in front of the bank of four hundred people.

There is a direct line as he looks back up the hill, now full to the brim with this mass of humanity. He begins talking. "This is a moment in time. You can set your clocks by this moment, the moment of totality. A once in a lifetime experience."

Who understands? Me not for sure, Sparks and Myrthin give each other blank looks. We have been thinking ever since of the meaning but have not arrived at it yet.

Crowd hush as the loud P.A. system takes Ken Kesey"s voice way out above our heads and way out to sea. John Swan the court jester is up on the wall trying to blow away the clouds with a sharp pointed dagger.

"Come on, if we all focus really, really hard we can blow these clouds away.."

He shouts invoking the power of humanity. No one believed in it, the clouds stayed and suddenly a helicopter whirrs overhead, filming everything. Kesey tells us that we are all happily to 'middle finger' the pilot, which we all do smiling.

"Merlin, we call on Merlin." Swan invokes.

Merlin stays well hidden. The sun too.

Kesey then starts with the story of Tricker the Squirrel and big bad Double the Bear. The Bear, an analogy for dumb power, eats up everything in the woods. Kesey has us twittering as birds, feigning shock and the audience laps it all up.

Kesey "ROARRRRRRRRRRRRRRRRRRS!"

We all jump in our seats. Tricker leads Double the Bear up

a tree.

"I can fly." Says Tricker.

"I can fly too!" Says, the big boastful three-hundred-pound bear.

Tricker leaps from the tree to another.

Big Double leaps. Down, down, down does the power of gravity take him.

"SPLAT!"

"I can trick too!." Says the squirrel, to wild cheering from the gathered audience.

The big, bad, dumb guy could be anyone driven by blind religious zeal.

Anyhow the squirrel had done the big guy, he'd been beaten by sheer quick thinking and the power of a trick, a goof, a prank.

The message was clear.

We then continued to drink wine and Kesey introduces the "WheresMerlin?" pageant. A historical piece with the Arthurian legend given a Prankster slant. The cast read like the pages of Wolfe's long before classic.

Kesey was Sir Kay, which was okay with all of us as he introduces the play to cheers from the audience.

Well, some of the audience at least, others were too busy munching and rumbling in jumbo packets of salted chips.

But hey, that was fine.

Do your thing man! Do it loud!

We understood that much by that point.

Fly your bag around your head, even if it was merely a bag of fried potatoes.

So go Ken go. Tell us about the play. We all know the name Merlin, there's even a European bird of prey that carries the name, who came first we know not, but anyway here comes a Prankster program seller.

"Programs, WhereMerlin? Programs. Get 'em while they're got." Hollered one of the American bandits close to where we sat.

None of us initially fell for thinking of buying such a commercial cookie on such a mystical outing, but we all did and mine was upside down. The cover was the wrong way around, it was the last one left.
"You can have it for half price!". Says the guy laughing at my shoulder.

"Naw, I'll just read it upside down huh, full price or bust!." I said giving over an amount of English sterling.

The program we all hid away somewhere for some time later, much later. Indeed I still haven't really dissected the thing, but it included, still does, the whole of the script for the "WheresMerlin?" performance, other Kesey writings, Prankster profiles and a long winding epic by one Ken Babbs.

264

Priceless the program is now, and the upside-down cover is now safely upright on a wall somewhere close to home.

Close to the eclipse is where we were at that point a merry moon and a lifetime ago. Out to sea the scene stayed the same, the sky a soft powdered gray cloud zone and the sun was nowhere to be seen, as if already eclipsed by the clouds.

Now back to Merlin and his whereabouts. The play begins with a lack of professionalism which catches us all cold.

There is Ken Kesey at the side mouthing each and every word of the script, the ultimate prompter. It strikes me that the play must be important if he has gone to such extreme care to memorize word for word. Others of the Pranksters though, well somehow, they appeared to be less diligent, for there is Kesey prompting the next line and telling the actor to speak louder into the microphone.

"They can't here you! Speak louder!"

And we watch on baffled, not sure what to make of all of this.

Mountain Girl is dressed up as someone called Queen Mab and is talking of some child that was taken from somewhere and hidden behind a rock for twenty years.

Then on comes the John Swan guy, the younger American, the one who had been up on the bus way back in Brighton. He carries a lute and is apparently the fool, the blue fool.

There is some dialogue between these two characters and then on comes the woman we met after swimming two days before. This was just to really confuse us. The cast then ham it up about this and that and I drink of the wine which is running low and look to the sky which is as it always was. The major difference was that I began to feel the moon's shadow speeding across the Atlantic at an enormous velocity. On its violent way directly towards us.

Kesey has to prompt one of the thespians again and the first rumblings of discontent begin to emerge from the gathered crowd. Which was understandable somehow, for even we, we who thought we knew what to expect, failed to make sense of what was going on.

Now there weren't any specific cat calls or loud yells of consternation, but you could sense the rising unease amongst some of the audience. The family behind us, well at least they were happy, still unpacking sandwiches and slurping on their endless hot tea.

We the wine drinkers must have cut a strange sight too. Our wine was waning, and our spirits were attached to our souls by only a thin, thin cord.

Kesey then takes up the story line as narrator as the fool sits down to play his lute. Kings, Queens, Lancelot, a lot of names we knew but couldn't possibly place in our perspectives. Indeed, by this point my mind was feeling the imminent eclipse in the way one feels a train approaching.

It was the excitement, the dread, the drinks the drugs or everything spun into one. The eclipse was coming and only ten, fifteen minutes away. For the three of us it was a nerve wrenching time.

Swan the blue fool began with a song. It was immediately beautiful, almost too beautiful for me to listen to.
It turned out to be the words of W.B. Yeats and it had

me almost holding onto Myrthin for fear of breaking down in tears.

What I was feeling was strong emotion, a feeling of love for a lot of things. I couldn't properly explain why this was happening to me, but I realized that there were so many bright things about to be cast into a shadow.

I loved and feared for the way the innocent birds were busily following their jaunty day's work blissfully unaware of the coming doom. I felt sad for them, for their lack of preparation.

I loved and feared for the way the sea played it so solidly, as a mass of stoic energy slowly girding its loins against all that stands in its way.

I loved and feared for the way Myrthin and Sparks sat silently listening to the tender folk music, with intense concentration etched in their weathered features.

I loved and feared for the way that it was all one huge living collage happening not at a de

layed time but right in that moment just as it should. There was no concept of late or early for we knew that at 11.11, there on the 11th of August it was going to be pretty dark.

What I loved most was that by 11.15 it would be light

again. I hoped so at least.

The Swan song came to a close and I had been biting my bottom lip for the whole scary episode, trying to maintain, trying to keep an aspect of control. I lit a cigarette as the last notes died against the rocks and as below us lovers wrote messages in the sand, oh so temporary, but oh so profound.

The song finished and Kesey announced that they would be stopping the show for the eclipse.

The mysto rose a notch as the temperature seemed to fall a couple of degrees.

Kesey and the Pranksters then placed themselves in positions looking out to sea there was no more theatre show, no more commentary.

From that point on it was the self versus the darkening surf. No one, and that I mean, no one was talking. Everyone eyed the sky cautiously for signs of huge dark eagles bringing with them an unholy blanket of night, or was that just the way I was looking at it?

The three of us had super eclipse glasses that we'd been given by some compassionate Daily newspaper. They were made out of orange cardboard, with silver lenses.
Looking around back up the hill was like looking back in time, back to those Fifties' 3D cinema shows with the audience all looking 'so' futuristic in their wacky glasses. But it was out to sea where the action was brewing.

We'd been told that the birds would start roosting and that the animals would begin to lay for sleep, all completely baffled by the effects of the sudden darkness. What they hadn't told 'us' was the eclipse's hidden effect on our 'own' animal instincts, we being not 'so' far from the animal kingdom.

Well looking into the clouds, a gray, white, gray patchwork

it was possible to see a change, a slight decrease in color, like before a storm hits the coast, but this was different for the clouds were still there it was just light that was going.

"Oh my god, look it's happening!". I whispered to Myrthin.

The Roving Reporter to his credit was busy with his camera, photographing the occasion.

Soon it was really going, with a lot of hooting from the crowd, some hisses and a general gloom surrounding us all.

Our light was being sucked away, taken to be placed in some dazzling chamber for the next five minutes, or eternity, nobody really knew for sure.

My mind clicked into thinking about the ancients being caught by these things, man what a feeling. They would be caught with ideas that their gods were not happy and who's to say that maybe we too should not be thinking exactly the same thing.

Down on the stage the Kesey clan are close together, Ken, Faye, Zane and his son Caleb. Others of the Americans stand alone or in pairs with cameras, videos and eyes behind aluminum glasses. I thought for a moment about the meaning of the day glow band, they that celebrate the power of color in all their work. I mean just check out the bus, for them it meant no more color.

So darker it gets, it keeps getting darker.

I shuffle a little closer to Myrthin as the light seems to be filtered into a thinner shade. The clouds were our judge for there was no yellow sun in the sky, so our darkness had to be measured against the gray.

Even the eating family behind us take a break from the long running feast and listen to the silence. It's only the wind that is picking up in volume.
So darker it gets, it keeps getting darker.
Now it is approaching the type of light you get when the sun dips behind a distant horizon, when there are still colors, just about and your eyes begin to acclimatize. Not at this speed though, this was like a fast running movie film.

I though, was feeling calm now, assured that this was only temporary and that this was as close to as dark as it would get.

So darker it gets, it keeps getting darker.

Yet that was the thing, just as you thought that was the peak, it would get even more Gothic. I had no benchmark to work with, no comparison was possible and just as you thought the whole show was over and as dark as it would get, the darkness would twist deeper.

It was now getting so overcast that you lost all sense of color and the sea, and the sky were becoming one unit.

So darker it gets, it keeps getting darker.

There was not a sound to be heard, though the energy you could certainly feel. It was a mixture of fear and delight. Dark enough now that the flashlights were tiny impish explosions through a curtain. I grabbed hold of Myrthin's arm in the need to feel something solid for this darkening has been going on for so long. The matter of minutes that had passed begin to feel like a matter of hours. We all there know it's the sun that's being stolen and that we are deep in the midst of a world without light, temporarily.

Finally, our world is pitch black.

So dark that it is awesome, a deep velvet blackness has swamped our senses and all of us just look out to sea and stare blindly into our world without the sun.
It is all so sadly dark, quite eerie.

Then to our left some freaky Ghoul type, a big, bearded maniac guy rises to growl at the photographers. He curses them for using their flashes.

Then another weird high pitched howling witch is up inciting strange and terrible spells. The atmosphere is getting intensely disturbing as these black magic high hats are coming on all wound up about the quality of darkness.

Out to sea on the horizon there is a thin line of orange where somehow the sun still manages to plead for its worth, but orange on an intense black sweep background is in no way a comforting color combination, not when you have a dozen demonic negative freaks wailing and dancing their arms to the bleak power of the dark side at your shoulder.

Well, down with you and your failure in trying to make negative gain!

Just as soon as the tension was about to spill over into
 chaos, it started getting lighter again, and as everyone knows, the journey back sometimes can seem like a breeze.

Within a minute it was light again and soon it was back to the gray clouded pre-eclipse skyline. It was over and I looked around for the wound-up wizards and witches but somehow, they had melted once more into the clouds.

We were back into the play without really noticing, the eclipse had been and gone. It had left us to move on and was now about to terrify the next million eyes on its chaotic path.

But yet it hadn't really been that terrifying, it had been unusual yeah, but it had happened so quickly that it was like driving through a tunnel, but without ever leaving your front room.

It struck me that we had just been deep into an oddity of nature but safe in the arms of advance scientific knowledge. We'd all known it was coming, good god even the exact time! Ultimately though it, the total eclipse, had left us to carry on and that was the most important thing.

Color was back and so were the Merry Pranksters, as was their search for Merlin.

On the stage people in flowing robes dashed here and there battling with their rhyming couplets and Kesey was there, always prompting. It was a curiously vivid mix. The drift of the story was a take on the Arthurian legend, but thrown through a telescope in reverse, so the outcome was like wild blasts of color that exploded into the gray morning as if paint had been spilt on a plain piece of paper.

It was way beyond all of us, all so far out of the thick end of the glass that one could only make vague connections. When the severed head which had been resting on the huge throne began speaking, the initial effect was disorientation and then it turned out to be Ken Babbs, who I immediately knew had been curiously missing from the whole proceedings.

All in all it was an absolute chaotic attack on the senses. Too much for some, and soon behind us several lunch boxes were being slammed shut for the final time and the disgruntled theatre goers were leaving. The enthralled in the audience however continued to look on in amazed confusion.

Meanwhile the three of us, well we were happy to finish our wine and grope around desperately for the floor. I recall feeling for my hat, then for my head just as something to ensure my world was still in place, it was.

Then things really livened up!
The closing scene of the play went something like this. Don't ask why it just did. Well actually do ask why, think about it hard.
Sir Pelvis, a take on Las Vegas Elvis, all fussed up in a classic white jump suit comes on stage with a goblet containing what he claims to be a magic potion.

Microcosm - The dawning of Rock and Roll, the awakening!

Sir Kay, Kesey, is now in the Thunder Machine controlling a talking skeleton who demands some of the magic potion.

"Give me some for my aching bones! Need a good hit to get out of my skin! Haven't been feeling myself lately!"

Microcosm - The tired world of the late Nineteen Fifties, in desperate need of a shake down.

So Sir Pelvis hands the skeleton some magic potion, which is then sucked clean through the straw.

"Yes, yes! That's the stuff! That's the stuff!" Speaketh the skeleton.

At which point the band and the whole cast commence playing a killer version of

"LOVE POTION NUMBER NINE!"

Microcosm - The start of the psychedelic wave of the Sixties.
The goblet gets passed around the group as the dynamic groove just keeps building and the chorus goes like a steam train funk right out of the James Brown school of liquid movement.

"Get off your Leery ass! Get on the bus!" Sing the troupe to a man, woman and child.

LOVE POTION NUMBER NINE!

Could have been Leary's ass. Who's to say? Whatever, as soon as the goblet begins doing the rounds things get wild and immediately there's a mania of dancing and pranking and all-around fun.

I then find the scientific drug version of myself thinking quickly of the nature of this potion. Its effect was so rapid in changing the mood down there on the stage that I decided it had to be either S.T.P., which is a high speed hallucinogenic, or LSD or maybe no drug at all.

I figured it could have been just pure dramatic experience and the power of the occasion. To this day I haven't found out, I suppose it doesn't matter. One thing though was sure, there was suddenly a completely, c*o*m*p*l*e*t*e*l*y spaced atmosphere out there in front of us, out of nowhere.

"Love Potion Number Nine! Just another hit of Love Potion

Number Nine!"
The goblet is passed willingly on to anyone who is interested and the song dissolves into a wild jam which includes Kesey playing wildly on a Theremin. "What's a Theremin?" You might ask.

Well, it is a weird electronic sound wave maker that works with the movement of hands through a magnetic field. The sounds are freaky enough straight, but Kesey had his machine flying through several effect pedals and so it was soon.

"Love Potion Number Neeeeeeeeeeeeeeeeeoooooooooooooooooooonnnnnnnnnnn!"

Chuck Kesey was now walking around as a wizard complete with a wild pointed hat.

"Merlin, look! There's Merlin!"

"But wait, no there's Merlin, another Merl................".
Suddenly it was quite the most magical buckaroo of noise and visuals taking place high over the Cornish sea in the Atlantic Ocean.

It goes on and builds up and kids appear from nowhere and more and more until the stage is alive with color and youth and wisdom and noise and people blowing bubbles and Kesey

"Treeeeeeeeeeeeeeeeeeeezzzzzzzzzzooooooooooooooooh!"
on the Theremin looking like a wild magician weaving dangerous potent shapes over the cauldron.
"Love Potion Number Nine!"

People are leaving and people are staying, and some are going wild chasing kids who are chasing Pranksters, who are chasing shadows chasing the light.

We are caught in all the shape-making above the waves, just feet away from the action, the shackles are off and there is no more performance just pure Merry Prankster ethos alive and kicking.

"Rat Poison Number Nine!" Screams Babbs at the end of his chorus and I find myself thinking a little about the deeper meaning of all of this.

The reason was simple.

In 1964 the Merry Pranksters set forth on their psychedelic exploratory journey, their drive was pure L.S.D, a completely legal drug. It was like aspirin still is in the new era, but this was acid straight from the rainbow factory and crystal clean in its formula. This quality allowed their trips into their inner space to be taken on a level ground, it was like fueling a rocket on pure helium.

The journey was fast, enlightening and guaranteed to be white in its light.
Sure, it could get hellishly confusing, but it was always just an extension of the inner you.
It brought up inner struggles with the pesky doubts that had run silent within you, yet had always been there. KAZOOOM! It was now suddenly possible to confront these ghosts and take a grip of these tremors in your personality and uproot the dangerous weeds.
It could get amazingly inspiring this new "investigation" of new inner ground but it was always just an extension of the inner you.

Yeah, if you were clean, with no demons to pull you down, then sweet Jesus how you could suddenly take things into a different sphere and learn how to fly. KAZOOOM!

It was suddenly possible to confront the godlike within you, that suspicion of greatness that you'd always carried around with you yet had been constantly told not to express.

Whatever way up, in the early 1960's acid had brought on an explosion of what was already running around inside the 'national' closely guarded self, and soon it was possible to find out as much as you needed to know.

This was the era of Hoffman, rye extract Sandoz chemical experimentation. The drug was largely factory produced under strict quality control. It was a clean drug.
What then happened is that one began to see through the whole world. To see that the whole of society was in fact only running around, merely pretending to be in control, mainly because that was the way it was supposed to be.
Suddenly in 1965, who really cares about dates, the Pranksters, Kesey, Babbs and others see that through doses of this very unusual potion, it is possible to see through people, into and beyond the smiles, beyond the frowns, above the clothes, deep past the words. To really see inside.

This was the clean L.S.D experience, the ability to take on a different view, in a way the ability to cut away from the need for twenty years of meditation in the search of insight. There it was right before you and a tiny dose would teach you as much about you and your surroundings as you ever wanted to know.

This revolution was a personal one, a universe beginning from your own central head space and really spreading out in a billion miles from where you stood. It became clear that you were indeed at the center of the universe, indeed your own universe.

But then, crash! Hold on!

Babbs screaming about rat poison is Babbs screaming about what then happened. What happened when the shit hit the cosmic fan, the cosmic fun.

The government under the driving force of Ronald Reagan deemed that L.S.D should be made illegal, and on the 6th of October 1966 it was ruled as a criminal offense to possess, take, and especially manufacture the danger drug. The number of the beast connections that run through that date speak for themselves? From that point on it was all over for the clean psychedelic wave.

Enter the illegal acid scene and immediately the purity of the drug was lost. Suddenly there were strychnine laced versions of L.S.D running around on the streets.

Paranoia slammed closed the doors of perception, freak outs spilled onto the streets, and enter the strong-arm police tactics.

The Merry Pranksters' experiments had been hijacked by the very people that had instigated the whole psychedelic wave itself. The CIA who had seen fit to develop the drug and dish it out in great quantities for research purposes. These maniacs were now suddenly back peddling like crazy, trying desperately to keep control of the innocent but untamed animal it had created.
In a way they managed.
"Rat poison Number Nine!."
In a way they failed completely.

A year later was 1967, the so called 'Summer of Love', now looked back upon with so much nostalgia it seems ridiculous. By 1967, Kesey was in prison and the Merry Pranksters had fled the scene under a lot of pressure.
See the Minack Theatre, Cornwall thirty-three years later.
"Love Potion Number Nine!"
I was beginning to get the impression, for now I was really thinking a great deal, I was getting the impression that the whole of this latest Merry Prankster tour was all about passing on the information. Trying to ensure that that which had started, continued and that there was never any giving up the hope even in the face of extreme adversity.

It was a passage of rites.

It was a challenge to take up the gauntlet, to take up the spear and try to drive it straight through the heart of the ever-omnipotent traditional beast of conformity.

It was clear in the way that they jammed and in the way that we laughed. Kesey then started a game with the kids which involved bursting balloons and seeing who conquered all before them.

The winner was the last kid with their balloon intact. It was a fierce battle, and I was so pleased that quite the most beautiful little girl came out as victor, a little four year old angel.

Even Carlita, remember her, the bully girl, even she couldn't win despite her brute force and devilish cunning. So you see there is hope that the good will out, and that was becoming the point of all of the experience garnered over the time in these people's company. I realized that there is a desperate need to keep fighting the dark side, and to keep fighting it with all the power of your god given heart.

Back on the stage Caleb Kesey was now on the Theremin, there with his grandfather making shapes and strange sounds just as a true family should. Then Zane, Kesey's son was on the music busy twanging holy sounds out of the thunder machine. It was all out circus and it was an all out gang of mighty clowns. It was superbly uninhibited.

Later, after some further thirty minutes of wild musical jamming, I seem to remember they even played 'The Magic Bus' without a hint of irony, rightly so, it was over with the first part of that crazy day. I remember a rising feeling, quite a magical feeling of how good it was just to be there at that moment in time.

The eclipse, Jesus, these guys had already well and truly eclipsed that, easily. So, after a while they finish, we finish and all in one big clump of crazed humanity we walk the way back up to the camping field, like a lunatic army returning from a thousand personal wars.

We'd survived the eclipse together and we would survive a lot more, forever. Myrthin was there busy carrying equipment, all of us are busy laughing about the show, and it is finally became clear to me, it is all of us humankind through everything together.
You are truly what you are and you truly don't need anybody's permission to be that most worthy being, you should just be yourself and with all your might.

This I now feel was the learning of the second most important lesson in my life! The first major lesson I learnt was on amphetamine a long time before. It's learning told me quite simply.

"You do not, absolutely do not, need to be liked by everyone."

That had been a real brain opener. See we are always told this and that and how to behave and how one should be unconditional in our respect, but no, that just ain't right.

Forget the rules!
Respect is earned and is not a birth right.

"You do not, absolutely do not, need to be liked by everyone."

There in Cornwall on the morning of the eleventh of August 1999, I learnt what I considered the second of the major lessons of acquired wisdom.

I suspect that there nay well be at least twelve of these lessons, but I have time to be hit with the others. This second major lesson of my life, a thing to always carry with me at all times was another simple motto. In my subconscious I now had a new ideological non-truth.

The words were simple, their meaning immense.

"Forget it!"

Very straightforward was the message, basically it was as Neal Cassady had once said, "Worrying is the biggest waste of time."

Indeed, indeed!

Almost Buddhist in its world view but that is old religion and we, I suddenly see, are in the midst of a completely new religious meaning.

The clown religion of the Merry Pranksters, a non religion that simply says you should be 'out front' and honest, at all times.

By the time we had returned to the field it was early afternoon. We were told by Zane Kesey to come down to the bus in an hour and that there would be an afternoon of wild entertainment. Indeed, indeed!

At our tents we sat under the now quite overcast skies as radiant neon human post eclipse beings for the first times in our lives. We opened more wine. There was Myrthin, beaming a huge grin across his now weeklong blasted features, his hair tight in a pony tail under his ever present straw hat. And there was Sparks with his blond hair and sunglasses, his vibrant blue Hawaiian shirt, all glowing. He was truly on fire. And there was I.

I remember seeing deep meaning in everything. In the wind. In the shape of bushes, even in the clouds. We were somehow stronger than we had ever been, and we really couldn't explain why!

It was just simple fact.

From that point on the rest of the story would run on a different plane and with a wholly quicker pulse. It was from this point on that other lessons started running thick and fast. We began moving at hyper-speed ourselves.

There was no turning back and there was nothing to lose, for in the hands of fate and fortune it became really easy to trust that nothing really turns out wrong. Everything is success unless you have the fear of failure.

But who fails? Who's the judge?

Grow the trust and just watch how the big clockwork machine provides unseen patterns for your world. A world which takes you to places you could never have dreamed of. Then you begin to learn to even take notice of your dreams. And then your dreams actually come true for they have already existed in that other perspective called sleeping.
In my dream we weren't sleeping, we were heading back down the field towards the bus.
This dream had real legs!

HIGH HEAD.

Down at the bus all crazy hell was being cut loose.
First it started to rain and so the whole thing moved inside a large marquee and then it began.

There was the Merry Pranksters, there were us and the other campers.

There was about two dozen of us in all.

It was becoming in loose terms a free for all musical jam, a continuation of the end of the show.

It was as if the theatre was being taken back from the side of the cliff.

There was no end, there was no beginning.

There was though one big funky sound blasting out into the rural Cornish air.
The Merry Prankster band was blowing it out in big time freak and roll.

On trombone ladies and gentlemen, one Ken Babbs!

Six feet two, with crazed but placid eyes, with unkempt hair under a flat cap, wearing denims and a blue bomber jacket.
"BAAAAAA!!! BAAAAAA!!! BAAAABBS!"

Babbs would play the trombone like others would chase an elephant, wailing loudly, defiantly, fearlessly and what's more in a key from another musical planet.

His thing was stressing important moments with sound, being in traditional tune was not important for Babbs. He was taking the music back from the musicians and setting up puzzles. He was fantastic to watch and really, really funny to listen to.

At some point I remembered the tape recorder we had with us, and I urgently asked little Josie, a friendly ten year old boy who'd begun hanging around with us.

"Josie, can you go up to the tent and get the tape recorder, its somewhere inside!".

With which Josie blasted off with that superb energy of the child running off up the field. Within minutes he was back again his heroic task completed.

"You're a star Josie!" Said Myrthin who like me was lying merrily on the grass.

So that it is how we then managed to capture for eternity thirty minutes of this whole crazed performance. The tape recorder was set up where we lay to record the goings on for posterity. Babbs' trombone has since become legendary amongst all those who have heard the tape.

"What the hell is that?". They ask before breaking up into laughter.

"Good question!." I reply. "Good question!."

Anyway, back to then, back on the field.

On Theremin, in the corner, Ladies and Gentlemen, one Ken Kesey.

ZZZEEEEEEEEEE   WEEEEEEEEEEEEE
KEEEEEEZZZZZZZZEEEEEEE!

Alone and intense. Kesey there with his hands flying through the air. The strangest high pitched sounds imaginable pinging out across the field, like fishing colored magic out of the gray sky!

All in all, there were instruments of every description.

There was the Swan guy, now dressed in a wild zebra jacket playing a vicious 'flying V' electric guitar.

There were drums, a new-age type with dreadlocks was busy banging out a jungle rhythm. There was Neal Cassady's son, already an old man, on an old electric guitar busy chopping out blues chords.

There was a really funky bass player, young and strung out, hamming it up like a superstar.

Finally, there were all the jazz players from the eclipse show, all playing piercing melodies that sounded like lucid birds. This was a feast of the finest art, well the finest 'non-art', for the Pranksters have always had this thing about taking the art back from the artists.

That was their main drive in painting the original bus, reclaiming art for the common man. This is somehow a very important and a very worthy aim.

It is all too often a stifling feeling to feel that one must have a certain amount of proficiency in doing something before one can even begin to enjoy it.

Why?

Well the experts like it that way! They like having to sculpt the next generation of artists in the mould of what has gone before! And what does that achieve? Well, it places limits on how good you feel about what you create, it lays down comparisons.

But what does this taking the art back from the artists actually mean? Well, it means just getting up there and having a molly fudging go! Just trying to make noise, paint splashes, act out your role, without fear of comparisons to drag you back! It is an invocation of that child like ability to try without fear. Anything that brings satisfaction to the non artist is already art and who's to say any different? Not the hulking frame of Ken Babbs who is now playing a ludicrously out of tune, tuned in version of the old "Summertime" jazz classic.

There is a microphone there too and I have an urge to get up and rap back and forth, but don't as I am not sure whether this is a time for saying something or listening to everything. Anyhow Babbs is soon at the microphone busy telling us of a new world order.

"The New World Order!" He repeats in-between blasting on the trombone.

"The New World Order! BAAAAAAAAAAAAAAAAAA! BAAAAAAAA!"

"The bus came by and left the lizard in its path! The New World Order!."

He intones to the holy mess of sound.

I got what he was talking about, it was the same message as always and that the 'new world order' would be the ones that wanted the world in a different state to its current disrepair. The new world order would place humanity and the stars first and the dollar bill last.

Kesey still fizzes away on the Theremin, rather background to the whole sound but totally there and totally deep into the waves of noise and energy.
It all goes on and on with incredible intensity, yeah and just remember some of these guys are sixty years young. Age, it really seems, has totally nothing to do with it.

Sparks decides to do a roving report from the roof of the bus, so off he goes up the ladder that runs up at the back of old Further, and in a minute, he is sitting giggling at the front of the bus.

'On the bus.' for want of a more elaborate explanation. Myrthin and I wave, and hoot then take a photograph for posterity, a great shot too.

The sky lay heavy lead gray with the colorful bus as a counterpoint, in the middle was Sparks. Back on the ground we watched everything and still we were busy talking to Josie our favorite ten-year-old elf.

"Guess what we do for work?" I ask out of the blue.

"Don't know!"

"Something to do with school!" Say I as a form of a clue.

"What you still go to school!" Replies the cheeky kid.

"Yeah, we're teachers you fool!". Says Myrthin before giving him a playful dig in the ribs.

Josie then told us how much he 'hated' school and

Carlita.

He told us how his and Carlita's families were close friends, travelers, all living out of Glastonbury. We tried to tell him that Carlita was just that way and that he should give her a chance.

"No way! She's a real witch!". Protested the ten-year-old. At which we left the subject for another day, a day which would never come.

Back to the music and the mysto took over once more. It went something like this.

At the end of one song, already twenty minutes long, they have a change in drummers. Off goes the one drummer who was forty years old with flying hair and on comes a young guy in his early twenties.

He was fresh faced, had shoulder length hair and was dressed in untypical clean-cut denims. He reminded me of the look many bands were carrying with them at the time, from Oasis down to the Beastie Boys. It was the 'well dressed street gangster' look.

Immediately, a new jam starts, something a little bit too Bruce Springsteen for my taste, but still entertaining in the big picture.

Yet after a mere couple of verses Babbs stops the whole thing in its tracks, he stops the music to tell the drummer he's playing too loud. Babbs who was calm and very well meant oozed with some kind of hidden authority. He spoke slowly.

"You're playing too loud man!"

With which the drummer drums down a little bit and the song continues.

And Sparks still sits perched in the sky on the bus and Josie and we still lie on the damp but comfortable grass.

Again off we go into that vague American land of rock music that somehow seemed a tad traditional to me but still it's an overall bundle of fun. Kesey flies through his instrument with vigor, pulling tiny notes from here and howling thumps from there whilst Babbs blasts away on the trombone, elephant loud and twice as proud.

Everything seems to be well with the world but oh no it isn't!

"Hold up! Hold up!" Says Babbs interrupting the flow once more. Suddenly there was a touch of tension amongst the proceedings.

"Man, you are 'still' playing too loud."

Babbs laughs, the drummer shifts nervously, and all eyes are on Babbs and the young drummer. Just who this drummer was, we didn't know. He could have been one of the Prankster second generation kids. He could have been a passer by. It didn't really matter for he was playing too loud for Ken Babbs and Babbs had something important to say.

I got the impression the whole unease was borne out of the fact that the music should have all blended together as one. That there should be nothing louder than anything else for that knocks off the music's equilibrium. A jazz ethic that is a rudimentary fact is that you really have to be able to hear all the instruments at all times.

It was not nasty this little interlude, it was more like yet another of the Prankster teachings. So, I look at Myrthin who looks at me and we both try to understand the situation and take it in.

The music starts again, once more it is the rock and roll from somewhere else but still it is great entertainment and shit man, everyone, just everyone was now listening to the drumming.

The drummer though was seemingly not listening to anyone else. From where we lay though it seemed to be all somehow perfectly in order, it was not too loud, but then again, we were actually listening from a different perspective, that of ground level.

Sparks was the exception but he wasn't even listening to anything as he was now talking to two women wrapped in blankets up on the top of the bus.
Ra, ra, ra rock and this time it looks dangerous because Babbs is not even playing his magic trombone, he is just listening.

The rest of the merry band they continue to play, Jesus do they play, a hundred tails to the wind. Babbs though, he is now a tiger stalking the stage and you can feel 'it' coming from a long way off.

"IT'S COMIN.' IT'S COMIN.' THEY MIGHT BALL YOU! THEY MIGHT HAUL YOU! BUT THEY WILL NEVER STAB YOU IN THE BAAAAAAAAAAACK!"

The confusing thing however was that you just had no idea

'what' was coming.

Again, Babbs stopped the musical flow, for the third time in so many minutes, and everyone held their breath.

Kesey stands silent whilst the rest of the band twitch and twiddle around on their instruments.

"It's still too loud!" Says Babbs to the now physically withered young drummer. "TOO LOUD!!!"

Then Babbs said something quite subtle, quite mild but something absolutely pivotal to our whole week. First he took in a deep breath and then proceeded as calmly as possible to ask the drummer a quite awesome question. "Can you hear what Kesey's playing?"

From where we lay we could see the drummer shake his head ruefully.

"Well then!" Says Babbs.

"You are playing too LOUD!"

A shiver squiggled its way down my spine, and I didn't really immediately understand why. But then!!!!!!!!!!!!

Enlightenment.

It was in simple terms Babbs merely saying that only by really listening to Kesey was the young drummer going to truly nourish himself in the occasion.

Kesey had something 'really' important to say, important even in the squeaks and blips of his Theremin playing. It hit me hard and drove home just how much reverence Ken

Babbs held for his long-term ally and perennial companion.

He was passing on a forty year 'best friendship' in the way that was saying, "Look if you can't actually hear Kesey then you are missing the point and believe me his message really does have that much value.." Now if a friend holds you in such high esteem, a person that knows the absolute ins and outs of the other guy, then it is credence is in my mind beyond questioning.
"Can you hear what Kesey's playing?"

With a so called rational logic one might question all this and even feel a touch of sympathy for innocent drum playing newcomer. Remember Babbs was only trying to help, only trying to offer a true 'once in a lifetime' experience to a young man who would probably never again play with the Merry Pranksters. Not on the day of this eclipse, or anywhere else, ever with such potency.

So I was astounded by this, and once more the mysto rose a notch because I realized again that Kesey was in fact passing on gold. It struck me that he himself would never tell you when to listen. It was never him blowing his own trombone, the information was just there to be taken on by anyone who found it valuable to take it.

Babbs hadn't been simply ego tripping, he hadn't even been power tripping. He had just felt the need to insist that Kesey was worth listening to.

It bugs me just how unappreciated the work of these guys still is. Yet it is only unappreciated because we are told it is not safe to listen, not worthy of comfortable appreciation. We are told this by people who have a confirmed antagonism towards the works of the Merry Pranksters.

These are the devious people who have the biggest say. This underdog fight is the Merry Prankster's essential, to have to battle for the smallest piece of ground, to have to fight even to have your say because no one wants to give them any space any longer. Their ideals are not politically correct. Well, forget you all and forget you with a smile.

The Merry Pranksters are morally sound, they played the correct role and as Ken Babbs so rightly put it that long gone afternoon.

"If you can't hear Ken Kesey you're playing too loud!".

Our world is unfortunately saturated with unnecessary noise.

I can't hear myself think!

You are playing too loud!

Who was playing and who was watching?

We were still under the cloudy sky where the field was dampening down. The improvised set was thrilling us still but then just as things were beginning to repeat back on themselves and mosey off down into another blues jam,

Kesey leaves his Theremin, pinging on a permanent 'YEEEEEEEEEEEEKEEEEEEEEEEEEEZZZZZZZZZZZZEEEEEE EEEEEE!." He slowly walks over to the microphone and calmly announces that he wants to tell us something. Tell us something? Who us?

Well, that is what it seemed like. He says he's going to talk about teachers. Myrthin and I listened hard for we were teachers, and it did seem like he was talking directly to us.

Kesey's charisma though always made it seem like he was talking directly to you and you alone.

"I want to talk about teaching!". Says Kesey standing directly opposite us about twelve feet away.

He then begins telling us the importance of education and that everyone needs to learn and to continue learning.

"There's nuthin' worse than those who claim to know it all!!!!!!!!!!!!!!!!!!!!!!". And the word all, repeats and repeats into infinity as all, all, all, all!

"Nuthin' worse! Worse, worse, worse, worse!"

There was a digital delay effect on his voice that caused the last spoken word to repeat itself several times.

At least that is what we assumed. Of course, we and the gathered dozen were immediately gripped by this turn of events, it was now a personal Kesey insight, the like of which only happens on very rare occasions.
"I was up in New York one time, at a school for unruly teenage guys………………………" Kesey says and everyone listens, all remembering Babbs and that it was important not to be playing 'TOO LOUD'!

"Trying to convince these kids the value of education, tion, tion, tion!.."

I drew a mental picture of the younger Kesey making his way into a gray, awful, brick building, and winter time with rain in the air. He was there to prove something to the cynical, the ultra cynical, the troublesome teenagers of the American wilderness.

"They paid me 1500 dollars for the day, a lot of money, money, money, money!"

Kesey then goes on to say how he talked, taught and ducked his way through a morning with a hundred eager listeners. Well, out of the hundred there were ninety nine eager listeners at least. At the end of his presentation talk a kid, a real cynical, teen king comes up and tells Kesey that he isn't convinced.

This tough, wrong side of the tracks kid faces up to Kesey with questions flashing in his eyes.

"Why should I bother learning anything?" The kid asked stressing the word 'anything.' "They can't tell me what I need to learn. I ain't interested in their stuff!."
Kesey then comes up with a deal, the kid knew deals he was from the street.

"Look if I can't prove to you why education is important then you can take the money I'm getting for being here today! All of it, all 1500 dollars".

The kid is immediately taken aback by the offer as this guy certainly isn't playing by the usual rules.

"Go on then do you take the deal?." Whispers Kesey secretively.

The young guy looks confused but there is no malice in the youngster's eyes, for in truth he really does want to learn, or at least see a reason to learn.
And in the slight drizzle on a field in Cornwall the dozen or so sitting, and the dozen standing listen intently.

"So, you know what I did?" Asks Kesey. "I read him a poem,

a poem by Yeats, a wonderful poem that explains a great deal!"

Kesey fell silent and then recommenced by reciting the following words.

I went out to the hazel wood,
Because a fire was in my head,
And cut and peeled a hazel wand,
And hooked a berry to a thread;
And when white moths were on the wing,
And moth-like stars were flickering out,
I dropped the berry in a stream
And caught a little silver trout.
When I had laid it on the floor
I went to blow the fire aflame,
But something rustled on the floor,
And some one called me by my name:
It had become a glimmering girl
With apple blossom in her hair
Who called me by my name and ran
And faded through the brightening air.
Though I am old with wandering
Through hollow lads and hilly lands.
I will find out where she has gone,
And kiss her lips and take her hands;
And walk among long dappled grass,
And pluck till time and times are done
The silver apples of the moon,
The golden apples of the sun.

Sun, sun, sun, sun, sun.

We were all spells bound. I'd never heard such a poem before.

I'd hardly heard a poem read aloud before, but from that

moment on, some inexplicable thing that had long since been confusing made infinitely more sense. So much so that we tracked the poem down some weeks later not even knowing it's title.

We remembered the words vividly, Myrthin, Sparks and I really remembered the words. The poem was called 'The Song of Wandering Aengus' by W.B: Yeats.

A copy of this now hangs on the outside of Sparks' front door as a gift of wisdom to anyone who should pass through the doorway.

For me, it had deep meant some time later in the year 2000 when I first met my now wife. I at some point offered her the poem as some form of explanation, instinctively she understood and that was pretty much proof of a very important thing.

The poem has everything. It has recklessness, adventure, poignancy, and of course the power of a glimpse of true love. I still have trouble reading it without feeling strongly emotional such is it's sweep.

Needless to say, the street guy back in the story couldn't take Kesey's 1500 dollars and 'had' found a reason to learn.

So simple and so effective, it struck me as proof of how powerful the use of a gentle magic can be. What had worked on that nameless New York doubter many years before had worked on us too. The proof that everyone is reachable when one uses the most honest techniques, the quality of truth.

When I look at Yeats' words now, I see that it is a precious explanation of that which we were actually searching for that week back in 1999.

No, it wasn't only a search for true love, though should it have arisen none of us would have turned it away, no it was a search for mystery, a search for some form of, let's call it guidance in catching the flow. Ken Kesey had laid it all cold with a mere poem, a poem by an Irish man of another era, though that was probably the point. The point being that there are things that are eternal and that our emotions are always the key.

There 'are' no new emotions, they are universally submerged in the subconscious, omnipresent and ultimate in the fact that we all have to deal with the same flights of fancy.

That was what we were learning. We were being taught by that which we were experiencing.

A hazel wood!

He must have meant a mystical place of hidden shadows, one of silver trees and mossy banks that rose soft underfoot. He meant the natural inspiration to walk and to travel through.

A fire was in my head!

There's no need to explain to myself that feeling of explosion in the cranium. There can be an absolute confusion and fire in all that you see.

Yet one often fails to understand that it is all driven by the eternal flame, the spirit. To a varying degree or other I think that all who have lived have had a fire burning deep in their head. Some though have it burning in their heart.

There is a difference.

So there in this poem's words was a further gift.

The Yeats' poetry was in a way a written explanation for a lot of that we were experiencing that week. It was about the desperate need to explore new territory simply because it lies beyond your doorstep. About the mountains of such inexplicably wonderful things that are waiting to be found, just off the main path, just away from the center.

Look, over here! The three of us, we had come away to the eclipse with little expectation, maybe a head full of questions but we were carrying a certainty in the company in which we were traveling, our own company.

The three of us were blind romantics of the lost generation and we had just been handed our love letter for the long journey.
'The Song of Wandering Aengus' was without doubt a psychedelic classic!

But hey enough nostalgia for the moment, there is a story to be told and this story was getting increasingly into the center of the vortex.

Kesey left the microphone still echoing to the words "Sun, sun, sun, sun, sun!", whilst we three, for now Sparks had returned from his bus rooftop experience, we sat there and wondered a while. We wondered about things that were probably not to be wondered about, the cosmic track that can send one hurtling too quickly into inner space.

Had Kesey really told the story for our benefit? Well of course he had, it was I'm sure something that he knew we needed to hear.

Then why was young Josie off busy chasing dogs who were chasing their tails. Was he too young to have got the message?

No, he was too young to need the message, he already understood. The others who were around listening whether they took anything deep on board?

I knew not, but there were few only, maybe fifteen at the most.

This was a highly personal moment, one which the three of us shared and would never forget. As I have said once before, things started getting faster still from that point onwards.

"DO YOU WANT A FIGHT?"

It was Ken Babbs dealing with the coming on, coming on, forever questions, forever closer, moves of one of the previous night's 'disgraces.

An old Hippie dude without shoes was demanding something and plainly annoying everybody but himself. Babbs was losing his patience.

"Do you want a fight?" Says the ex Marine, only joking of course but the message was clear, back off dude, you are bugging us all!

The time after the Wandering Aengus poem, went at a pace, at times an unhappy pace.

Kesey moved back to the noise of the Theremin but then

slowly he seemed to lose interest and later we all met in the far reaches of the marquee.

Outside there were quite heavy scenes taking place. Some people, some people.
Ones who had not been listening were talking really loudly. One strange guy, English, in his late twenties, was berating the Merry Pranksters for having cordoned off the bus for the week.
"I mean you call it open, it's just the same hierarchy as always. You guys up there, the rest of us down here!". He complained.

No, one answered him, which of course just made him worse.

"Arrogant Americans!" He spat as he stomped off up the field.

It reminded me a touch of myself way back in Brighton, way back when the bus had originally come and left us all waving at spaces.

Yeah, somehow I could see what the English guy was saying, but he was missing a crucial point, a point that had become increasingly obvious during the week.

The Merry Pranksters have somehow managed to develop almost a mirror existence whereby they totally reflect what is projected onto them. They themselves are apparently extremely grounded in who they are and have the ability to bring out both the best and the worst in anybody.

The ability to bring it all out front, with no hidden agendas. At Kesey's farm back in Oregon it was well known that the place was generally open to anyone who made the journey, Kesey had written much about the ethos of being 'open' in his book, a great book, called 'The Demon Box'. Many travelers would turn up out of the blue with often dubious reasons to be there on this working farm but there was no hiding away from the stranger at the door.

It was a selfless karmic attitude, but hey, again it would be a mirror that was awaiting you. Turn up with some positive agenda and that would be returned in kind but turn up with some negative growl then that growl would be amplified so strongly that it became loud enough for the culprit to hear. Then the person would be forced into dealing with the dish he was kicking out.

The Merry Pranksters were never into being used as other people's karmic scapegoats.

'We are what we are, and you have to be what you are to even begin to understand what you might really be.'

This ideal went right back to the beginnings, the beginnings on the 1964 bus trip when the only way to cope was to be brutally honest and not to allow things to smolder dangerously inside your own soul.

On the original trip, nine totally different characters had made a brutal trip across the United States in a blundering old school bus. One Prankster, a troubled young student named Sandy Lehmann Haupt, had suffered most of all. He had been unable to 'bring it all out front` and had ended up being surrounded on all sides, by himself. Ultimately, he had been caught up in violent paranoia and confusion, just unable to ever ask for the truth or even for guidance. He feared the power of Kesey and was constantly challenged into hiding his own feelings, which was a mistake.

That this guy Sandy eventually passed away only one week before Kesey was another of life's ridiculous coincidences.

So back to ourselves in the midst in this crazy post eclipse, heavy vibration. We wandered around talking to whoever we bumped into.

 My, we were into the third, fourth or the thousandth bottle of wine of the day, but we were making sense out there in that alternative universe on the field. We waltzed next to the vibrating bus and Sparks had a long, intense conversation with the whole gang.

Then we three met Kesey who after dealing the poem of wondrous words asked a strange question.

"Hey guys, what's a googly?"
Sparks began trying to explain that it was a certain type of ball delivery in the game of cricket. one that was really slow but with a wild spin.

"Really! Well let me tell you a joke!". Says the legendary man, still sparkling under his hat.
"About Australians!" The three of us stood around while we were asked.
"What's the difference between a buffalo and a bison?".
We looked on dumbly on then shrugged our shoulders.

"Well you can't wash your face in a buffalo!"

We all laughed at the play on the Australian accent, you know basin and bison and buffalo!

Then Kesey told us he'd been to Australia and Sparks told Kesey about Perth, his hometown, whilst Myrthin and I talked a little about Wales.

Back outside the heavy vibrations were diluting a little and as the four of us walked into the slow drizzle, all smiling, it was late afternoon. Ken Babbs had not had a fight, the music was still going, the sun still hid behind a water-colored sky and we three left the marquee madness and headed up to the tent for some wine. It had already been a long day and it was somehow just beginning.

At the tent we sat down on the damp grass and watched a little. What was in the air was a freaky kind of desperation, an intangible ill at ease within nature.
As if the eclipse was causing aftershocks and that things were taking time to settle back into a routine. Or more fancifully, a new routine was here and not to go away. The eclipse might have been a standard bearer of change, the beginning of another time.
One constant though was the wine we were drinking, our stocks were depleted but of the seven bottles purchased in Penzance, three were remaining.

Enough! We sat and talked like excited children, eager to recount our observations of the day, of the Kesey experiences, the play, the eclipse and a hundred fascinating other things.

The general mood was one of real learning. We'd learnt from the apparent amateur nature of the play, most certainly from the poetry and above all how well the group dynamic seemed to carry the Merry Pranksters even after nearly thirty years.

As we sat, we watched. There were more and more tents being put up, cars arriving regularly until there was nearly double as many campers as there had been. It was the amphetamine debris of the festival crowd. They arrived with tales of a stand off with the police, illegal parties being shut down and with a great interest in the crazy colored bus.

The tent a couple of tents away from us was where the dog lived, our friend, the Rastafarian terrier. His owners were a sweet couple, in their early forties and had used the camp site as a convenient location from which to visit Cornwall's wonders and winding ways.

We had been on friendly terms since the day we'd arrived, but they were suddenly somehow on edge. I think they were a little uneasy with the influx of new arrivals. Somehow, we knew what they meant; each new arrival brought with them a bass heavy boom of music that continued booming from that point on. But hey it's only rock and roll and we like it!

After a while and a tepid dab in the last gram of amphetamine, I'd made sure that there was still at least half left for my own consumption, or for sharing, well at least there was some left for later, we made our way out to the 'Arena of the Middle Ground' to join in the game of cricket that was going on.

It was the usual teams, us, the kids and a few other fathers. My god it was fun, I did a running commentary.

"Coming into bowl, the legend from the East, young and spicy! Watch that arm action, over and out! Only six years old but heading for the top. Here she comes! Here she comes! And yes, it's hit away over the fielders, over the field, over the fence and away to the sun!"

Myrthin came over laughing! "Cut it out! You're putting the bowler off!"

"I'm putting the bowler off but the boy with the bat loves it. Did you see that shot?" I continued before Myrthin leapt on my back and I took off on a run across the field.
"And here they come, the Celtic horse riders, coming to storm the Arena!" I managed to scream before I or rather we, plummeted to the floor in a giggling heap!

On struggling to our feet with most of the wine in tact we gulped in deep breaths and questioned each others sanity.

"Hey, you maniacs we're showing some videos down at the bus a bit later make sure you come down!". It was Zane Kesey, Kesey's son telling us about the next stage of that momentous day.

"Yeah great, we'll be there!." I say before jumping on Myrthin's back for a shot of revenge.

"Yeah the Celtic horse riders of their own apocalypse are going to be there! They are already on their way. They are way out West, like Laurel and Hardy once said. One flew East and One Flew West and One flew over the Cuckoo's…………………"

Crash we collapsed again covered in a maroon crystal shower of wine as the bottle arced upwards above our heads.

"No matter!" I spluttered, "There's more of that where we come from,"

"Well, you can ride off and get it!" Counters Myrthin.
Brushing ourselves down we dragged ourselves to our feet, picked up the wine bottle, still almost half full, then waltzed back to the game laughing. Sparks had failed to

take his eyes off the intricate batting and bowling, such is his enthusiasm for the sport.

Meanwhile, yes, there's more and more cars turning up. After talking to a group of newcomers, all male, in their late teens, wild eyes, short hair, we find out that there is to be a huge rave party on the beach that night.

"Coming from all over the place!." Says one of the guys in a strong London accent. That we personally were already all over the place was of no concern!

"Rave on!." Shouts Myrthin in a false accent, the news of another party had his spirits raised.

"Cuckoo's Nest!" I scream back finishing the sentence from earlier.

Now the news of the beach party had me in two minds. On one hand I knew that the day after was the day to get back to dry land. Sparks was flying back to Vienna early the day after that.

The Dancing Driver was required to guide the troops the three hundred miles back to the of the living. But the amphetamine was the main part of my plan, the way to ensure a certain awake type of vibration at any point. That's why I was glad to still have a hefty half a gram left either for the coming night or the morning after. A beach party well let's wait and see.
Somewhere over our heads the sun dipped bleached puce down to the horizon.

Night was approaching quickly for the second time that crazy day.

KOOL AID ACID TEST

It was now dark on the camp site, approaching ten o clock and the main buzz was sitting watching the original Merry Prankster's videos with the Merry Pranksters.

They had a video projector with them and were projecting colored images onto the white canvas of the marquee. It was the 'Kool Aid Acid Test Videos.'

Original footage from way back when, from when the world was still black and white, and psychedelia was a secret government baby. We three, well we had continued to dive into our endless wine collection and now close to the Chai tea tent, we were fidgeting with joy.

I had at some point frazzled down a great portion of my remaining amphetamine and was riding on quite a flying high jagged rise. The other two they were oblivious to my personal self doping and were content to ride with whatever else we could muster. Joints and drinks were still

doing the rounds, as were inevitably a couple of the lost cases, the shoeless desperadoes.
"Give me a hit of that man! Just a tiny bit! Go on!" Says one remarkably persistent character, a Dickens type of downbeat.

He was blessed with no teeth, hissing breath and arms which always snaked their way around your shoulders. He was almost amusing but certainly not a long-term proposition.

After whatever type of plunder, he could get he kept appearing at regular intervals. I heard from someone that this flake was actually Josie's father and that filled me with me a mild sadness. Josie though, he was a fine fellow and was still with us. He'd been virtually a constant companion since the afternoon. Indeed, he was really cool company and appealed to the child within us. He was our surrogate son for the day without sun.

We talked for a while with Carolyn Adams, the original Mountain Girl, she'd started telling us that she remembered us from Stonehenge.
"Are you guys' musicians? You look like musicians."
We told her we were vaguely musically inclined and then we discussed our specific vehicles.
"You should have seen us getting the bus up the lane!". She giggled. "It was like squeezing a dart out of a toothpaste tube!"

"Good god," I interjected, "Our car it's been a hell of a thing. It's got a mind of its own. It only starts when it feels like it! We've been ridden ragged by engine failure all week! We call it Norm! Like you call yours Further!"

"These!" She said giggling cryptically. " Are very weird

times."

No kidding! We were sitting chatting with a key character out of a key book under a thousand scattered stars.

On the marquee vivid color flashes into the dark night. Scenes of wild dancing from a 1965 Acid Test jives the night. The lady at our side is the younger lady on the screen, dancing madly whilst at the same time in 1999, laughing comfortably.

"Man look at George!" She says as the image of a freaking dancer in a blur of movement rises green into the purple shot. This was the young version of George Walker who was standing watching silently to the side.

"I still move that fast when the moon is full, you know what I mean!". He suddenly shouts across the noise. A soundtrack played by The Grateful Dead winds away at a tuneful chaos and we all laugh along with each other between staccato psychedelia. Suddenly in comes our lost soul albatross guy.

"Hey Mountain Girl!"

Carloyn Adams is fifty years old and I don't think anyone, even the closest of Merry Pranksters refer to her as Mountain Girl any longer.

"Hey Mountain Girl, you know what? We should get married, you and me!"

Somehow even in the midst of all this opened out looseness, this shoeless wonder was still an embarrassment.

"Not on your life man! You're too soulless!." She replies pointing to his bare feet.

This amused our desperate friend but inspired him to seek solace in our wine.

"Hey guys can I have just a little hit. It's lovely wine that, umh, lovely wine!"

We were beginning to know his ingratiating routine which involved asking for something, a joint, a drink, a cigarette, anything, then declaring the quality of that which he was seeking.
I was truly relieved my amphetamine was well hidden from his grubby grasp so I disappeared to take a piss and to lick some more chemical energy into my system.

On returning with a renewed fizz in my step to the open air Prankster cinema, I took time to take in the scene. These films were real precious historical artifacts of the counterculture and watching them in the company of those main protagonists was a special feeling.

According to Zane Kesey the program was going to run until eleven o clock, when everything was going to stop and Channel Four were going to broadcast their Merry Prankster 'eclipse' special directly from the field out to the nation. They had a mobile studio set up in a small truck and the program was still being edited as we sat there. Nonstop all this stuff and of course there was the 'Beach Party' still to come.

There was no sign of Ken Kesey, he was probably resting, or eating or doing his thing away from the crowds. Babbs too was missing, but one who was now always with us Desperado Dude Number One.

His shambling, barefooted aura was suddenly bursting onto the scene with wild excitement and for once he wasn't seeking something, he was bringing ominous news.

"Guys, guys, quick. You've got to come with me. There's this cat with a whole bottle of liquid Californian! Come on! I've already had five quick hits. Amazing man!" With which he grabbed hold of Myrthin's arm and refused to let it go.

Now liquid Californian is acid, LSD. It is the real deal, a screwy, mind warp drug! It is the top of the roller coaster, and it can introduce you to 'heaven and hell, both.'

In the dark, in the midst of the night, following our one-time Nemesis to find this bottle of strong, magic potion, I could just about see the panic in Sparks' eyes. Just as I could feel the doom in mine.

Myrthin though, he was just as fast as lightning, he held no fear.

In an instant there we were. In front of us stood a vision, a king dealer acid-head of the sparkling American stars.

This guy could only have been thirty if that. He was shirtless, lean and had the scrawny features of one who dismissed food for religious reasons. To top it all he had a carefully plaited pony tail that ran three feet down his back, it twisted like an evil wind as he turned to the tramp with little empathy.

"Hey no more man! It'll kill you!." The guy spoke with a slow, doped out Californian accent and was obviously tired of giving our fried companion free hits.
"No not for me man, no, for my pals here!".

Meaning us three, hapless victims.
"Yeah, okay I see!." Captain Trips smiled as he turned to look at us.

"Hey, no problem, there's enough here for everyone!"

With which this mysterious little guy lifts up a small, brown medicine bottle, on which a skull and cross bones was painted on the front.

"Okay guys hold out your hands!". Says Captain Trips with an almost evil glare in his dark eyes. "Hold out my hand! Yeah, sure and lose my mind! Forever!"

I was not at all into the idea of succumbing to this unknown chemical entity. I was already in the throes of a strong amphetamine high; it seemed bordering on the irresponsible to take this guy up on his deal.

Not Myrthin though, for he was already there watching the clear liquid form a tiny pool in the palm of his hand. I could then see the shuffling outline that was Sparks.

I could also see the sniggering imp of a man that was the Desperado. In my mind I could see the three-hundred-mile-long journey ahead of me the day after and I could also see the jagged white lines of the powdered speed.

"You next!" Whispered the dealer in the direction of Sparks' shadow!
Sparks had never ever had a real LSD experience! Therefore he was unsure and seemed to need help or persuasion.

It was Myrthin who grabbed hold of the scales. He busily encouraged Sparks to jump on the psychedelic ship with him, which he did with great panache, a similar palm full of clear liquid and with a rolling eyed laconic shrug of the shoulders.

"Here we go then, away, away!". Says Sparks with an air of confusion.

Then it was my turn.

"Hey man!", Captain Trips whispers as he stared through the darkness deep into where I stood. "Shall I dose you?"

The guy's demeanor alone was enough to drive me well away from following suit. His question just seethed with a desire to drag me with him on his spiral to nowhere land. He was one of those of a rare breed in these nonpsychedelic days, an acid guru. But so was I in a different way and I answered simply with a quiet determination.

"No thanks mister! I've already dosed myself several times around. You know what I mean?"

And that was that. The guy turned away disinterested Sparks and Myrthin were about to embark on a journey through the dimensions and I wondered about my decision.

In fact, I still do!

Should I have joined in on the big eclipse LSD trip?

It strikes me even now that the personal danger that awaited me that evening was a danger I didn't need to confront. So too the potential personal joys!

I was actually in no need of a further doped out experiment when one was already flying in my soul. One time, a long time before I'd mixed acid and amphetamine in a night club experience. My god, there were three of us and we'd kept blacking out for five minutes at a time. We'd lose consciousness whilst dancing and that was not the kind of 'high' that rested easily on my eager shoulders. So Californian Liquid Acid, not really, not when Welsh amphetamine was already sending shivers to my brain.

As compensation I finished off the rest of the speed and prepared to watch the amusing disintegration of my two friends, yeah disintegration and then their inevitable resurrection.

It was going to be a time for those two musketeers to ride a fast train through dawn and beyond. It was going to be a time for me to take it onwards from there. My priorities lay elsewhere and that involved guiding the battered Norm back to London then Wales in one piece. I'd had a valid reason to forego the kaleidoscopes behind the eyes. I needed to remain sharp or at least not completely mad.

So, this is how the next hours began.

Sparks and Myrthin managed to keep some form of focus for a short while. We spent time helping fix the Merry Prankster's video projector, it had given up the ghost whilst we were meeting the acid ghost of summer's past.

There was George Walker, there was Zane Kesey and there was us. Oh, and of course Desperate Dave who was now like a second skin.

"Hey is the plug in the back?"

"Sure, as damn is. I think the motor's gone."

With which suddenly the machine started to work and all

of us cheered as one.

The film flickered back into action on the makeshift screen. There were shots of acid light shows and the continued dancing marionettes, the Watts Acid Test from 1966.

Though somehow it was no longer quite all so fascinating! Not with the Sparks and Myrthin show beginning to warm up. What really kicked off the mayhem was the beaming of Channel Four's eclipse special. To watch this in a field was unusual enough, but to watch it with my two friends coming apart at the seams as well, was just way weird!

There we stood a huddle of original Pranksters, some old enough to be from the Sixties and some younger ones, the ones born in the Nineteen Sixties. The portable studio had a small monitor on which the program could be seen. Television was a strange enough concept after the week spent in no time land but being at the very center of thirty minutes of actual 'on air' broadcasting was a new one.

For thirty minutes we watched a review of the day that was still going on. We saw the theatre performance, the eclipse, the camp site and a short Kesey interview.

And do you know what I really saw?

I saw in one clear flash the ultimate difference between living something yourself and watching it edited down for you. The day that I was going through was a glorious Technicolor event. A cliff hanger, a thriller, the breaking news headlines all thrown into one multi sensation.

The television program we'd just seen was a pitiful bedfellow to that which had really happened. It was a very poor representation and though it is plainly impossible to show the truth through an edited perspective of what has been. I felt that with a bit of imagination, it must have been possible to have captured the fundamental spirit at least.

And therein lies the problem! The problem of how to get across what the Merry Pranksters' world view and what it is really about!

There is no easily explained philosophical dogma, it is a non philosophy that they represent. I tell you it is not surprisingly that it is they themselves that have truly come closest to capturing their own spirit.

In two films they have put together, "The Journey to the East" and "North to Madhattan", both taken from the original 1964 bus trip, you learn more about their special take on things than in any of the books written, theories expanded, or photographs taken. It is an indefinable something that runs through those films, call it magic for want of a better word.

But getting these films to the public is no easy task.

Sparks and I have been recently pushing to get them screened in an underground cinema in Vienna. It is almost impossible.

"Do you think these things are suitable for the cinema?."
Asks the theatre owner. Good god!
And when he asked us both.
"Why do they always film themselves!"
We answered simply.
"Because no one else would do it!".
There has been rumors for many years of a Hollywood blockbuster version of Wolfe's 'Electric Kool Aid Acid Test', but so far no one has been able to pull it off. One day maybe but it is difficult to catch the essence of mystery

with mere money.

On the field, on the hill with a god given opportunity, Channel Four had tried and failed. They had failed by filming without imagination. Though it didn't really matter, imagination was running wild up on that field. We were all mad and some of us were about to get a lot madder!

It finally all got irreversibly crazy after one in the morning. I had lost my two companions losing the plot. They were tripped out in a spaced way, making little sense and busy giggling with Desperado Number One.

I myself was now way too gone to adopt any judgmental role. I couldn't really get a hook on their temporary madness, so I left for the sanctuary of my tent. There I lay under a canopy of my own silence. Though it was hardly a calm escape. There were strange noises exuding from every direction.
Some crazed hound busily taunting the night from somewhere down by the ocean. There was also a gentle rumble from the beach party as it pounded down on the night.
There was a wind that blew evil draughts through the flapping tent door.
I felt alone on that windy moor, but I preferred it that way. I was alone to lie and ponder in my own amphetamine cocoon.

Yet hold on I was fooling myself! After mere matter of minutes, there came the tripping Sparks and Myrthin walking by. You could clearly hear them as they walked stumbling up the field claiming to each other that they had gone each gone blind first.

"Oh my god Sparks, I can't see a thing! Give me your hand.

Haw !"

"Here I am! Where are you?"

And there I lie, mildly panic stricken! The two of them are flying on LSD and are heading my way, albeit slowly, but they are coming my way!

I thought quickly, I thought clearly, and this was my plan.

I was going to try to remain silent and listen in to see how they were pulling through. LSD has the effect of forming a huge bond between those on the drug at the time, it is by its nature a very group orientated thing.
I, being the one not on the trip, though not exactly excluded from the experience, could certainly never really join in on the wild fantasy. They were embarking on a double voyage through a tunnel of the most colorful sensation anyone could ever encounter.
I worried a little as I didn't really fancy nursing the two of them through a hallucinated night adventure, but that would only be needed should it all get too hairy. Then of course it would have been my very duty to play the calm role.

But hold on!

"Look at the fence!". Screeches Sparks, "It's fizzing white electricity! Look!"

So there they were both blind yet seeing barbed wire fences as electric currents!

Oh my god, it looked like a long night ahead of us all! Though that made me even gladder to be in a clear amphetamine state of mind. It gave me the ability to listen in on their enjoyable psychedelic madness. I was tripping by proxy in the second dimension.

"Are you there?"

I lay quietly as if asleep.

"He must be asleep!" Says Myrthin.

'Sleep' I thought to myself, 'Jesus God! Some chance!'
I lay silently as they managed to burst their way into the car and commence skinning up whilst listening to music. Even though I was fearful of mania it struck me that the music was playing really quietly out of the speakers.
"SSSSSSSHHHH! Turn the music down!". Says a paranoid sounding Sparks. "It'll wake up the whole camp site!"

I began to wonder about Sparks. He was venturing down the psychedelic road for the first real time and I hoped with all my soul that it would be a heavenly experience that was awaiting him.

Myrthin though, he was less of a concern as he'd been on that psychedelic lemonade road many times before. He was capable of controlling it all. Sparks though? I wondered!

In my sleeping bag with my eyes wide open, I lay and listened to the mild hilarity building up in the car.

"Hey, turn the lights off someone's coming!" Sparks panics.

"Just close your eyes, they won't be able to see you.." Answers Myrthin calmly.

Then wild laughter from both of them and amused giggles from inside my tent.

After a while of this routine. Sparks panicking, Myrthin calming him, then all of us laughing, I heard something that made me doubt my own sanity.

"I am." Announces Sparks unsure but determined. "Going to get my head down and get some sleep!."
I shot up in the tent.
Now a mere two hours into a strong twelve-hour LSD experience means you are just not going to be able to, 'Get your head down!'

No, your head is going to be exploding with a cacophony of the most amazing colors. Exploding with a concert of the loudest of voices and the purest of angelic music! There is no place for sleep! Not for at least a dozen hours more. I sat in trepidation as I heard the car door slam shut then Sparks' tent zip open up! I started counting in my head.

And remember the barking dog.

Well, in literally only one minute of time I heard Sparks bursting out of the tent and back into the car.

"Did you hear that dog? Every time I turned over, it started howling. It was the king of the hounds of hell, and it was after me!." Sparks said sounding startled.

"It's been barking all night!" Advised Myrthin.

I lay there listening to all this and I acknowledged that I was for the first time getting a true hook on the psychedelic experience from the outside. This was second hand. I was learning big lessons through listening to the two acid matadors. They were at a place that I had been many times myself. The room of LSD confusion and wisdom. The room had Sparks and Myrthin lost amongst themselves busy falling through all the classic LSD experiences. I knew that there was no way that I could successfully join them on their journey.

Not that the journey seemed to be a particularly pretty one at that early stage. It seemed for Sparks at least, to be quite an ordeal. I could hear a panic in his voice above the timid music. He was absolutely convinced that he had been the reason for the barking dog. He was convinced too that he had been in his tent for a lot longer than the one minute of time.

Though it is another perspective that this drug allows, a chance to see further than one normally can. A chance to see colors as you normally cannot. A chance to feel sensations more strongly than you can do under normal circumstances.

I recall one mountain-side experience flying on LSD.

It was dark and we were staying at an old cottage high in the Alps. It was all jolly psychedelic mayhem until I saw an unbelievably beautiful white moth get hypnotized by an electric light bulb. This large moth was a snow-colored representation of purity being trapped by the awful power of false light.

I had to save it. In trying to free the doomed thing I caught its wing awkwardly and carried the creature out to the dark with huge gloom. I had killed what I was trying to save. Or so I thought. With great care I placed the probably stunned white flash on a nearby wall then left it in tears.

A while later I returned to find to my enormous pleasure that the moth had flown off, free!
Or had been eating.

I stood alone in the dark with tears of joy running down my cheeks.

It was in this state that two other party goers, non-LSD takers turned around the corner to find me.

"Jesus! What's the matter?"

In my wild-eyed state with a real tear-stained stained complexion I turned towards them smiling.

"It's the moth." I announced to the utterly confused twosome. "It's flown. It's flown!".

Both of them looked at each other and left. They could never have understood, yet I easily understood how strange they must have thought I was behaving.
It was though, and this is the point, all amazingly logical to my acid perspective. I'd had to save the moth and had managed.

So, who in fact is to say that Sparks was not right in his assumptions? It is only the way of the majority that says these things are the way they are.
They say that you can't see an electric white emanating out of dull, gray barbed wire fence.
They say that one minute is always one minute of time, every time.

They say that music is quiet when it is actually loud. Turn it up, no turn it down.

That which Sparks and Myrthin were living through was the amazing sensory perception change which LSD can bring on.

That this brings with it a danger lies only in the fact that the individual is expected to conform to society's expectations. The danger lies in the fact that society defines our colors and states the ways of behavior. Yet it does this to suit its own aims in maintaining the status quo. In the early years of the new era there is no space for the altered state. The elders of our governments tell us that they already know how it should be. That they know best.

They have no need for psychedelic warriors, yet they need gray suited, gray heads by the billion.

But as the years pass by, as hours to some and as centuries to others, there is ever greater threat in being stuck alone away from the crowd. It is almost inconceivable to run around the new era with a head full of acid. They have eagerly put people far away from the system for such things. Locked up and out of sight.
When the Merry Pranksters first began their psychedelic mission, the drug was legal. There were no guideposts, and the society was crafted in its stiffness. It was only when the drug became illegal that the stakes rose, and the risks took over.

But the idea of a widespread LSD wave in this critical phase of our existence does carry some hope with it. Even if the idea of a completely acid drenched society is obviously as frightening as the worst of the alternative philosophies.

There is an inherent danger emanating from any that have made it to the top. 'Acid for all' is not taking into account that some people just do not have a head for heights.

The idea though that there is a positive strength in the ability to be different is important. It is the insight, the different insight that the drug allows is that that is significant. Though there is the danger that the insight reaches such a level of frightening reality that it becomes too great for most minds to comprehend.

There is a need for an education into the ways of such narcotics as there will always be those who wish to explore, escape or merely live. LSD is quite the most extreme of all the drugs, so it is the one with the most hideous reputation.

We all know the stories about people jumping out of windows. It's propaganda and has never happened to any the wide cross section of people that I've known. What I have seen though is the terrible effect of a bad trip turning into a long term impediment. This just shouldn't happen! It is often kids that are caught this way. Kids too young to be forced into dealing with such wild swings in reality. It is these poor guys that are the victims, victims of having had doors opened too quickly.

They are left dangling in mid air without a support net. This is probably my complete intention in writing this story of mine. To provide some kind of reassurance, to provide some loose form of guidance into driving your way beyond the day to day.

Drugs only heighten what is already lying beneath and where there is confusion there should be no drugs. Certainly, no LSD!

"Let's go down to the party!" Says Myrthin.
"Oh no!" Says Sparks.
"Oh my god!" Whisper I.

The drug was forcing things forwards, Myrthin was once

more chasing the night and I had the feeling that Sparks would inevitably be chasing him. From where I lay, I wondered. Should I jump out of the tent to warn the two musketeers? I realized it would probably only panic them. I saw that I had to let what was going to happen just happen!
Happen it did!
The two of them stumbled away from the car clinging to each other and slowly their voices faded away into

the distant night.

I was alone.

There was a silence.

The five hours that followed and led me into the next day went like this.

The two musketeers made it to the beach in a flashing, wild vision. LSD in its heaven and hell mood swings makes the banal seem dangerous and the dangerous almost impossible. Because the two men had been flying wild on the drug.

Sparks had had huge reservations about the wisdom of turning up uninvited at a religious, sit around a fire, sing song, beach party. Yet despite any doubts they had somehow made their way down towards the lethal cliffs above the beach.

Myrthin and Sparks, there they were, sticking firmly to the middle of the darkened lane for fear of falling off either side. Sticking closely to each other too, literally in an arm in arm psychedelic huddle. Suddenly the two guys are in a jungle, a prehistoric jungle of dinosaur leaves, huge, great heart shaped leaves, and that these leaves rumbled and didn't rustle made it all just a little too much.

"AAAAAAAGH! HAAAAAAAA! HAAA!" In hysterics Myrthin and Sparks collapse to the sandy floor to contemplate from a safe place, for laughter on the floor is indeed a very safe place.

Then in a stab of surprise a tongue of vibrant white light pierces the black space above where they lay. They were both still howling with laughter. It was a line of illumination sent to cut the dark and to paste frightening images on the Dinosaur leaves.

"Do you guys need help to get to the beach?"

It was the light speaking. No it was behind the light that was speaking. A voice that was leaking out from the shadows of night. Two dark shapes emerge holding a torch, the Night Watchmen of the Dinosaur Lands.

Gulp, Sparks jumps, and Myrthin, he tries to giggle his way up onto his feet.

"You!" Says one of the Night Watchmen, "You come with us, we'll lead you to the beach. Two hours ago two guys coming through here slipped off the bridge and cracked their heads open!"

"Bridge!!! What bridge?" Asks Myrthin in his blissful confusion.

"Ah man, there's a bridge to the beach and, it's a narrow mother, only half the size of the path!".
The two tripped out warriors hold onto each other tighter and laugh into the realization of the avoided danger. And

within a matter of steps the torch bearer illuminates the way and there is amazingly enough a very, narrow, totally dangerous bridge. It is all too much for Sparks who suddenly in a wave sees that the week's lessons are continuing and that once again fortune is smiling down on the intrepid journey.

In strange unfamiliar ways the two were told that the night was to be known as the "Night of the Shooting Stars". At which point Sparks and Myrthin look to the skies and gasp at the sight. There above their heads hung a dark canopy punctured with a million tiny holes.

Each of these holes was letting through minuscule threads of golden light. Yet stranger still was that many seemed to be moving at speed, flashing across the sky, like a celestial explosion or a tunnel full of fireflies.
Inspired by what had been seen the little group moves across the bridge. They move over furious sand dunes to reach the golden cove which was alive with manic color and light.

Music circled around the warped shafts of green, blue and reds, all mingling in one before their very eyes. A mass of elongated people changed shapes before their eyes as shadows melted out of the sand, into the sea then back as hued curves.
"Jesus!" Says Sparks, totally taken aback,

"It's Las Vegas by the sea!"
But back at the tent.

It is amphetamine dark. I lie and try to pretend to sleep whilst strange voices dip out of the mist to howl into the wind.

I was tired too, but behind my eyelids things were alive with a velvet dark movement.

Comfortable it was not. I was too concerned about Myrthin and Sparks to rest easy. Cars would screech past carrying people to and from the party.

The hounds of hell of Sparks' imagination continued to howl away into the night. I watched the tent door flaps fly in the breeze. It would soon be dawn and it would soon be time to leave on the long trek East.
But back on the beach.

Sparks is caught in the most amazing sensations near the waves. He sees his footprints glowing in the sand like radio active steps to the future. He watches as the green glitters then twists through several shades into a dark puce, then green again.

"Did you see that!" He whispers amazed to no one but himself. Then runs off to catch Myrthin who is also sitting busily on the sand.

"Look at the footsteps, they glow! And!" Sparks bends over to press his hand into the sand, the sensation is a tingling, a star-light tingling. "Look it happens with your hands too.".

"Jesus! What's happening?" Remarks Myrthin before testing the phenomena for himself and sees that his imprint throws up a rouge color.

"What is happening?"

What was happening was that the two guys were deep into the trip and the drug was throwing out some remarkable visual sensations.

"Let's go and dance!" Suggests a now laughing Sparks and off the two head into the mass of warped shapes that are the dancers.

"Its time for the sand-floor dance-floor! Myrthin my man. The sand-floor!"

The music, an electronic trance explosion becomes way more intense as the two move closer to the epicenter of this earthquake on the beach. The drums and bass boomed off against the rainbow-colored cliffs and echoed deep into the brains.

And it was easy to move, easy to move in and out of the music for it was like a written language of instruction. Arms moved in cyclical motion and fingers spread out as if capturing the energy or shooting out even more. There they dance like wired windmills, rooted deep into the soft sand seeing traces of color move through the stroboscopic lights. It looked like so many versions of a moment trailing off behind each other. There are hundreds of dancers, hundreds and all moving in real fine proportions across the colored music.

But back at the tent.

Someone blasts on a car horn and screams out of the car window.

"Hey John. Johnny man! You've got to come on down. It's fantastic! Come on!"

There is silence. Then once more and louder.

"Hey man! Come on! You've got to come. It's great."

Again, silence reigns before the unknown night caller once more blasts into the night sky!

"Johnny! Come on!"

Johnny, who I assumed from where all this was going on, close to our tent, had to be the middle aged guy who was camping in the corner. The guy with his wife. The quiet couple with the dog.
This confused me, for the voice that was calling just throbbed with the insistence of drugs, ecstasy or coke's high pitched insistent whine.
Suddenly from nowhere I heard the screaming voice of the most certainly non drugged Johnny. He was not too pleased. He was wild with temper.

"Listen you, will you just LEAVE ME ALONE!"

With which the car sped off into the dark.

Johnny I guessed was angry and seemed to be on the edge of explosion. Me, I shivered a little to myself and decided to go and sit outside the tent and smoke until the daylight returned.

But back on the beach.

After a bundle of dancing Myrthin needs to roll a joint but his fingers are no longer connected to his nerve control center. They are rubber and hollow. He still intends to fight on with his plan watching as the white papers bleach out into a kite flying in a petrol sky, then run through the blaze of orange flames that seem to tickle the underbelly of the dark night. But the cigarette papers fly away and oh woe, they are the last in the packet.

A slight crisis on acid is likely to turn into a huge dilemma so Myrthin is up on his feet and off on a search.
"Did you see that?" He asks to the shadow at his shoulder that is Sparks.
Sparks did see it and what he also sees is Myrthin approaching a figure that he recognizes as a guy called John Swan, the young Merry Prankster guitarist.

Now Myrthin is on the search for cigarette papers and he finds more, something much more. Sparks from his vantage point sees John Swan whisper something quietly to Myrthin who moves closer.

After mere seconds they both seem to be in a mutual trance and are jumping up and down as one, chanting something at the top of their voices.

It is as Sparks would later describe as the "tightest, most loving embrace I've ever seen between anyone". Sparks sits watching completely amazed by it all and when the two guys finally break off leaving each other with huge knowing smiles, he is sure that he has just seen some form of amazing instantaneous understanding. The likes of which that is so rare as to be almost extinct.

"That was incredible!" Says Myrthin as he flops down to the sand next to Sparks, "Absolutely Amazing!". He then commences telling of how the two strangers had felt an enormous spiritual connection, one which was so difficult to explain. When they had hugged each other there Myrthin explained there had been an almost unbearable explosion in Myrthin's heart. Like a huge, piercing electric bolt. John Swan had apparently been talking about pure love, and its importance. Myrthin had felt it. Pure, first-hand, a beyond borders rejoicing in love for all.

Sparks understood and could see the emotional glare in Myrthin's eyes. They were both close to tears as they both hugged each other with glee as a feeling of pure joy pulsates around them. The two explorers have for the first time and forever bonded their connection.

But back at the tent.

The only bonding going on is between a speed head and the stars, but its a strong one, a strong bond. For between the wisps of cigarette smoke the stars are becoming familiar. See Sirius there in its flashing green, white and red, as always prominent.

Old Sirius, the Dog star. I liked that star the most for it looked like a jazz star, a glitzy place that stays open night and day.

There were shooting stars too, every minute one would blast silently above the tent, every minute, until I began to wonder if it was not just a reaction to tiredness.

No, they really were there, really, just beyond the glowing tip of my cigarette. I even picked out a satellite on its silent orbit. It would faithfully trundle on its lonely way, so far from earth. Out there in near space forever sending images back to land, spinning endlessly on its fixed path around the globe. My friend the satellite took only twenty or so minutes to make it right around the world, I was convinced of it.

Look here it comes again! Oh, look a shooting star! And there is the Great Bear! Its easily identifiable shape that looks more like a cooking pan than a bear to me. And the little bear, the same, a small cooking pan.

Stars, stars, stars!! Billions of them. I even had a great view of the constellation that I had always believed to be the scorpion from which I am most influenced, being of that specific star sign.

The scorpion really does look like a menacing desert stinger, but I have been told by someone who knows, that it is actually not a scorpion at all and in fact a completely different constellation. For me though and especially that night in Cornwall close to the Merry Prankster's bus, it was definitely a scorpion, a proud one too.

It was peaceful that sleepless night slowly approaching dawn. It was close to four or five in the morning and it made me wonder about Sparks and Myrthin.
But back at the beach.

Myrthin is off and away still sparking from the revolutionary encounter with John Swan. He drops in and out of small scenes with a huge smile on his face and a wild glare in his eyes. As always supremely sociable and supremely confident. Whilst Sparks who is now strongly confident on the trip and not at all fearful is busy dancing himself into a hole just on the fringe of the main sand-floor dancefloor.

It is only after a while that he notices he has burrowed himself shin deep in the still glittering green sand and this he finds remarkably amusing.

After all he is Australian and after all as all school kids know if you keep digging down, it's to Australia you're going. Sparks was going home, but hey he was happy here, he didn't need another beach, so he skipped out of his hole still laughing to himself. He sees a stranger coming directly towards him.

Yeah, he's coming directly over towards where Sparks now stands swaying in the glitter. Slight doubts and mild panic surface through the joy as the Australian wonders 'why?'. 'Why is this guy now looking directly at and through my eyes?'

"If I was you mate!". Says the guy in a strong English accent. "I would go up there!" pointing into the melee of movement that is the main body of dancing.

"If I was you!." With which he was gone off down to the sea for reasons best left alone. With which Sparks is vaguely confused but gives the guy some credence and takes his advice. So it is off into the mass and it is time to be sucked away into the tubular musical rainbow experience. It did all sound even better from the middle, really better and Sparks was pleased to have moved on someone else's suggestion.

But back at the tent.

A thin line of light is spreading out over the ocean and me and I suddenly have company. A stray dog is sat up with me, it is the hound from hell. It was friendly though in its eyes I see a reticent fear, an unease in being alone.

So that is the reason behind the constant noise, only loneliness. As it sits down, I think we both feel somewhat more comfortable. The hound from hell is actually sent from heaven to keep me company. It was that primeval link between wolf and man, a link that has been forged over a long, long time. It was a wild relief to be with this friendly animal for the drug of speed had me on edge.

It had me in no man's land awaiting the next move. In the company of a wise old hound suddenly things seemed to be a little bit easier to fathom. I could see dawn was coming as the sky lay bruised over the dog and me. The dog though, it cared not, for soon it was twitching in sleep, content with the company. Dreaming of endless runs over rich pastures in pursuit. In pursuit of hares or love or its own tail.

Or even the master that whistled him on. I felt envious in a way as it was only me doomed to sitting through that sleepless night alone. Though it was nobody's fault but the drug and without the drug I would have slept through it all. I looked down to the bus it was slowly throwing off the dull cloak of night and beginning to glint once more. It seemed to want to invite me down into its magic for one last personal moment. I thought of being inside a pyramid surrounded by colors that would literally leap off the walls and overwhelm you.

The pyramids used to be a blaze of color inside, and it is a very fine analogy for the mystics emanating still from the Merry Pranksters and the bus Further.

If you were to visit a pyramid five thousand years ago, it would be a wholly different experience to now. In place of the crumbling finery would be a fierce rising plane, sharpened at its pinnacle by polished metal. Inside throughout the hidden chambers instead of faded reds you would find a psychedelic explosion of piercing images and effigies. Created this way in order to ensure the safe passage of one who was greatly revered. Their work would be of such minute detail that its meaning would be quite baffling and known only to those who were clear in its purpose.

I walked down to the bus with the dog for company, he'd had no trouble in rousing from his dreams. I walked down with the intention of watching the sunrise cast color onto the artwork. I intended looking for secret passages on the outside looking in.

But back at the beach.
It was also just about to dive into morning. No ordinary morning though for Myrthin and Sparks are still lost in the violent orange surges of the psychedelic in their system.

It paints the rising tide red and the sand green.

It has the sky blasted purple and it has the horizon as the thinnest line of yellow. Images of nearby people wobble and vibrate as they move past and the pulse of pounding blood in their ears refuses to relent.

A cast of summer clouds dance slowly in the summer sky, tinged ever so slightly with green at the edges. Myrthin and Sparks sit together on the sand and watch the persistent hundred or so dance through into morning. It is not a conventional tired that keeps them seated no, it is more a sense of awe at how different things can be. No matter how hard their traditional logic whispered away, there was no denying this new way of seeing things. No denying these new versions of how things seemed to look.

It was almost the time to move back, a time to return to the tent and the camp site. Almost! This beach thing was somehow just to all consuming to leave. The music still leaked like velvet out from the surrounding cliffs. The dancers still created obtuse shapes that seemed to flow into some huge, coordinated performance. A huge show that was being put on just for Myrthin, just for Sparks!

Close by someone spots a couple deep in an embrace, a young pair hugging and kissing life into the new day. It all seems just too idyllic, just too perfect. The world 'is' on the way up. The world 'is' going to win.

But then, just when this feeling of euphoria was about to explode into a very deep meaningful something, someone approaches. Someone approaches very quickly and very determinedly. Yet this is no welcome visitor.

This is a portent from the wrong side. A reminder of some of the less savory truths along the drug way. A warning from the brutal side, a warning of what can go wrong!

It was dark around the edges this vision.

It was the unmistakable shape of the desperate tramp, the ingratiating tramp of the forever free bum ride who had secured the free Californian acid the night before.

Fear it seemed had clotted his system and he looked close to death as he wobbled his way up towards Myrthin and Sparks. He looked like a character from the pages of a medieval horror novel. His knees close to the sand and his hunched back pressing him down. He stopped about a yard away from where the two sat. The early morning did his wrecked, frightened face no favors. His lined features were grimed over dark, and his eyes were like splattered ink wells.

"Hey guys!". He coughed desperately. "Have you got a joint! I've had a hell trip! A real bummer. I've been going mad! Seeing my death, my death!! A spliff quick! I need one! It's my nerves." He whispered desperately as if afraid of which lurking demons might be listening.

In tears he asked once more. "I need a hit!"

This was all that he said, he said no more. He then just seemed to hang in the air like someone's soiled clothing on an invisible washing line.

It was a pathetically sad sight and Sparks couldn't take it at all. He thought of Josie, this man's son, a lovely child who deserved more than this from his father. He thought too of the tramp, and how he was letting himself down tragically with this desperate lifestyle of his.

Sparks who was close to tears couldn't stop himself.

"You!." He said pointing an uneven finger at the crumbled human being before him. "You are a disgrace! A disgrace to yourself and to your son!"

Someone burst into inappropriate laughter! Someone covered up with embarrassment! Someone else cried. It was the truth, and everyone knew it. This tramp was gone, he was way too far across the divide. It was obvious in his movements as his dark silhouette slipped away.
Away to where though?
Away to a new beginning?
Away to a tragic morning of fighting death?
Away to his son?
Away to the waves?

Sparks didn't know where, but he was in tears as he watched the thin specter take his terrible, desperate act elsewhere. A hundred musketeers watched the guy leave before deciding to make the long journey back up the hill.

The sad appearance had ruined the purity and had prompted movement and escape from the beach. Wearily and arm in arm Sparks and Myrthin made their way off the sand, even finding Myrthin's missing sunglasses on the way.

It was the end of the night and the beginning of the day ahead.

But back at the tent.

I spend time touching the bus and following the intricate patterns painted on its bodywork. Looking closely at the paint work it was possible to see tiny detail in the huge collage.

There were miniature painting of jesters, magicians and symbols of archaic origins. There were lightning bolts crashing out of orange clouds. There were spider webs woven intricately into patterns too complex to decipher. A row of stamp-sized American flags ran in waves along the side of the bus. If you followed them around the whole crazy vehicle, you came back to where you started from.

There were dozens of multi colored hot air balloons. Some in red white and blue, some in blazing yellow. Stars of course there were hundreds of stars and stripes too. At the front of the bus, on the hood cover, there was a sculptured court jester figure pointing his wand and leading the way.

Doves of peace and even a cow were also taking pride of place. Dolphins too, dolphins painted in paisley colors diving into a deep ocean of orange diamond design.

A huge whale tail splashed in a shimmering arctic white ocean. There were plump bunches of grapes dangling from vines at the top of the bus. A huge white spiral spun its way across the roof from one side of the bus to the other. Totem poles too, carved in blue paint against a red background. Above the windscreen there was a third eye peering down, piercing the dawn.

Above that was the destination plate. The place the bus was going. The bus was going further.

I understood something quickly. I understood that it was crucially important to look closely at any big picture just to be able to see the smaller composites that make the whole. To go further you need to be overwhelmed. To go further you need to go with color. It made me break down in tears the effort and care that had gone into the whole of this venture by the Merry Pranksters. Their only message was a lethally naive message from another age.

"All you need is love." Is what they were saying.

This is what Kesey was passing on.

"Love is all you need."

It was easy to scoff such dumb optimism. But the Merry Pranksters were immune. They had made themselves untouchable by making themselves absolutely approachable and swamped in fun.

Above my head the sun was back with us.
So were Myrthin and Sparks.

I heard them coming before I could even see them. It was the two acid wanderers, and it must have been close to six in the morning. They made their happy but haggard progress over the fence and close to our tents.
"Get in the car! It's London next stop." I shouted happily.
"Great, unbelievable! Let me dose you!" Says a wild eyed Myrthin making no sense. Sparks he just stood limply to one side.

It hit me in a flash! It hit me hard and true! I had to get them away from their beds and into the car. We had to pack up. We had to leave! There was too much riding on this to be able to spend a day lazing around a field in Cornwall.

Sparks needed to be in London by the next day, the Friday. He had to be there early the next day. His flight for Vienna was at ten in the morning. My last strands of wisdom told me to herd the two of them in the car and drive them out into safety.

"Get in the car!" I shouted politely. "Get the tents down and off we go!"

The acid in their system complied with my demands. Myrthin bundled our wet tent into Norm's boot whilst Sparks somehow managed to fold his tent into a tiny bag.

It all took a bit of time but at least it kept us moving. While this was going on I was busy trying to kick start some life into the engine. Dormant for three days as it had been it was unwilling to wake but after twenty patient shots at the ignition I managed to rev it into action.

That was that. We all took a long, silent look around the field, poignantly but also alive with a determined madness. The next leg of the journey was upon us. We left the bus and the Merry Pranksters and the field. We would from that point on carry them with us wherever we went.

Now I won't try to describe how we scorched across Southern England in one manic blast. Stopping only just the once for gas! I won't try either to describe how deeply Myrthin slept and how Sparks stared blankly out of the window, for hours.

Now I won't even try to describe how we moved faster than ever before and never seemed to leave the fast lane of the motorway. I definitely won't try to describe what made us think of hitting on a friend of Sparks's. Our plan was to ask him to let us stay the night at his North London flat. Jesus God!

What I will tell you though is that at three in the afternoon on a Thursday in August we were stranded in Watford. A suburban modern nightmare in a shopping mall. We three, forcing chicken burgers down our throats. It was impossible madness on all sides and none of it made sense.

Not the shops selling bags!

Not the kids with their dads!

Not the polite signs or even the overpowering neon lights. We were lost and desperately looking for any help.

Later we happened across a book shop, a Dillons or a Waterstones! One of those huge places with a million books. We'd walked in like refugees from a psychedelic war. Our hope was to find a clue leading us to somewhere to sleep for the night, anywhere that was not a tent.
The original idea of staying with Wolfram, Sparks's man had gone awry. Sparks and we two especially had been unable to even speak on the phone without dissolving in hysterical laughter.

Ultimately, we were homeless and looking for a way out. My idea was to hunt down a travel guidebook for the local area!

"A travel guides! But which county are we in? Which

town?"

Five hours earlier we'd been in a field in Cornwall and it was that confusion which brought me to ask the greatest question I have ever asked.

Quite innocently I moved towards a passing young shop assistant.

"Excuse me!" I said lowering my sunglasses a little. "Could you tell me where we are?"

She didn't even answer! She just walked away!
The true answer lay in a bookshelf on the floor above us.
After some lost minutes we made our way up to the popular fiction section. There I happened across a book written by Hunter Thompson, he of 'Fear and Loathing in Las Vegas' fame. This book I had in my hand was a magic link to what had just gone by.

Out of vague desperation and deep interest I flicked the book open and scanned the contents page. It was a large collection of short stories, rants and prose written by the author in the late Sixties and early Seventies.

I skimmed through with only half focussed intensity. Suddenly I saw words that stopped me breathless in my tracks and took me immediately back to the day before, back to the total eclipse.

It was only a title to a short article, an article about three pages long but still it was final proof of the existence of magic. Proof that we truly had been in the presence of eminent company for a week.

'KEN KESEY. WALKING WITH THE KING!'.

Read the title of Hunter Thompson's words before my eyes.

I slammed the book shut without reading the article, I didn't need to. I span around three times and lifted my arms to where the ceiling hung silver above me. To my side I saw the familiar shapes of Myrthin and Sparks.
"Walking with the king!" I shouted happily to their confused faces. "That's it! That's it! Indeed Hunter! Indeed! Walking with the king! We've been walking with the king!!"

I dragged the two musketeers out with me and back to the car. I had a great idea.

"Let's go to Aylesbury!" I giggled insanely. "It must be a great place!"

So, it was to Aylesbury we went. To a Travelodge motel after we'd got flagrantly lost in the town centre.

Little was making sense but ultimately, home was a box room for fifty pounds.

Myrthin coughed his way onto the floor whilst Sparks and I lay glassy eyed staring at a blank television screen.

Every so often Myrthin and Sparks would explode in hysterics about some event from the beach party. Their Californian LSD trip was still in full swing. We drank some beer and faded into evening as hollow shells. Hollow but bleached clean by the events of the week. We were hooked into the life of the moment and didn't think too much, just existed in the huge cosmic flow.

A day later we were all back where we'd started but as changed men!

Sparks had arrived in Vienna to a feast of unwanted joints, fed to him by eager youngsters in the back of a car.
The youngsters were eager for tales of the week. Sparks could hardly speak. At one point the cops had flashed blue lights in a car behind them and then sped away into the distance. Sparks had smiled blissfully at what no one else could possibly have begun to understand.

Myrthin and I we got through hundreds of miles of traffic virtually unscathed. We moved with our pistons steaming! We moved with our wallets cleaned out! We were absolutely broke!

We laughed our way through a one hour traffic jam and reached North Wales just before the banks shut. Norm was returned to the Jocars Corporation a broken but a wiser car!

His efforts in allowing us to maintain progress had been monumental. It had certainly been one of his last ever journeys. His ailments seemed to be incurable, but his bravery had been overwhelming! I laid a tender hand on his roof and kissed him farewell.

Within two hours it was back to the Dark Place us in a fever. We told everyone of tales which no one could ever understand. The others on our table assumed we had gone mad and stared at us with enormous empathy!

TRIP OR TREAT TOO!

The months after Cornwall sped past.

Kesey and the Pranksters were safely back in Oregon after their three-week search for Merlin. Had they found him? Quite probably but they didn't seem to be too keen on telling anyone.

Myrthin was safely back busy teaching the infants in his classroom. Safely back in the Dark Place too and busy singing songs to anyone who would listen.

Sparks and I dove into another Viennese season with stars in our eyes as I returned to the board game with a huge enthusiasm for everything mildly circus.

Sparks was once more doing his money changing game but with a new-found incredible level of tolerance and patience. Things were once more what they had been once before. But no!!!!!!
Things would never be the same again.

WHERESMERLIN?

By Ken Kesey

In Vienna at the tail end of 1999 there was a violent psychedelic invasion going on!

Each weekend seemed to be spent in a haze in a vibrant corner of some room or other. The search it seemed was only just beginning and then came Halloween. In 1966 the Merry Pranksters had held their Acid Test Graduation ceremony on the 31st of October. It was heralded as 'The moving on from acid' spectacular. Kesey under intense pressure from all sides had been cornered into making a proclamation about the evils of LSD.

Under huge media coverage and with a court case looming he was about to tell the world to leave acid behind.

You shouldn't keep going through the same door of perception was what he meant.

On one level it looked like Kesey was controversially

turning his back on the whole psychedelic revolution.

On another level it was obvious he was saying something else. He was telling the world not to get trapped in believing in the world of the hallucination.

It was, he claimed, important to move on from the constant dependence on a drug to show you the way, though only once you had at least found that way.

The Acid Test Graduation ceremony was to be held at San Francisco's large Winterland Venue. But the promoter Bill Graham panicked and backed out at the last minute! Then came the rumors of what the Merry Prankster's had actually planned for the evening. The super prank!!

The following day, the 1st of November, the jolly clean minded folk of California's Democrats were due in the same venue and the word on the street was clear. Kesey had planned to saturate the building with liquid LSD. A dozen thousand good thinking Californians would have been dosed out of their narrow little minds and the world would have changed forever. Kesey may well have been locked away for a long, long time. So went the rumor. Ultimately though the actual graduation ceremony eventually took place in the Merry Prankster's warehouse. It was the low key last gathering of the whole gang. Neal Cassady handed out the diplomas and by three o clock it was down to the core of the pranksters gathered in a tight circle. The mood was heavy and filled with vague regret. It seemed as if the battle had been lost and that the powers of evil had won. Kesey was on his way to prison. The bus 'Further' was on the way to retirement on the Kesey farm in Oregon. It was the end of 1966!
Sparks realized in 1999 that there were big numbers at

play. Halloween in 1999 was 33 years after the 1966 Acid Test Graduation ceremony.
Three three!
Six six!
Nine nine!
From that point on our own Acid Test Graduation Graduation ceremony came into being!

The plan was that we as a large group would fly into an LSD Halloween in honor of the Merry Pranksters and in honor of the numbers. It was intended to prove that the psychedelic movement was alive and well as we approached the new millennium. Kesey had taken the mission to the eclipse to prove the very same thing.
There were fifteen of us in total, men and women of all description ready to blast into the Celtic New Year.

The LSD was strong blotter acid and served in a golden goblet. The Halloween evening commenced with a video about animals' unusual survival techniques.

Then we spent an hour listening to randomly selected music, all of which had huge meaning. By the time the goblet had done the round several times, it was the streets that were calling. We grabbed a tennis ball and kicked it out into the streets of Vienna.

It was the ball that was king. Wherever it landed we went. We were immediately dragged in a giggling mass into a terribly traditional Viennese bar.

The atmosphere inside was turgid. Within minutes San Fran Ron, a fifty-year-old Californian, had thrown his hat James Bond style at a pair of antlers hanging off a wall. The hat and the antlers had tumbled to the floor.

The atmosphere changed immediately! There was much laughter! Then there was a careful game of placing Ron's collections of crystals in intricate patterns across the huge wooden table.

It was a collective sculpture that continually evolved. It was a game without competition, a game without losers but a game with many winners. Around the table the intensity is immense. It is Halloween and the spirits are rising! There is though no animosity and even the most olden and conservative of the customers rise with us.

Then gone. Our tingling group mind follows the ball back through the archaic, cobble stone streets.
We were moving further as a collective.

And the acid is rising!

In the next venue the ball takes us to, peanuts are the problem.

Sammy the drummer, a twenty-five-year-old Austrian, is convinced the peanuts are made of wood! Then he tries to cling to explaining what he is feeling. "Everything feels so small, yet the universe is so huge!". We all tried the peanuts and found him to be correct. The peanuts did taste of wood, whatever wood might taste like!

Lenny, he of Brighton in the summer, is caught in a hurricane. The music spins him round but he is only seated! Some youngsters that Sparks has brought with him are deep in conversation about!!!!!!!!!!!!!!!! No, one knew! It was as if they were merely deep in personal monologues.

I sit next to Sparks flying with a metallic high that has us communicating answers to questions that had only been thought and never voiced. It was too loud to talk so we thought out our conversation. It was a strong feeling of a higher force. Whilst McDougall, a twenty-six-year-old Irish guy, was opposite us looking to the ceiling with a huge smile on his face! He hadn't spoken for a long time! Yet what was a long time?

How long had this madness being running on?

We finally left the club and its music to hit one further ball race!

The ball takes us to another club.

This club is specializing in Sixties music. This club is beaming videos onto walls. This club is perfect.

On plush velvet seats we sit in a large half circle. Beamed onto us and behind our heads is the film 'Fear and Loathing in Las Vegas.' Hunter Thompson again! Kesey's long time counterculture companion! It strikes no body as being weird this perfect coincidence! It is as it should be!

I think back to the end of the Kesey week and the return to civilization. How hard it had been to make sense of all that modern madness. But not anymore, it was fine! Fine to be sitting in a completely hallucinated state in the midst of 1999 Vienna! No, one chased us down, no one even suspected anything more than over exuberance on Halloween beers and wines.
It 'was' possible to carry out psychedelic experiments crash bang in the modern age!

There were still limitless possibilities!
At five in the morning, it was down to Sparks, a guy called Gentle and I!

We were sitting in my apartment fishing out a couple of remaining blotters from the goblet. We were invincible! Give me more!

At seven in the morning, I was in bed fighting the pictures behind my eyelids. A panic was rising within me as I feared that maybe, just maybe this 'Graduation Graduation' was about to spin me into crazy land. Had I graduated too far too quickly?

I was alone with my fears! These fears had not existed at all within the previous hours but now in my solitude they flew in like heavy eagles.

Yet there was amazing insight too! I saw that it is how you interpret things that makes them what they are? It is all down to perspective.

I saw that the ability to see the positive in everything is key to a healthy mind.
Then I panicked about my breathing as my chest was tight but that was soothed away for it was easy to cope with the light. It was only when I shut my eyes did things get intense! Colors would catapult in strange waves forming images from another dimension.
I saw Chinese faces struggling in violent floods, fear etched on their faces. I saw the world as a lonely woman, without company and stricken by disease. There were explosions of purple mushroom clouds into a darkened sky. Airplanes falling in flames from clouds.

Where these horrific omens of the new millennium?
Where these mere horror flashes of the deepest mind?
Whatever. Just as the panic was rising to sweep over the riverbanks!

Just as I was going to rise back into the daylight as a terrified man. The memories of the total eclipse dragged me back onto dry land. I remembered Kesey's crucial words about 'love'

"You've got to show it! You've got to be able to look it in the eye! You've got to deal it! Love! Love! Love!"

And in an instant, I was becalmed. It was that simple. It was time to 'deal it.' In those terrible images of destruction, I'd been shown the awful consequences of a world without love.

I dragged myself up to begin clearing away the mess from the night before. Outside was the first day of November 1999.

Winter was on its way, yet the sky was deep blue, but a frost had sparkled the rooftops around the place where I lived.
Slowly I began washing up the mess, carefully replacing the jigsaw pieces of the night before. I looked up to the wall and saw Kesey there watching me with a wry grin. It was as if he was watching my psychedelic house work with mild approval.

I smiled back. Halloween was over and we had tamed the ghosts. It was a time to move forward. Forwards took me out onto the empty streets to buy cigarettes to calm my nerves. It was a public holiday and Vienna was trapped in a dull Sunday vibration.

I strode down the pavement past store fronts advertising the unnecessary, the gambits of our greedy society. I walked past a couple of strangers who shuffled their way home in the bright sunlight. Church bells clanged a sharp, metallic reminder of the ways of the forced religion of non fun.

Then with a clean, new packet of filthy smoke in my hands I returned to the safety of my apartment.

With a cigarette glued to my bottom lip I started, tentatively at first but then in a torrential flow, I began to chronicle the story of Ken Kesey, the Total eclipse, the Merry Pranksters, Myrthin, Sparks and I.

It felt strongly that the energy had indeed been frozen within me, but now that the thaw was setting in, there was a liquidity once more stirring a long forgotten frozen lagoon of psychedelic sense.
It was time to document the truth, or the non truth, but certainly not the lies. It was time to set the record straight! Time to take it all a step further!

"The answer is never the answer. What's really interesting is the mystery.".

POSTSCRIPT

Just two years later Ken Kesey died. It came out of the blue and shocked us all deeply. It was my father who told me, via a text message on a cell phone. In clinical computer lettering his message was simple.

"Sad news! Ken Kesey died yesterday! Love Dad :("

I left the noise of the bustling bar room and drifted off into deep reflections of the small amount of time that I had spent close to Kesey's sparkling charisma.

Once upon a time on a cloudy week in the shadow of an eclipse we had walked with a king. We would never forget!

Though the king might well be dead. His vision rides further.

THE KING IS DEAD! LONG LIVE THE KING!

Printed in Great Britain
by Amazon